Also by Knud Erik Jørgensen

The European Union and International Organizations (*editor*)
European Approaches to Crisis Management (*editor*)
Reflective Approaches to European Governance (*editor*)

International Relations Theory

A New Introduction

Knud Erik Jørgensen

First published 2010 by
PALGRAVE MACMILLAN

Palgrave Macmillan in the UK is an imprint of Macmillan Publishers Limited, registered in England, company number 785998, of Houndmills, Basingstoke, Hampshire RG21 6XS.

Palgrave Macmillan in the US is a division of St Martin's Press LLC, 175 Fifth Avenue, New York, NY 10010.

Palgrave Macmillan is the global academic imprint of the above companies and has companies and representatives throughout the world.

Palgrave® and Macmillan® are registered trademarks in the United States, the United Kingdom, Europe and other countries

ISBN 978-1-4039-4699-7   hardback
ISBN 978-1-4039-4700-0   paperback

This book is printed on paper suitable for recycling and made from fully managed and sustained forest sources. Logging, pulping and manufacturing processes are expected to conform to the environmental regulations of the country of origin.

A catalogue record for this book is available from the British Library.

A catalog record for this book is available from the Library of Congress.

10 9 8 7 6 5 4 3 2 1
19 18 17 16 15 14 13 12 11 10

Printed and bound in Great Britain by
CPI Antony Rowe, Chippenham and Eastbourne

Contents

List of Boxes, Tables and Figures

Boxes

Tables

Figures

List of Abbreviations

ACP	African, Caribbean and Pacific countries
ASEAN	Association of South East Asian Nations
CAP	Common Agricultural Policy
DIY	Do it yourself
EBA	Everything But Arms
EU	European Union
GATT	General Agreement on Tariffs and Trade
HST	Hegemonic stability theory
IGO	International governmental organization
IMF	International Monetary Fund
IO	International organization
IPE	International political economy
IPT	International political theory
IR	International Relations
ITO	International trade organization
LDC	Least developed countries
MBA	Master of Business Administration
NATO	North Atlantic Treaty Organization
NGO	Non-governmental organization
NIEO	New international economic order
ODA	Overseas development aid
OECD	Organisation for Economic Co-operation and Development
PPT	Post-positivist theory
RIPE	Review of International Political Economy
UK	United Kingdom
UN	United Nations
US	United States
USA	United States of America
USSR	Union of Soviet Socialist Republics
WTO	World Trade Organization

Preface and Acknowledgements

It is a key feature of mature disciplines that they engage, from time to time, in critical self-reflection. While such reflections are intriguing and rewarding in their own right, an important motivation for writing this book is my conviction regarding the importance of incorporating them into the textbooks used to introduce the discipline and its theories. The design and conception of this book has, therefore, been strongly influenced by the fruits of my own research on the genesis and development of the discipline, in particular on the trajectories of European IR theory, the genesis and origins of IR theory more generally and the benefits and pitfalls of aspiring to make IR a truly global discipline.

The book styles itself 'a new introduction'. Its novelty from an intellectual and pedagogical viewpoint consists primarily in the following six key features which I believe will make it a distinctive and helpful guide to grasping international and global affairs in the 21st century:

- **A broad notion of theory**
The book adopts a broad yet not boundary-free conception of theory introducing all main *categories* of theory (explanatory, interpretive, normative), and illuminating the distinctions between them without privileging one or more.

- **A clear differentiation of types of theoretical reflection**
Theoretical reflection on international relations is all too often subsumed under the catch-all umbrella concept 'IR theory'. For newcomers to the field, such an aggregate is particularly unhelpful because it means they are introduced to a *ratatouille* without realizing that different components have different forms, functions and limits. In contrast this book provides a new way of structuring theoretical reflection distinguishing between theoretical traditions, currents of thought and specific applicable theories.

- **A focus on the 'shaping' of theory and its philosophical underpinnings**
The book illuminates as a running theme throughout how applying different meta-theoretical commitments (e.g. behavioural, formal, rational choice, critical or social constructivist) to particular traditions, currents of thought and theories will shape them in different ways.

- **A global and de-centric approach**
The absence of a substantial non-Western challenge to the Western dominance of international theory is particularly disquieting for a discipline carrying the name of 'International Relations'. While it is probably unavoidable that we view international affairs from where we are situated, it only takes some effort to imagine how horizons would look like from elsewhere. Which theoretical perspectives on issues of world politics will we find in, for instance, Beijing, Kinshasa, Brussels or Brasilia? This book attempts to take a less parochial and more genuinely international approach by adopting a 'de-centric' perspective.

- **A commitment to 'do it yourself' theorizing**
Theorizing is not just for theorists. The book encourages students to do their own theorizing by developing the analytical competences it takes to think theoretically. To this end, in the best traditions of 'do it yourself' (DIY) home maintenance and construction, it includes a handy user-friendly manual and provides and introduces a wide selection of analytical tools.

- **Broad-ranging coverage of the field and key readings**
Inclusions of substantial quotations from a wide range of sources provide the flavour that only the original 'voice' of authors can provide. In addition, the citations function as an interface between this book and the wider literature that is available for further reading. Hence, students who want to know more or to follow a given line of argument will know where to go for the original and extended version of these arguments.

Few books are produced solely by the author and I owe a great deal to all those people who have been part of the dispersed team behind this one. My publisher at Palgrave Macmillan, Steven Kennedy, as all who have met him will readily confirm, is one of a kind. Throughout the long process of developing this text, he has been patient, committed and encouraging – in short a perfect editor. I am also most grateful to Palgrave's anonymous reviewers, especially those who commended the original proposal and thus helped get

---

Box 0.1   The International Relations Theory website

The companion website for this book provides a range of additional material including case studies of 'real world' illustrations of IR theory in action, a glossary of technical and contested terms, PowerPoint slides for each chapter and web links.

http://www.palgrave.com/politics/Jorgensen

the project off the ground and, in particular, the one who provided extremely detailed and helpful comments on both the first and a semi-final draft typescript. I am also indebted to my colleagues Tonny Brems Knudsen, Jørgen Dige Pedersen, Mehdi Mozaffari, Mette Skak, Georg Sørensen, Anders Wivel and Clemens Stubbe Østergaard who kindly devoted precious time to commenting on drafts of individual chapters and in particular to Morten Valbjørn for his very thorough, helpful and sympathetic comments on the whole book.

Teaching teaches the teacher (too). This book is based on what I believe are the most valuable lessons I have learned from teaching both introductory and advanced courses. The ideas behind the book have been tested in courses both at my home university and at the ECPR European Summer University in Grenoble, France. Though it is difficult to measure the direct impact of such experiences, I am fairly convinced such experiences have been crucial for shaping the book the way it is. Finally, I should mention my involvement in designing a new two-year master's programme, International Studies, at Aarhus University. I would like to thank all students involved for their most valuable feedback.

I presented papers at the 2006 and 2008 Annual Convention of the International Studies Association outlining the key principles behind the text and incorporating draft material for feedback. I was very fortunate to have Edward Weisband, Virginia Tech and Dan Lindley, University of Notre Dame, as my discussants. All were merciless and meticulous in pointing out a number of weaknesses, yet, at the same time, very supportive of the project overall. I would also like to thank Carmen Mendes at Coimbra University for testing the chapter on theory building and informing me about her positive experiences. Last but not least, I would like to thank my secretary Anne-Grethe Gammelgaard and research assistants Stine Wolf Randrup Andersen, Laura Landorff and Yazgülü Sezgin who did an excellent job in bringing the bibliography, index and other book features into order.

Knud Erik Jørgensen

Note: Figure 7.2 in this book was previously published in the volume *The Social Constructon of Europe* that I co-edited with Thomas Christiansen and Antje Wiener; it is reproduced here by kind permission of Sage. It was also published in the *Journal of European Public Policy*, 1999 special issue, and is reproduced here by kind permission of Routledge.

Introduction

Theorizing is a process through which we refine knowledge, producing a concentration of insights into international affairs. This nature of theory explains why theory is a prime shortcut to knowledge about international affairs. Of course we can, in principle, spend a lifetime building such knowledge but usually we cannot wait that long. Sometimes we only have one term at our disposal to grasp the essentials of one or more aspects of international relations. In this context, theory can basically do two things for us. First, it can in a very efficient fashion simplify what is otherwise a very complex world that many people find almost incomprehensible or at least difficult to grasp. Second, theory functions as a guide to the analysis of international actors, structures or processes. The guide points out who are or what is important, so that we can focus our attention on that and legitimately ignore other unimportant beings and doings. This sounds relatively easy and is only complicated by the disquieting fact that, as in all areas of social science, there are several contending theoretical perspectives and approaches. There is nothing we can do about the fact that the social sciences are characterized by more approaches than arrivals. What we can do is become acquainted with the major perspectives and approaches. It is therefore the aim of this book to introduce the main traditions, currents of thought and numerous specific theories, that is, the main layers of theoretical reflections on international relations.

Main theoretical traditions

This book introduces the six main theoretical traditions:

- **International Political Theory**
Theorists within this tradition analyze international affairs by means of concepts that belong to the field of political theory, including terms such as rights, justice, obligations, norms, ethics and community. International political theorists examine normative issues, interpret the writings of political philosophers, such as Kant, Hobbes and Grotius, and discuss what these political philosophers might have to say about contemporary international affairs. Finally, they critically examine political reasoning, that is, justifications or explanations of choices and political action.

1

- **Liberalism**

The liberal tradition is cultivated by theorists who believe that not only change but also progress is possible, although progress does not necessarily come easy. According to liberal theorists, human reason and rationality explain why human beings are capable of making progress possible. They also believe that international politics need not be characterized by anarchy and war. Anarchy can be moulded by means of international institutions, and economic interdependence reduces the benefits of war and therefore the likelihood of war. Because democratic states tend to be more peaceful (at least vis-à-vis one another), the increasing number of democratic states leads to an enlargement of the global zones of peace.

- **Realism**

Theorists within this tradition are characterized by a strong focus on the role of power politics and by their professional pessimism concerning international progress. They assume that history repeats itself endlessly and can therefore be said to represent a circular conception of history. Realist theories are strongly state-centric, focus primarily on conflicts and dismiss the importance of international institutions and non-governmental actors. The heyday of realism seems to have been the Cold War and it has had a particularly strong position in the United States. The tradition should not be confused with realism in art or philosophy.

- **The International Society Tradition**

Theorists working within the international society tradition – also called the English School – reject the simple opposition between liberalism and realism, arguing that the inclusion of a third (alternative) tradition allows us to do more nuanced studies that more accurately describe today's complex world. They claim that though the international system is anarchical, that is, it is lacking a global political authority (world government), key features of an international society – for example, rules and institutions – do exist and have important ramifications for the nature of international affairs. They highlight the sociological dimensions of international relations, for instance, behavioural conventions. The tradition has been most prominent in British academia but has increased its global spread in recent years.

- **International Political Economy (IPE)**

Objecting to the widespread separation of international economics and politics, theorists within IPE are keen to theorize linkages between international politics and economics. It is the tradition that most directly includes economic dimensions of international relations. Apart from this shared feature, theorists conceive of IPE in most diverse ways. Some consider IPE to be simply the employment of economic approaches and research techniques in the study of politics. Others draw on the Marxist tradition, emphasizing the determining effects of economic factors on politics. Still others extend (political) realism by adding attention to economic factors. As we find IPE theorists on most continents IPE is one of the truly global traditions.

- **The Post-Positivist Tradition (PPT)**
While positivism is a philosophy of science that has underpinned a major part of IR scholarship in the past, it also functions as a kind of negative point of departure for post-positivist theorists, who aim at going beyond positivism and explore the analytical potentials that emerge when positivism is left behind. While post-positivists share this feature of going beyond positivism, they are going in three different directions. Some explore the options offered by Critical Theory, a quasi-Marxist strand of thought that can be traced back to the 1920s. Others examine the options embedded in social constructivism, conceived of as a set of commitments to social theory, including theories of international relations. Still others explore the benefits offered by post-structural approaches. Given that positivism was mainly cultivated in the West, the shadow of Western positivism shows in the fact that also the post-positivist tradition is mainly cultivated in North America, Europe and Australia.

Understanding the 21st century by focusing on the 20th century

It is indisputable that international relations theory has a long and winding pedigree. Some like to quote Renaissance analyst Machiavelli and his focus on the ubiquitous role of power; others prefer to go back to Greek historian Thucydides analyzing the timeless features of warfare. Still others find it useful to trace the discipline's genealogy to ancient Chinese texts written by Mo-Ti or Confucius, or they go back to the Indian analyst Kautilya who seemingly outlined an early balance of power theory. However, this book deliberately focuses on developments in the 20th century, not least because the contemporary discipline of international relations has been profoundly shaped during the last century. While each of the six theoretical traditions has historical examples of thinkers and theorists, all six traditions have been shaped by 20th-century world affairs, by the general dynamics of the social sciences, by the growth of academia and by changing trends and fads in the production of knowledge. Rather than superficially skating centuries, the chosen focus enables us to be more comprehensive and to explore more deeply and widely the world of contemporary theoretical reflections and debates.

The structure of the book

The book is structured in a simple yet compelling fashion. In the introductory first chapter, the scene will be set and the defining features of the following chapters will be described. These features underpin the book and should therefore be explicated in some detail. Five basic principles have particularly guided the preparation and design of *International Relations Theory: A New Introduction*:

- A broad notion of theory
- A clear distinction between theoretical traditions, currents of thought and specific theories
- An aspiration to be truly global, that is, to avoid ethnocentric perspectives
- A focus on both theoretical substance and form
- An invitation to become not only consumers but also producers of theory ('do it yourself' theorizing)

The employment of these novel analytical and heuristic principles is bound to make a distinctive and truly new introduction to international relations theory.

After the introductory chapter, six chapters on theoretical traditions follow (Chapters 2 through 7). Each of these chapters is structured by means of the same template (see below). The purpose is to introduce and provide overviews of six theoretical traditions. This feature makes it easy to identify differences and similarities along a number of key parameters. Subsequently, the book turns to two thematically cross-cutting chapters, each designed to introduce crucially important dimensions. In the first place, Chapter 8 outlines major inter-tradition theoretical debates. The reason is that theorists do not only operate within a given tradition and thus cultivate theory in perfect isolation. Rather, they often engage in lively debates across the boundaries of traditions. These debates are excellent tools to strengthen our understanding of the essential contestation of theoretical reflections. Second, Chapter 9 provides a tool-kit to be employed when engaging in 'do it yourself' (DIY) theorizing. Finally, Chapter 10 summarizes, concludes and outlines perspectives.

The structure of each chapter on theoretical traditions

All six chapters on theoretical traditions (Chapters 2–7) have the same structure, consisting of seven parts. You will first encounter a brief *introduction*, setting the scene and sketching the main characteristics of a given tradition.

Then follows a *genealogy* – that is, a description of the origins and development of traditions, essentially outlining the main phases through which the tradition has developed during the 20th century. As each tradition is characterized by a varying number of main *currents of thinking* within each tradition, the respective characteristics and dynamics of these currents are outlined. Each tradition is also shaped by several *kinds of theory*, that is, types or forms of theory. The diversity of forms can be explained by different meta-theoretical commitments, for instance commitments to rational choice or constructivist formats. Additionally, each tradition is home to several *variants of theory* – specific theories that can be applied in empirical research. Whenever the task is to prepare a theory-informed analysis of an empirical research question, we should look out for specific and applicable theories. In this respect, it is useful to know that the six sections on variants of theory, when combined, constitute a comprehensive catalogue of such theories. After the presentation of specific theories, each chapter will outline the main *intra-tradition debates*, underlining the main positions and their dynamics. Finally, the chapters will include a section summarizing the *contemporary research agenda* of each tradition. As theorists cultivate a range of contending traditions and specific theories, they tend to ask different questions or address different issues in different ways. Hence, the research agendas are partly different and partly overlapping.

Chapter 1

Why Theorize International Relations?

Progress is marked less by a perfection of consensus than by a refinement of debate.
                                                        (Clifford Geertz 1993: 29)

Why a book on IR theory rather than a book on the substance of world politics? After all, many superficial policy pundits or journalists would argue that theory is useless and basically a waste of time. Others regard theory as an unwelcome 'must do' activity: 'So much for theory, now to the real world!' Still others simply cannot figure out why theoretical debates seem inconclusive, contemplating what makes Clifford Geertz's statement above both accurate and appropriate. Questions like 'Why theory?' or 'What can theory do for us?' therefore pop up all the time and require upfront and convincing answers. However, different answers have been given to these important questions and, in the following, I summarize five major sets of reasons for engaging in theoretical reflection (for an extended summary, Box 1.1 shows ten different yet overlapping reasons).

- Theorists tend to agree that a prime function of theory is guidance of research. Despite the widespread assumption that data speak for themselves this is hardly ever the case. Hence, engagement in interpretation is unavoidable and different lenses lead to different interpretations. Theories can be seen as such lenses; competent analysis requires knowledge of the potentials and limits of the different options.
- Theory is an excellent tool to challenge prejudices, traditional world views or conventional wisdom. In addition, theory produces intriguing questions to analyze and enables examination of implicit assumptions and perspectives.
- Theory makes it easier, or at least possible, to grasp the modern world, not least because theory conceptualizes the world, simplifies complexity and outlines feasible avenues of enquiry.
- Theory can play an important role when we want to evaluate political practice. Politically convenient reasoning can be challenged by means of theory-informed investigations.

6

- The field of study we label 'International Relations' happens to be a discipline that is defined by its theories, knowledge of 'its theories' is thus a precondition for becoming acquainted with the discipline.

So there are convincing arguments on the importance of theory, but how does it actually guide research in practical terms? What can theory deliver? A very neat answer is provided by Lisa Martin in relation to the sub-field of international institutions which, she observes, has long been in favour of studies that are:

> quite policy-oriented and descriptive, lacking an overarching analytical framework. This lack of a theoretical foundation meant that, although individual studies generated strong insights, they did not cumulate to create a coherent picture of, or debate about, the role of international organizations in the world economy. This situation changes with the publication of an edited volume called *International Regimes* (Krasner 1983) and of Robert Keohane's book *After Hegemony*. These books cast international institutions in a new light and suggested a novel explanatory framework for studying them and patterns of international behaviour more generally. (Martin 2007: 110–11)

This is a beautifully concise description of what theoretical reflection can do in terms of significantly upgrading research in a given field of study. It simply takes theoretical reflection to summarize and synthesize the findings of empirical studies.

What is theory?

But what actually is a theory and which theory should we use? On this there is a range of views. Some authors take a narrow view, starting out by selecting one particular category of theory and then systematically introducing it in the following chapters. Some teachers and students like this method, because they can subsequently avoid having to bother with other conceptions of theory. Moreover, the reasons for choosing a given conception of theory and neglecting the rest can be presented in just a few sentences. James Rosenau and Mary Durfee thus explain:

> Aware that our own expertise, such as it may be, lies in the realm of empirical theory, the ensuing discussion makes no pretense of being relevant to thinking theoretically in a moral context. All the precepts that follow are concerned only with those mental qualities that may render us more thoroughgoing in our empirical theorizing. (1995: 181–2)

Box 1.1   Ten perspectives on the function of theory

1. Theory can be seen as a guide we need to conduct research, not least when we aim at analyzing rather than merely describing world politics. In order to help us upgrade our studies from description to analysis, theories guide us through the upgrading process. This first reason appears to be strong, because we all know what unguided research and mere description looks like. Not very attractive!

2. Theory can help us because data do not speak for themselves. We need a device that can help us interpret data, understand the symbolic dimension of data and put data into perspective. Theory provides just such a device, suggesting we focus on important actors, processes or structures and warning us not to waste time on unimportant phenomena. Theory points out how things hang together, what key terms mean and how valid arguments are composed, for instance arguments in favour of or arguments against humanitarian intervention, free trade or international institutions.

3. Theory can help improve our analytical competences, especially because theory serves to question or challenge our existing world views. We all tend to create rather impressionistic views of the world, generated by media coverage, movies, political engagements or travel. Theory challenges or confirms such self-made images. Knowledge of contending perspectives simply leads us to recognize that our individual image only constitutes a part of the full story. In this fashion, we broaden our horizons, and because we can now play more than just one card we expand our analytical competences.

4. Theory is sometimes presented as lenses through which we perceive the world. This take on the value of theory emphasizes that there is one world but different interpretations (lenses) of it and, finally, that the role of theory is to make us conscious of perspectives that otherwise might be implicit or taken for granted. However, lenses can be coloured and changing from a grim, dark one to an optimistic green lens seemingly makes a significant difference, not least concerning our observations. But has the world actually changed, or, is it just our perceptions of the world that have changed?

5. When we attempt to understand world politics, we are usually overwhelmed by data and other informational material and subsequently in doubt about which material to select. We must therefore resort to theory, as theory is foremost a simplifying device. This type of reasoning is a good example of the 'keep it simple' doctrine at work and also highlights selection and prioritizing as prime functions of theory. Put differently, theory helps us to determine what is important and what is not. Some of the most parsimonious theories help us considerably in terms of simplifying. Rather than analyzing the security dynamics of the world's 192 officially recognized states, we can usefully keep it simple

by focusing on the handful of states that are great powers and nevertheless make claims about global security dynamics. Put differently, simplifying is of great help. The bad news is that blinkered visions also simplify. In a best case scenario, believing that your blinkered vision is the full horizon is a risky assumption; at worst, it is dangerously naive.

6. Knowledge of contending theoretical perspectives is, of course, possible, yet also simply a precondition for grasping the modern world. Theoretical knowledge is simply a must. Hence, we do not have a genuine choice between theoretical and a-theoretical analysis, and we do not have a choice between knowing about one or more theories. In order to grasp all of the important aspects of the modern world, we simply need to draw on the entire theoretical repertoire. Any suggestions to the contrary seriously lack credibility.

7. All theories can be recognized by their three fundamental dimensions: ontological, epistemological and normative. The first dimension identifies 'existing things' (whether material or ideational), whereas the second reflects on how we can know about these things, and the third tells us what we should make of them (see also section on meta-theory). It is difficult to imagine one of the three dimensions being left out, so with this conception we are dealing with the very foundations of theoretical reflection.

8. Many warn insistently against downplaying theory because, in the words of Stanley Hoffmann and Robert Keohane, 'attempts to avoid theory not only miss interesting questions but rely implicitly on a framework for analysis that remains unexamined precisely because it is implicit' (1990: 284). Serious analysts would obviously not like to miss interesting questions or rely on unexamined frameworks.

9. IR is a discipline that has largely been defined by its theories (Neuman and Wæver 1997). From this observation, it follows that without understanding the theories it is next to impossible to understand the discipline, for instance, how it has evolved and where it is heading.

10. Many examples of theory serve the dual function of providing both critique of foreign policy and prescriptions or recommendations for a certain course of action. The critical function can be illustrated by John Mearsheimer and Stephen Walt's (2003) criticism of the Iraq War in 2003. Based on a realist perspective on world politics (see Chapter 4), they claim that there was no emerging genuine balance of power problem, for which reason the decision made by the Bush Administration to launch war was wholly unnecessary and unwarranted. Mearsheimer has also presented an example of theory-informed policy prescription. Based on his theoretical position, he is highly critical of intensive US engagements with China, instead recommending a policy of cautious, limited engagement. Obviously, realist theories are not alone in having such a dual function.

In this manner, Rosenau and Durfee claim that they do 'empirical theory' and leave the rest basically untouched. Stephen van Evera is also brief in his indirect dismissal of broader conceptions. He simply defines theories as 'general statements that describe and explain the causes or effects of classes of phenomena. They are composed of causal laws or hypotheses, explanations, and antecedent conditions' (1997: 7–8). In this fashion, he opts for an exclusive focus on causal or explanatory theory and does so by means of a narrow definition of theory.

The two quotations represent a very widespread yet narrow conception of theory that implies an unfortunate reduction of the research and teaching agenda. In contrast, this book favours a relatively broad conception of theory. But this raises immediately the problem of how broad should such a conception of theory be? Is there a boundary somewhere? In his introduction to *Theories of International Relations*, Scott Burchill points out that:

> one of the purposes of this book will be to argue that the term 'theory' is not limited to its 'scientific' or positivist formulation and that explanatory theories, of the kind which flow from the adoption of a positivist methodology, are only one type of international theory. (2001: 1)

In a similar fashion, this book introduces not one but several avenues of theorizing. But if there is more than one conception of theory, how many conceptions should we cover – and which ones? In this context, Chris Brown's understanding of theory is most helpful. He goes beyond a narrow monist conception, which would highlight one conception as the one and only, and claims that there are essentially three categories of theory:

> [T]here are explanatory theories which attempt to explain why, under what circumstances, wars happen and normative or prescriptive theories which try to tell us what our attitude to war ought to be – whether for example we should volunteer to participate in a conflict or conscientiously object to it; to this pairing we can add theories which interpret events, which attempt to give meaning to them – something that the carnage of the First World War seemed especially to require. (1997: 13)

Each of these categories of theory comprises numerous specific theories and is cultivated by theorists in all of the major theoretical traditions. According to Craig Parsons (2007), explanatory arguments follow four major and most different avenues: structural, institutional, ideational and psychological avenues. Interpretive theory also comprises a broad range of more specific theories, a feature emphasizing that we are talking about a category of theory rather than a specific theory, as such. Concerning normative theory,

Andrew Hurrell (2004) alerts us to the fact that students of international relations cannot avoid engaging in normative reasoning. Given that they often have not been introduced to international political theory, it follows that they are unable to avoid 'barefoot' normative reasoning. It appears obvious that an introduction to international political theory represents a feasible solution to the widespread serious problem of barefoot normative reasoning. This presumption explains why an entire chapter is devoted to international political theory (Chapter 2).

Theoretical traditions

Intellectual research traditions can be defined in different, yet partly over-lapping ways. According to Timothy Dunne, 'intellectual traditions share, to varying degrees, the following four attributes: classification, continuity, abstraction and exclusion' (Dunne 1998: 55). Whereas classification provides a certain order of intellectual currents, continuity is in charge of demonstrating that patterns of thinking have evolved over time. Abstraction and exclusion imply that we aim at understanding the larger picture of affairs and leave nitty-gritty detail for another time. Dunne continues by pointing out that the notion of 'tradition' is often a means to reduce complexity and to upgrade teachability by means of simplifying and empha-sizing various heuristic functions. Concerning intellectual traditions, inter-national political theorist Luigi Bonanate provides a most helpful definition, 'a corpus of centuries of research, characterised by classics, schools of thought, original proposals and a specialised debate' (1995: ix). As we will see, the chapters focusing on theoretical traditions (Chapters 2–7) demon-strate that Bonanate's definition is an apt way of characterizing the key features of traditions. Though philosopher of science Larry Laudan (1977) is not dealing with international relations, he has important things to say about what he calls research traditions, which are nevertheless also relevant for international relations theory. According to Laudan, 'a research tradition is a set of general assumptions about the entities and processes in a domain of study, and about the appropriate methods to be used for investigating the problems and constructing the theories in that domain' (1977: 81). He further explains that a research tradition is not explanatory, predictive or testable, yet provides the guidelines for theory building. In summary, the definitions of theoretical traditions vary but are first and foremost variations around a common theme.

If the above outlines the contours of the characteristics of intellectual research traditions, then which traditions does it make sense to include in our selection? Once again, the answers vary. Mark W. Zacher and Richard A. Matthew point out that '[i]n typologies of international relations theory, liberalism, realism, and Marxism are often presented as the three dominant traditions of the twentieth century' (Zacher and Matthew 1995: 107). Martin Wight (1991) provides a second answer, suggesting that the main traditions are constituted by three Rs: Realism (Hobbes), Rationalism (Grotius) and Revolutionism (Kant). This book will not follow any of these suggestions, being characterized instead by its own way to structure the material.

In order to achieve an adequate balance between inclusion and exclusion, this book includes six theoretical traditions:

- international political theory
- international liberalism
- political realism
- the international society tradition
- international political economy
- the post-positivist tradition

These six traditions are widely acknowledged as the major and most important theoretical traditions in International Relations; it is within these traditions we find the leading theorists in the field of world politics. Furthermore, these traditions have proved capable of spinning off numerous currents of thought and specific theories; hence, when seen as a whole the traditions constitute the main and most dynamic centre for theoretical creativity. Moreover, theorists belonging to the six traditions engage in theoretical debates to an extent that is simply unmatched by any other tradition. Finally, there is no shortage of references to the six traditions, a fact that highlights their recognition in the field. Some write about 'returning to the roots of the realist tradition' (Gilpin 1986: 308), others simply about 'the realist tradition' (Donnelly 2000: 6–42). The English School is variably said to belong to the Grotian tradition, the Rationalist tradition or the international society tradition (Dunne 1998; Linklater and Suganami 2006; Bellamy 2005). Scholars practising international political theory are in the process of creating a new tradition. In doing so, they are partly resurrecting an older tradition and partly drawing on a range of political theory traditions (Brown 2002b). There is no shortage of studies within the rich international liberal tradition, although Zacher and Matthew point out a surprising fact: 'a systematic presentation of liberal international theory is not offered in any well-known texts' (1995: 107). The international political economy tradition is unified by its focus on interfaces between international economics and politics, yet is otherwise somewhat dispersed, with some versions having strong affinities with other traditions. Characterizing post-positivist theorists as belonging to a tradition is surely contestable and anathema to some. As James Der Derian has pointed out, however, the fruitfulness of philosophical traditions is to be found in their 'ability to condense and simplify ... complexity into uniform, comprehensive, teachable expressions' (1988: 190). The post-positivist tradition is no exception to this heuristic option of condensing and simplifying. In summary, the aforementioned six traditions will be introduced in the following chapters.

Currents of thought

If traditions are the main branches of the IR discipline tree, then the currents of thought are the smaller branches of the tree. Individual currents are thus part of a tradition but are more specific and dynamic than traditions *per se*. For illustrative purposes, a few examples suffice. It is widely agreed that there are two main currents within the international society tradition: pluralism and solidarism (Knudsen 2005; Jackson 2005a, 2005b). Both currents have distinct characteristics and comprise numerous specific positions (cf. Chapter 5). Three major currents can be identified within realism: classical realism, neorealism and post-neorealism (also called neoclassical realism). The liberal tradition has been categorized in a number of ways. Some talk about weak and strong liberalism. Others identify ideational, republican and commercial liberal theory (Moravcsik 2003a). Robert Keohane includes three currents: neoliberal institutionalism (his own creation), republican and commercial liberalism. He distances himself from the two latter currents, emphasizing that 'my arguments diverge from those of much liberal international political theory' (1989: 11). This suggests that when reflecting on intellectual traditions, we should also include a dynamic perspective, that is, keep in mind the evolution of traditions and currents over time, including attention to factors that are capable of explaining such change. Finally, we should not expect watertight divisions between strands of international thought. Changing patterns of overlap occur, and some currents are only distinctly different along a few dimensions.

Currents are excellent for purposes of orientation and overview but are not directly applicable in empirical research. This is simply because they have emerged over time and without an eye to application. They are too broad and general to serve as specific guides to research. A guidebook to South America does not tell you much about Lima, Peru. It might provide some general information, but it is highly unlikely that this information will be enough to guide you through the city.

Though the various currents of thought represent parts of different traditions, it is easy to find examples of individual theorists who over time have shifted from one tradition to another or from one current to another. For decades, Martin Wight was a rather typical English classical realist before co-founding the international society tradition, where he can be situated

		Table 1.1 *Theoretical traditions, curr*

Traditions	International political theory	Liberalism	Realism
Currents of thought	Cosmopolitanism Communitarianism	Interdependence liberalism Republican liberalism Neoliberal institutionalism	Classical realism Neorealism Post-neoliberalism
Theories	Just war theory Theories of identity Theory of international justice Theories of community *Dependencia* theory	Democratic peace theory Transnationalist theory Constructivist liberal theory of cooperation Liberal intergovernmentalism	Balance of power th Theories of alliance Power transition the

within the pluralist current of thinking. Hence, it is no coincidence that aspects of realist thought can be found in Wight's writings, even in his studies produced as a member of the English School (Molloy 2003). Furthermore, it is no coincidence that members of the English School end up as realists (if they end up at all) in texts that exclude the international society tradition by means of squeezing prominent members of it into the category of realism. Actually, the precise relationship between the English School and Realism remains a hotly contested issue. Raymond Aron's position is a different difficult case. Some regard him as a (French) classical realist (Giesen 2006; Waltz 1990), whereas others tend to see him as a kind of French representative of the English School. Still others speculate that Aron probably is un-'boxable' and constitutes a school of his own. Aron is far from being alone in this category of 'difficult to box' thinkers. Other examples include E. H. Carr, Chris Brown and Takashi Inoguchi.

Variants of theory

Theoretical traditions and currents can first and foremost be used for purposes of classification and orientation in the landscape of theories. They provide the broad contours of theoretical reflection, suggesting that an image of a long, slowly moving river is suitable. Most traditions and currents are capable of spinning off concrete, specific theories applicable in empirical research. The realist tradition has thus produced, for example, the balance of power, balance of threat, power transition and hegemonic stability theories. It should be noted that a liberal version of the latter theory also exists, and the two versions should obviously not be confused. Similarly, balance of power theory exists in both a realist and English School version. The exam-

t and specific applicable theories

ional society	International political economy	Post-positivism
n	Mercantilism (or economic realism)	Social constructivism
sm	Marxism	Post-structuralism
	Liberalist	Critical theory
	Eclectic	
of fundamental institutions	Hegemonic stability theory	Securitization theory
of hegemony	Classic theories of imperialism	Discourse theory
of humanitarian intervention	*Dependencia* theory	Theories of identity
	World systems theory	
	Theory of embedded liberalism	

ples clearly demonstrate that one ought to take context into consideration before jumping to conclusions about the nature of a given theoretical variant. Each of the following chapters on individual traditions will include a section on variants of theory, providing examples of important discrete theories and outlining key characteristics of each theory. When students are being asked to prepare a theory-informed, empirical analysis of a given topic, these sections are ideal for the task of identifying one or more potentially suitable theories.

Table 1.1 summarizes the above introductory sections on theoretical traditions, currents of thought and individual applicable theories. At the same time, it provides an overview of the six chapters on individual theoretical traditions (Chapters 2 through 7).

What is meta-theory?

Meta-theory quite simply means theoretical reflections *on* theory. Hence, knowledge of a range of the key dimensions of meta-theory promises to enhance our understanding of the nature of IR theory. However, because meta-theoretical explorations can occasionally be akin to travelling without ever arriving anywhere, the present book is characterized by a slightly pragmatic and instrumental perspective on meta-theory. Consequently, not all of the complex meta-theoretical issues will be introduced; rather, only a few, but important, basic aspects. Five aspects will be introduced in the following, simply because they are deemed to be at the top of a genuine 'must know about' list.

As seen above, *ontology* is about as basic and foundational as it gets in the social sciences. This is quite simply because ontology is the branch of philosophy that is concerned with what there is, that is, the existence of things, no matter whether these 'things' are of a material, institutional or mental nature. In other words, when we consider the 'international', we consider the building blocks or the properties of the international sphere. Part of the very rationale of theories is to provide an ontology of the international, for example, assumptions or propositions about more or less important actors, structures and processes. Each theoretical tradition is capable of providing answers to the question of ontology, but, significantly, the answers provided by various theorists vary immensely. As mentioned above, ontology is a philosophical branch, and ontological studies are concerned with issues of being and existence. Quite a bit of translation is required to make sense of the various philosophical positions on ontological issues. There is no escape from such translation, however, as ontology by definition plays a key role in how IR theory is developed. A suitable starting-point might be the philosopher John Searle, who has created a general theory of social ontology and social institutions (Searle 1995). Furthermore, according to Alexander Wendt and Raymond Duvall, the relationship between ontology and international theory can be understood in the following fashion: 'although social ontologies do not directly dictate the content of substantive theories, they do have conceptual and methodological consequences for how theorists approach those phenomena they seek to explain, and thus for the development of their theories' (1989: 55). In this way, Wendt and Duvall see a clear but loose linkage.

The term *epistemology* is derived from the Greek word '*episteme*', meaning knowledge. Hence, epistemology simply means theory of knowledge, or reflections on strategies of building knowledge. How do we know what we know? Common sense tells us that experience represents one avenue towards knowledge, but not always a sufficient or feasible strategy for building knowledge. This fact is perhaps particularly relevant in regard to international relations because it is very difficult for most students to generate knowledge about, for instance, nuclear strategy by means of experience. The philosophy of (social) science provides a range of different strategic options; however, there is no need to go into detail in the present context. Instead, we will examine linkages between epistemology and theory. Given that the role of theory is to guide us in the process of acquiring knowledge, it is rather obvious that epistemological assumptions and commitments constitute a key dimension of any theory, whether or not such assumptions are explicitly stated or implicit. The epistemological underpinnings of individual theories will therefore be highlighted, and each chapter on theoretical traditions will include a section on important kinds of theory and describe how variation in epistemological commitments has contributed to shaping the development of IR theory.

The *agent–structure problem* is among the perennial problems in the social sciences and, thus, by implication also in international relations. Essentially, the problem emerges due to an unavoidable analytical distinction between agents (actors) and structures. The problem is how we should weigh or relate these two components in our studies. Some analysts completely disregard structures and prioritize actors, resulting in a strong actor-orientation. This point of departure enables a class of questions – for example, questions about how actors view their situation, including their assessment of possible social or political action. Rational choice perspectives are also actor-oriented, but in this case actors' properties are predefined and preloaded with a specific kind of interest. In contrast, structure-oriented studies focus on structural phenomena first and actors second. Structure-oriented analysts take their point of departure from structural features, subsequently defining the properties of actors and determining their likely behaviour.

The *levels-of-analysis* problem is labelled as a problem but can actually also be seen as a solution, offering a way to order or categorize theories at different analytical levels. We often want to explain a certain phenomenon, such as the causes of war. The problem, then, is to determine at which analytical level we should identify potential causes. In this respect, the levels-of-analysis problem provides a most helpful typology. One bundle of possible causes can be identified at the level of individuals or small groups. A number of theories all operate at the level of individuals, explaining, for example, the dynamics of 'groupthink' (Janis 1982), individual belief systems (Goldstein and Keohane 1993) or the nature of human beings (Morgenthau 1948). A second bundle of causes can be situated at the level of states, pointing to state identity (e.g. democratic, middle-power, imperial or maritime), economic system (feudal, market capitalism or Marxist control-economy) and civil society characteristics (strongly or weakly developed). A third cluster of causes can be found at the international level, including causes such as the anarchic nature of the international system, the nature of international society, the development of the capitalist world market and its political ramifications. How many levels does it make sense to use? Some operate with three levels: individual, state and system (Waltz 1959; Singer 1961); others find four levels appropriate (Jervis 1976); others yet opt for five levels: individual, bureaucratic, state, regional and systemic (Hollis and Smith 1990). Basically, there is no 'correct' number of levels. The adequate number of levels depends on the question to which you want to find answers. In order to determine which typology suits your purpose, it often helps to think through a number of potential analytical levels before focusing on one or more suitable levels. In any case, it helps to consider possible alternatives before opting for a solution. (See Figure 1.1.)

Criteria for good theory

Which *criteria* characterize good theory? The various criteria that can be employed in order to determine whether a given theory is good or bad are

Figure 1.1   *Level of analysis and the agent–structure problem*

LEVELS OF ANALYSIS	AGENT-STRUCTURE
International system/society	Structure
Region	Structure-Agent
State	Structure-Agent
Bureaucracy	Structure-Agent
Individual	Agent

extra-theoretical and, thus, belong to the heartland of meta-theoretical enquiry. There are three major avenues concerning criteria. According to the first avenue, '[t]here are six criteria (all of them standard in philosophy of science) that are relevant for international relations inquiry . . . I label these, respectively, the criteria of accuracy, falsifiability, explanatory power, progressivity, consistency and parsimony' (Vasquez 1995: 230). Vasquez represents a model example of criteria for explanatory theory built on a positivist footing.

The second avenue is associated with political and normative theory. It is clear that most international political theories (see Chapter 2) would fail miserably if assessed by means of the above criteria. However, this is not necessarily a problem for international political theory, because it only indicates that the criteria for good political theory are different to some degree from those relevant for explanatory theory. Unfortunately, one of the features of political theory is that such criteria are rarely spelled out in concrete terms. One exception is John Dunn, who specifies the skills required to conduct political theory:

1. Ascertaining how we got to where we are and understanding why things are this way.
2. Deliberating about the kind of world we want to have.
3. Judging how far, and through what actions, and at what risk, we can realistically hope to move this world as it now stands towards the way we might excusably wish it to be. (Dunn 1990: 193)

Box 1.2 John Vasquez's criteria for 'good' theory

'"Good" theories should be:

... accurate;
... falsifiable;
... capable of evincing great explanatory power;
... progressive as opposed to degenerating in terms of their research programme(s);
... consistent with what is known in other areas;
... appropriately parsimonious and elegant.'

(Vasquez 1995: 230)

The three skills can serve as a point of departure for assessments of a given theory and its 'good' or 'lousy' qualities.

The third avenue concerns the criteria for good interpretive theories. Interpretive theorists insist that you cannot or should not avoid interpretation (Ball 1995; Geertz 1993). This general claim also applies to the field of international relations; perhaps more so than many realize. Nevertheless, when analyzing international politics, we do attempt to establish what is the meaning or significance of given texts, talks or other forms of political action. Examples of relevant texts include treaties, international agreements, diplomatic notes, official documents and reports – and this list is far from exhaustive. Furthermore, actors involved in international politics carry out speech acts and engage in negotiations across cultures. Standard ingredients in interpretive analysis – context, author intent and reception – are therefore no less relevant in the field of international relations than elsewhere. The criteria we use to determine whether or not an interpretive theory is good can be divided into two categories. The first category comprises the criteria that apply to all theories. Does the theory help clarify muddy waters? Does it assume the simplest possible form? Does it generate interesting questions? To which degree is it capable of addressing the future and for making predictions? The second category contains more specific features. As Clifford Geertz points out, interpretive theory is not built to 'codify abstract regularities but to make thick description possible, not to generalize across cases but to generalize within them' (Geertz 1993: 26). Basically, he claims that the relevance of criteria for explanatory or deductive theory is of little help when assessing the quality of interpretive theory. Furthermore, interpretive theory does not always draw a sharp distinction between description and explanation. Actually, the term explication is favoured, for which reason we can raise questions regarding the explicative power of given interpretive theories. Finally, theories should to some degree contain propositions about the relative roles of context, author and reception.

The important general lesson is that the criteria for determining whether or not a theory is good or bad should not be taken for granted or at face value. Their scope varies considerably, even if they are often presented in universal terms. Overlaps between different sets of criteria are limited but can be found. However, issues of limited applicability, complementarity and congruence remain contested, and students cultivating a critical approach ought to pay close attention to the position from which claims are made and criteria cherished. Finally, you will inevitably sooner or later encounter theoretical value judgements, such as 'this theory is clearly outdated'; 'and this is why we do not introduce you to the international society tradition'; or 'realism is so 20th-century theory'. Hence, it is important to critically examine the criteria for making such judgements.

Kinds of theory: a question of form

Having briefly introduced a range of theoretical issues, in this section we address their relationship to underlying epistemological positions. As we shall see the adoption of, for example, rational choice, constructivist, behavioural or other epistemological commitments can have a major impact on substantive theoretical traditions, currents of thought and on specific theories, effectively 'shaping' them into new forms. This is perhaps best seen by giving two examples of how this 'shaping' principle works out in practice and is used in this book.

First, the 1960s were characterized by a great debate between traditionalists (including classical realism and the English School) and behaviouralists. Against this background, one would possibly be inclined to think that the contrast between these two perspectives on world politics would be complete. However, John Vasquez (1983) demonstrates that this is not the case. In reality, some of the traditionalists' key assumptions were simply reproduced by behaviouralists, although given a new form. In other words, we have a case of traditionalist assumptions being shaped and re-presented in a behaviouralist disguise. Vasquez argues that by giving research a different form, compatible with the underpinnings of behaviouralism, many observers focused on the great debate and the theoretical rupture but forgot to pay attention to the crucially important dimension of continuity.

Second, the 'shaping' principle at work shows its impact right from the beginning of this textbook, that is, in the table of contents. Perhaps to the surprise of some, there is no individual chapter on constructivism. This deliberate choice does not imply that constructivist perspectives are absent. On the contrary, the choice is based on the claim that constructivism is not a substantive theory, competing or comparable with, or, for that matter, complementing substantive theoretical traditions such as realism, liberalism or international political economy. Conversely, it is argued here that constructivist perspectives can be combined with all substantive traditions. Hence, constructivist realist theories are imaginable (Barkin 2003), Wendt's constructivist theory of international cooperation should be situated within the liberal tradition, and the English School can be seen as a prototype constructivist international society tradition (Dunne 1998).

The two examples demonstrate that the issue of different *kinds* of theory has to do with form rather than substance. Each analytical form has its own distinct sources of inspiration. Some draw on some version of positivism, that is, a philosophy of science producing select criteria for good scientific strategies of enquiry. Positivist underpinnings often lead to the employment of quantitative research methods. Others draw on rational choice, that is, a social theory that has very explicit and distinct assumptions about actors, structures and processes. Still others draw on constructivist perspectives, for example, philosopher John Searle's (1995) general theory of social ontology and social institutions. We can occasionally encounter the very same substantive argument couched in different analytical languages or theoretical forms.

Any genuinely pluralist-minded scholar will know that every kind of theory has its own 'tool-box' of methodological procedures. The rigorous employment of normative theory does not require the employment of method tool-boxes that have been created for explanatory theory (see e.g. King, Keohane and Verba 1994; van Evera 1997). Similarly, interpretive theory has developed its own specific criteria for what constitutes rigorous analysis. Though discourse analysis and contents analysis appear to share some concerns about the subject matter, their assumptions, approaches and methods differ significantly. In summary, accounts of theories should highlight how given theories have historically been given different forms. This perspective on international relations theory will be further introduced in each chapter on theoretical traditions.

Theoretical debates

Contending traditions, currents of thought and theories trigger theoretical debates. Figure 1.2 illustrates how three of the six traditions relate to each other and how some of their theoretical currents are close and other currents are far from one another.

In addition, Figure 1.2 shows that there are both inter-tradition and intra-tradition debates. Numbers 1–3 represent intra-tradition debates, whereas numbers 4–6 represent inter-tradition debates. According to the figure, one

Figure 1.2   *Three IR traditions, currents of thought and six theoretical debates*

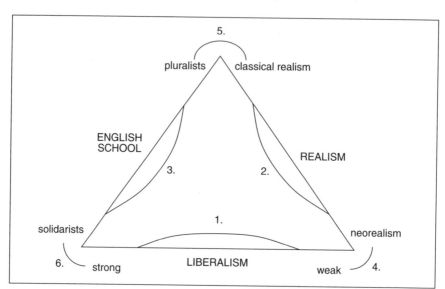

should expect a lively debate between weak liberals (neoliberal institutionalists) and neorealists. Indeed, Joseph Nye (1988) has not only identified a lively debate but actually a so-called neo-neo synthesis, in other words, there has been sufficient rapprochement between two formerly competing perspectives that they end up being almost completely congruent or alike. Robert Keohane's *Neorealism and Its Critics* (1986) and David Baldwin's (1993) volume on the 'neo-neo debate' include prominent contributions to the debate between contemporary neoliberals and neorealists. Concerning realism and the English School, Robert Jackson (2000) emphasizes the crucial differences between classical realism and English School pluralists, thereby contributing to inter-tradition debates.

In addition to inter-tradition debates, there have been a number of important intra-tradition debates. Kenneth Waltz's article, 'Realist Thought and Neorealist Theory' (1990), represents poetics on theory and, at the same time, contributes to an intra-realism debate (cf. the key notions in the title of the article: 'realist thought' and 'neorealist theory'). Basically, Waltz criticizes his classical realist colleagues for not developing proper theory. Rather, he suggests that they had certain ideas (thoughts) about international affairs but were incapable of doing genuine theoretical work. Similarly, we have previously seen how Robert Keohane (1989) does not subscribe to all liberal currents of thought. On the contrary, he deliberately bids farewell to two important strands of liberal theory. The argument demonstrates that at least some contemporary liberal theorists are eager to disassociate themselves from other currents within the liberal tradition. They are keenly aware of criticism directed at these currents and have therefore reformulated their position. Alexander Wendt's (1992a) launch of constructivism was essentially a criticism, from a liberal perspective, of the strong liberal position. It was not that he was unhappy with strong liberalism as such; rather, he was dissatisfied with the self-defeating research strategies applied by strong liberals and proposed instead the shaping of liberal theory by providing it with constructivist underpinnings. Nicholas Wheeler (2000), who represents a solidarist position within the English School, criticizes English School pluralism and, thus, contributes to an intra-English School debate. Karl Kaiser (1969) was among the liberal scholars who introduced the transnational perspective. In this fashion, he launched a perspective within the liberal tradition which was novel at the time. At the same time, Pierre Hassner (1968a, 1968b) published two significant studies, emphasizing the crucial relationship between civil societies, states and international relations. The timing of this publication was no coincidence, as '1968' demonstrated that the international system of states could be influenced by social movements.

In summary, inter- and intra-tradition debates are the lifeblood or dynamic dimension of a thriving discipline. They are the surf shaping the here and now situation and represent the trajectories of the traditions, currents and research agendas of tomorrow. The intra-tradition debates will be introduced in each individual tradition chapter (Chapters 2 through 7), whereas inter-tradition debates will be further explored in a cross-cutting chapter (Chapter 8).

To deal with the range of issues identified above, this book uses a standard framework for discussing each tradition component set out in the checklist in Table 1.2. There is a principle at work in the distinctions between the different layers of theoretical orientation. The book focuses on the structure of international thought, including how traditions, currents, theories and theorists link, intertwine and overlap. While traditions and currents represent the long-term perspective – and to a considerable degree also inertia and dogma – theoretical debates represent contending perspectives and the dynamic part of the discipline (though they can also degenerate into never-

Table 1.2   The structure of traditions

Introduction
Genealogy (intellectual roots, historical development, most recent phases)
Currents of thought
Kinds of theory cultivated
Main variants of theory
Main intra-tradition debates
Contemporary research agenda
Conclusion

ending stories and eristic dialogues). The focus on the structure of international thought will be balanced by a second focal point: the theorizing actors, that is, the theorists.

Centric and de-centric perspectives

Despite the claims to some kind of universalism prevalent in many contemporary introductions to International Relations and IR theory, most, in reality, have quite distinctive national characteristics. Students in the US will almost all learn about the subject from a range of more or less American texts, while other widely used English-language texts like *The Globalization of World Politics* (Baylis and Smith 2003) have a distinctively 'British' flavour. In Germany, Siegfried Schieder and Manuela Spindler's *Theorie der Internationalen Beziehungen* has been a great success in introducing contemporary theories of international relations. In Spain, Celestino del Arenal's *Introducción a las relaciones internacionales* has long been used. In the Czech Republic, Petr Drulák's *Teorie mezinárodních vztahů* (2003) aims at introducing the importance of IR theories in a largely theory-free zone in the heart of Europe.

In an attempt to be truly international, the following chapters in this book aspire to represent a 'de-centric' perspective. In this manner, they aim at addressing concerns that have been expressed in different ways, for example, *ex negativo* in titles such as 'International Relations: Still an American Social Science?' (Kahler 1993; Crawford and Jarvis 2001), or 'The Sociology of a Not So International Discipline: American and European Developments in International Relations' (Wæver 1998). Takashi Inoguchi and Paul Bacon's subtitle 'Towards a More International Discipline' (2001) represents the aspiration of the text (see also Friedrichs 2004; Schmidt 1998, 2002, 2006; Thies 2002; Holden 2006; Jørgensen 2000, 2003/4); from this follows that a truly novel textbook is bound to be more than a mere copy of copies of previous introductions. Therefore, it will not tell all the same conventional 'stories' as many other books on the market ('once upon a time, it all began in Aberystwyth, Wales ...'). Instead, it is based on contemporary research on the discipline and will introduce historical traditions as well as contemporary debates on, for example, the merits, outcome and very existence of the so-called 'great debates' (cf. Smith 1995; Schmidt and Long 2005; Kratochwil 2006).

Why all the fuss about centric and de-centric perspectives? There are at least three good reasons. The first is connected to the topic 'international relations'. Many point out a predominant Euro-centric way of thinking about IR. European power politics, vintage 19th century, basically functions as the default mode of the 'international', and deviant cases are usually neglected or treated as no more than deviant outlayers. In response to this poverty in conceptualizing the international, some explore non-Western perspectives on international relations (Puchala 1997; Aydinli and Mathews 2000, Tickner and Wæver 2009). In doing so, they go beyond the concepts many tend to consider as key and therefore taken for granted. Similarly, Amitav Acharya and Barry Buzan (2005) ask, 'Why is There No Non-Western International Relations Theory?' It is a fact that theoretical debates differ significantly in the sense that the configuration of theoretical orientations differs across regions and continents. Consequently, the fault lines of theoretical debates also differ. Xinning Song (2001) argues that some academics in China are prone to develop International Relations with Chinese characteristics, and Takashi Inoguchi and Paul Bacon (2001) emphasize that Japanese IR includes five traditions, most of which are home-grown. In this context of diversity, the general challenge is to find a prudent balance between reproducing 19th-century images and essentially giving up the entire well-known conceptual repertoire. In some intriguing way, there seems to be a parallel between the dynamics of international society and IR theory, both of which originate in Europe but have been globally extended. This extension has been profound in some places, whereas the extension has been thin and fragile elsewhere.

Second, perspectives on international relations – as presented to students – are sometimes fairly narrow. Many Western teachers teach students about the subject matter in a manner characterized by a range of biases. Andrew Hurrell (2004; see also Nossall 2001) describes how American syllabi in International Relations tend to put students in the cockpit of statecraft and view the world from within the Washington Beltway, that is, the epicentre of American power. Presumably in order to encourage students to think about international relations and perhaps to point out the relevance of such thinking, teachers sometimes ask, 'How should *we* handle crisis x?' or 'Why do *they* hate *us*?'. Obviously, this tendency is far from being an exclusively American feature. On the contrary, the tendency to cultivate ethno-centric perspectives is truly universal. However, understanding international relations should also be a question of reflecting on events and processes as they may appear in the eyes of others.

Third, there is a problem of biased coverage in the literature. A few illustrative examples will suffice. Ian Manners (2003) has observed how a state-of-the-art article on foreign policy analysis consists of 97 per cent articles written in the US and 3 per cent articles written elsewhere. Though foreign policy analysts based in the US are undoubtedly very important and numerous, there might be a selection bias at play in the article. European foreign policy analysts tend to display a different bias in the sense of hardly seeing anything in the world but European foreign policy. Likewise, a considerable proportion of European IR scholars stay strictly focused on Europe and see nothing but the European sub-system of international relations.

Theorists and 'do it yourself' theory

Theoretical traditions, currents of thought and specific individual theories can be presented in three markedly different fashions. In the first place, they can be presented as a kind of pre-given complex structure of ideas – something developed in the past by someone, somewhere. The outcome is a huge ideational structure, and it is ready for consumption, whether in terms of comprehension, application, celebration or critique. Thus, we tend to say, for example, 'Here we have the theory of hegemonic stability' and 'This is the democratic peace theory'. Newcomers to the field therefore have a mountain to climb, ridges of theoretical traditions and currents to pass and concrete theories to consider and possibly apply. Fortunately, students love to box traditions, currents and theorists, and they are not the only ones struggling with this temptation. For many there is nothing like a neat order, probably because such order provides peace and harmony in their minds. Unfortunately, this tendency leads to simplification rather than nuance. True believers are emphasized rather than renegades, and watertight distinctions are upheld rather than messy overlaps. It is somewhat paradoxical that there is a pronounced agency-orientation in many IR theories and a strong structure-orientation in the teaching of IR theory. This paradox leads to the next issue: the theory builders.

Second, theories can be presented as the creation of one or more individuals and as accomplished in a specific context of time and space; presumably – according to Cox's theorem – created *for* some purpose and perhaps *for* someone (Cox 1981). Disciplines such as Sociology, Philosophy and Political Theory (among others) are not afraid of theorists. Numerous volumes on specific individual theorists have been produced, and contending interpretations are put forward in ever-changing configurations. In the field of IR theory, things are altogether different. IR theory is a field of study in which we seem to be afraid of theorists; at least, we tend to display benign negligence towards personal endeavours at understanding international relations theoretically. Perhaps the individual theorist is a taboo? If so, a few examples of taboo breakers exist, including Iver B. Neumann and Ole Wæver's *Masters in the Making* (1997), Martin Griffith's *Fifty Key Figures in International Relations* (1999) and Timothy Dunne's *Inventing International Society* (1998). Schieder and Spindler (2003) also include reflections on individual theorists, although their book is generally organized according to traditions. The autobiography is a different means to avoid the collective taboo, but autobiographies are rare (see Kruzel and Rosenau 1989; Morgenthau 1984; Frei 2001; Haslam 1999). Once again, however, these examples offer exceptions to the general rule. This is bad news for students and the discipline alike. Bad news for students, because – compared to abstract systems of thought – it is relatively easier to comprehend the reasoning of individuals. It is bad news for the discipline, because the tendency downplays the creative role of individual theorizing. In order to counter this tendency, the role of individual theorists will be emphasized throughout the book.

Third, an important issue concerns whether students ought to be encouraged and taught how to build theory. Is DIY theorizing desirable? On the one hand, it is not difficult to come across professors and students alike who find the very idea of encouraging students to theorize an irresponsible – perhaps even dangerous – invitation to trouble. In this context, it is relevant to keep in mind that most scholars do not theorize. The predominant maxim appears to be that theories exist, should be understood and – on occasion – even applied. Theorizing should thus be left to the few mature talented senior professors who have unique skills for such intellectual endeavours, particularly because it is too serious or difficult a task to be entrusted to anybody else. Some even claim that not all people have the skills required to carry out proper theorizing. Conversely, James Rosenau and Mary Durfee point out that it does not necessarily take extraordinary skills, 'but rather a set of predispositions, a cluster of habits, a way of thinking, a mental lifestyle' (1995: 178). Most readers of this book presumably qualify in terms of one or more of these qualities, but would nonetheless refrain from engaging in thinking theory thoroughly, in part because they have never been trained in such intellectual endeavours. However, experimental teaching has found that students are generally quite capable of thinking theoretically (Shinko 2006).

Finally, even if not all *prima volta* student theorists manage to produce an advanced theory, those engaged in the process will arguably have a significantly better grasp of existing theories and the nature of theory once they have tested their DIY capabilities. Moreover, invitations to theorize force would-be theorists to carefully consider the linkages between substantive international relations issues and theory. For these reasons, the book cultivates the principle that students ought to be invited to actively theorize. Try out your skills as a theory builder rather than exclusively remaining a theory consumer. The present textbook therefore invites its readers to DIY theorizing, and outlines the virtues, potentials and problems of DIY theorizing, as well as presenting a guide to the art of creative theorizing (see Chapter 9).

What is the field of international relations?

If International Relations is a discipline and international relations the subject matter, that is the phenomenon we observe and analyze, then we should briefly address the relationship between the two. When the discipline of International Relations was less well established, this question assumed a crucially important function. It was part of the secession movement that 'liberated' the discipline from more historically mature disciplines, such as Sociology, Economics, History, Philosophy or Law. In order to create a compelling rationale for the emerging discipline, the students of international relations sought to identify the specifics of *international* politics and the *international* system. Once such specifics were identified, a more or less elaborate rationale could be established. Some point to the international system being separate from national political systems. Others focus on politics among states. Still others highlight relations between states not being covered by other disciplines. In this context, one should not forget that in many parts of the world, this disciplinary liberation struggle continues, while in others it has hardly been launched. The development of the discipline is therefore very uneven, and this book will necessarily reflect this unevenness. In any case, the question has to do with the *raison d'être* of the discipline, including the question of whether IR is a discipline or a sub-field of political science (or Law or Sociology), the distinctiveness of IR and its boundaries (to other fields), as well as the boundaries between different spheres of social action, for example, politics, economics ideology or sustainable development.

What, then, is the conception cultivated in this book? At this point, it is tempting to paraphrase the Belgian painter Paul Magritte by declaring that this book is not about international relations. Rather, it is a book about *theories* of international relations. Hence, there is no great need to define international relations as such. What really matters throughout the book is how various theorists theorize international relations differently and, thus, define the 'international' and the relations characterizing this sphere of social practice. Some theorists define IR quite narrowly as simply relations between the units – states – in the international system. Other theorists are more inclusive in terms of both actors and relations and focus on interstate, inter-society and state–society relations. Still other theorists include inter-region relations (e.g. European Union–ASEAN relations), relations between states and international organizations (e.g. relations between China or Mexico and the United Nations) or economic relations (e.g. patterns of Japanese foreign direct investment in different parts of the world). In short, though there is only one world, the actors, structures, processes and relations theorized are or can be very different. Our understanding of this rich variation in theorizing is a basic precondition for understanding the nature, function and scope of different theories. Furthermore, theorists make assumptions and claims about this world and thus contribute to constitute a 'world of our making' (Onuf 1989). This is an important and necessary aspect, because by constructing the world in a certain fashion, theories are subsequently able to guide and help us in our analytical endeavours.

Finally, international relations mean different things in different parts of the world and different things at different times. For the Taiwanese government, security, trade and international recognition are among the prime concerns when developing foreign policy. For the European Union, international relations have traditionally excluded brute military force, and conceptions of a civilian, normative or multilateral foreign policy profile have been widespread. For China, international relations have connoted colonial incursions, intervention and restored sovereignty during the 20th century. A fourth example is international relations in 19th-century Europe, characterized by multipolarity and conventional power politics (Kissinger 1957). In other words, the nature of international relations is historically contingent. In this context, try to think through, for instance, the difference between the international system with and without international organizations.

Conclusion

The chapter introduces some of the issues, dilemmas and challenges that are associated with a basic understanding of international relations. Such features and considerations are hardly new. Indeed, the question of how to teach international relations has been on the agenda throughout most of the 20th-century history of the discipline of International Relations (Zimmern 1939). The associated analytical challenges can be usefully divided into four sets of issues. One set of issues concerns the subject matter and its characteristics. What are the nature and specifics of international relations, and how has the discipline, International Relations, evolved during the 20th century and entered the 21st century? A second set of issues concerns the nature of theory, theoretical traditions and currents of thought, as well as the feasibility and desirability of active, creative theorizing. A third set of issues concerns meta-theory, that is, the framework of analytical commitments by means of which it is possible to reflect on existing theories or create new theories. Hence, key aspects of meta-theory were briefly introduced, including ontology, epistemology, the agent–structure problem and the levels-of-analysis problem. In addition, various criteria for determining what constitute good theory were outlined. Finally, due to the fact that students will intuitively think normatively about international issues, normative concerns trigger a profound interest in international affairs. In order to avoid rather uninteresting subjective 'barefoot' normative reasoning, however, an argument was made in favour of the inclusion of an introduction to contemporary international political theory, including reflections on the triangular relationship between political theory, international political theory and IR theory.

In the next six chapters, we examine in more detail how each of the six theoretical traditions have developed during the 20th century and into the 21st century; how they provide broad perspectives on world politics, have generated a range of specific theories and how the traditions have been shaped or formed by different underlying commitments to the production of knowledge. The chapters also examine debates among theorists within each individual tradition and outline their contemporary research agenda.

Questions

- How do different theoretical traditions define the field of international relations?
- What can theory do for us when we are attempting to understand international relations? Which different conceptions have been emphasized?
- What is meta-theory? How can meta-theory help us to better understand the nature of IR theory? Which key meta-theoretical aspects have been highlighted?
- What is the nature of theoretical traditions? Which traditions have been selected for the present volume?
- How would you characterize intellectual currents of thought, for example, in relation to traditions and concrete theories?
- How are form and content related? How do kinds of theory differ?
- What is the function of concrete theories? How are traditions and currents capable of producing ever-more concrete theories?
- Concerning theoretical debates, how would you characterize intra- and inter-tradition debates, respectively?
- What are centric and de-centric perspectives? Which consequences follow from the adoption of a de-centric perspective?
- Is DIY theorizing desirable or feasible? Would you rather prefer to leave the task of theory building to theorists?

Further reading

Aron, R. (1967) 'What is a Theory of International Relations?', *Journal of International Affairs*, 21, 185–206.
> In this seminal article, Aron makes the argument that a theory of international relations is basically not possible.

Brown, C. (1992) *International Relations Theory. New Normative Approaches* (New York: Columbia University Press).
> In Chapter 1 Brown makes an excellent argument in favour of a broad conception of theory, focusing on explanatory, normative and interpretive theory.

Giddens, A. (1984) *The Constitution of Society. Outline of the Theory of Structuration* (Cambridge: Polity).
> In this book, Giddens outlines a possible solution to the agent–structure problem, a solution that is called structuration theory.

Hollis, M. and Smith, S. (1990) *Explaining and Understanding International Relations* (London: Clarendon).
> This is a comprehensive and useful introduction to the use of meta-theory on International Relations theory.

Jørgensen, K. E. (2000) 'Continental IR Theory: The Best Kept Secret', *European Journal of International Relations*, 6, 1: 9–42.

Jørgensen, K. E. (2003/4) 'Towards a Six Continents Social Science: International Relations', *Journal of International Relations and Development*, 6, 4: 330–43.
> These two articles discuss de-centric perspectives on international relations.

Schmidt, B. C. (1998) *The Political Discourse of Anarchy. A Disciplinary History of International Relations* (New York: State University of New York Press).
> Probably the best book-length analysis of the historiography of the discipline International Relations, including reflections on the issue of theoretical traditions.

Searle, J. (1995) *The Construction of Social Reality* (New York: Free Press).
> This is an eminent and clear-cut introduction to the branch of philosophy that deals with social ontological issues.

Singer, D. J. (1961) 'The Levels-of-Analysis Problem in International Relations', *World Politics*, XIV, 1: 77–92.
> This article introduced the levels-of-analysis problem to international relations.

Smith, S. (1995) 'The Self-Images of a Discipline: A Genealogy of International Relations Theory', in K. Booth and S. Smith (eds), *International Relations Theory Today* (Pennsylvania: Pennsylvania State University Press): 1–37.
> This book chapter is an excellent and highly critical examination of ten popular self-images of the International Relations discipline.

Wallace, W. (1996) 'Truth and Power, Monks and Technocrats: Theory and Practice in International Relations', *Review of International Studies*, 22, 3: 301–21.
> This article examines the relationship between theory and practice and presents a fierce criticism of theoretical excesses and exegeses.

Waltz, K. (1990) 'Realist Thought and Neorealist Theory', *Journal of International Affairs*, 44, 1: 21–37.
> Based on a specific philosophy of science, Waltz points out why an international relations theory is possible, how classical realists failed to develop one and how neorealism represents an example of genuine theory.

Wendt, A. (1987) 'The Agent–structure Problem in International Relations Theory', *International Organization*, 41: 335–70.
> This article examines the agent–structure problem; Alexander Wendt points out how the problem can be applied in the field of international relations.

Wendt, A. (1991) 'Bridging the Theory/Meta-theory Gap in International Relations', *Review of International Studies*, 17: 383–92.
    This article discusses meta-theoretical issues and their relevance for international relations.

Website for further information

www.theory-talks.org

Chapter 2

The International Political Theory Tradition

The idea that the role of theory is to settle questions once and for all – to reach conclusions – is fundamentally mistaken, the product of a misreading of the nature of science and a misapplication of this misreading to the social sciences.   (Chris Brown 1992: 239)

International political theory (IPT) is an increasingly important member of the family of IR theoretical traditions. Thus, most thinkers in the classical political theory canon – Machiavelli, Hobbes, Kant, Grotius, Marx etc. – reflected on international affairs in more or less elaborate ways. Significantly, a prominent group of contemporary political theorists do the same, though often in a much more structured fashion. Importantly, compared to theorists in other IR theoretical traditions, these political theorists theorize about international affairs in different ways, using different keys to approach the topic and often ask questions that other theorists neglect. The avenues of enquiry are also different, as are some of the objectives, as Chris Brown argues in his usual concise fashion in the above passage. Essentially, political theory is a key part of political science, dealing with the structure of political arguments and justification for political action or preferences. At the centre of attention, we find issues concerning 'just', 'good', 'valid' or 'right' political ideas. Furthermore, as we will see in this chapter, political theorists examine the role of rights, responsibilities, duties and obligations. Whereas political theory usually examines these issues at the national level, international political theory goes beyond the national level, exploring their role at international or global levels.

It should be highlighted that the tradition is peculiar in being both a tradition in its own right and a set of systematic reflections on the normative or ethical dimensions that are present in *other* theoretical traditions (Chapters 3 through 7). In general, it has been increasingly acknowledged that by disconnecting IR theory and political theory – from the 1950s and several decades on – the discipline has been on a detour and it is time to reconnect IR theory with political theory and philosophy. The aim of the present chapter is to contribute to this endeavour by introducing the domain of IR theory that has the nature and form of political theory.

This said, it is no easy task to define or characterize the international political theory tradition. One way to approach the distinct characteristics of international political theory is to briefly consider six leading theorists and what they have to offer in terms of explicating the term and characterizing their field of study. Before embarking on this short explorative expedition, it is worthwhile to keep in mind that not all theorists use the same terms, even when they have fairly similar phenomena in mind. Some thus prefer to speak about normative theory; others prefer the notion of constitutive or ethical theory; and others make a plea for employing the term international political theory.

Among the leading contemporary international political theorists, Chris Brown offers one of the most succinct and straightforward definitions:

> By normative international relations theory is meant that body of work which addresses the moral dimension of international relations and the wider questions of meaning and interpretation generated by the discipline. At its most basic it addresses the ethical nature of the relations between communities/states, whether in the context of the old agenda, which focuses on violence and war, or the new(er) agenda, which mixes the traditional concerns with the modern demand for international distributive justice. (Brown 1992: 3)

Hence, Brown suggests that we will find the characteristics of the tradition within a triangle consisting of i) moral/ethical dimensions, ii) meaning and interpretation vis-à-vis violence and war, as well as iii) international distributive justice. In a later publication, he leaves the explicit reference to normative concerns behind and suggests that we talk of simply international political theory (Brown 2002b), even if this, in substantive terms, does not make much of a difference. As the chapter title above indicates, Brown's recommendation has been followed in this book.

Terry Nardin is rather cautious or slightly defensive in his characterization of political theory:

> The political theorist, as a theorist, stands apart from political activity and seeks to understand it in other terms, examining its arguments, defining its concepts, uncovering its assumptions and placing it in a wider context to bring its character, presuppositions and implications more clearly into view. (Nardin 2006: 465)

In contrast to many political theorists, Nardin is thus keen to emphasize that political theory can and should be carried out in a strictly analytical fashion. It does not necessarily imply a direct political engagement. In his view, it is the object of theory that is political, not the theorist or the theory. This is not a commonly held view, as many political theorists find it difficult to operate with a watertight distinction between political and scholarly practice.

R. B. J. Walker (1987, 1993) was among the first to consistently and systematically examine IR theory as political theory. If the distinction between the separation of political theory and IR theory became the norm in major parts of social and political science – focusing on national communities and international relations, respectively – Walker attacks the usefulness of the distinction head-on. He is deeply sceptical about the very feasibility of the project of cultivating modern IR theory in its own right, suggesting as an alternative that IR theory should be interpreted as political theory. In order to accomplish this endeavour, Walker employs post-structuralist deconstruction techniques, thus contributing not only to international political theory but also to the post-positivist tradition (see Chapter 7), indeed thereby demonstrating that the two traditions sometimes overlap in terms of both concerns and approach. Walker specifies his approach in the following way:

> In all of these readings of key debates, conceptual options and methodological injunctions, my concern is to destabilise seemingly opposed categories by showing how they are at once mutually constitutive and yet always in the process of dissolving into each other. (Walker 1993: 25)

The keyword in this quote is 'destabilize', particularly because Walker's endeavour is to destabilize concepts that often tend to be reified, albeit in different ways, in IR theory and in political theory.

In *International Political Theory* (1999), Kimberly Hutchings combines the criticism of mainstream, non-IPT approaches and an outline of alternatives. She criticizes mainstream IR theory for systematically downplaying ethical issues and then proposes an understanding of international political theory that combines normative issues and international ethics in the practice of world politics with the theorist's own ethical judgement. Moreover, she attempts to avoid conceptual antagonisms that – though widely employed – often produce endless or fruitless debates. More specifically, she draws on both Hegel and Foucault, in particular on their 'insights into the impossibility of disentangling ethics from politics and into the nature, scope, and limitations of normative judgment' (1999: xi). Ethics should therefore be considered an essential part of politics, implying that suggestions about a distinctly ethical foreign policy amount to nonsense. She believes we can usefully draw on the philosophies of Hegel and Foucault to gain insights about ethics.

Klaus-Gerd Giesen (1992) outlines the long and rich tradition of thinking international ethics theoretically, thus contributing to the cultivation of the IPT tradition in the French-speaking world (see also Bonanate 1995). Like many other international political theorists, Giesen claims that all IR theory contains an implicit or explicit ethical dimension. Mervyn Frost (1986, 1996) covers an intellectual landscape that is rather similar to Giesen's, but Frost has a slightly different take on IPT. In *Ethics in International Relations* (1996), Frost has a double agenda; in the first place, he has an interest in understanding why normative issues and normative theory have been consistently downplayed in the discipline. Second, he outlines the contours of a Hegel-informed normative theory, designed to be applicable in studies of specific normative issues.

Combined, these theorists make a strong argument in favour of abandoning the strict separation between political theory and IR theory. They argue that the key terms that are used in the study of international relations belong to the conceptual repertoire of political theory and, furthermore, that political theorists have a long tradition in specialized debate on the different and changing meanings of these terms. In this context, think of terms such as 'sovereignty', 'justice', 'duty', 'just war', 'ethics', 'responsibility' and 'obligations'. Concerning 'sovereignty', as early as the 16th century, political philosophers were making a career out of thinking about the – at the time – novel phenomenon that since has been known under that name. Regarding the notion of 'just war', doctrines of just war are as old as war itself, and the conceptions of just war range from crusades to contemporary practices of jihad and pre-emptive war. Likewise, many theorists have examined the relationship between power and ethics, and the notions of duty and obligation provide headings for extensive specialized literatures. In short, contemporary IPT examines contemporary variations of the meaning of these terms, explaining changing meanings and interpretations across time.

Genealogy

All theorists stand on the shoulders of those who came before them, often revisiting or evoking past traditions initiated or cultivated by classical political theorists. These traditions represent the intellectual roots or origins of contemporary theorizing. Martin Wight (1991) outlines three traditions of international thought as represented by Thomas Hobbes, Hugo Grotius and Immanuel Kant, respectively. Luigi Bonanate (1995) considers the deontological tradition, that is, the tradition of thought that focuses not on the rights but on the *duties* of states in international society. Michael J. Smith (1986) reviews the realist tradition in the 20th century, while Michael C. Williams (2005) reassesses the key features of realism, specifically the contributions made by Hobbes, Rousseau and Morgenthau. Besides invoking such traditions of thought, most major IR theorists have also engaged in interpreting or (re-)appraising classical political theorists. Illustrative examples include Kenneth Waltz (1967) interpreting the international thought of Jean-Jacques Rousseau, Michael Doyle (1983a, 1983b) analyzing Immanuel Kant and Hedley Bull (1969) examining Hugo Grotius. In turn, such studies have often been criticized for being misreadings of the political philosophers. As such charges are immanent to political theory, it is very important that research strategies for interpretation are explicitly specified, yet without becoming an independent end in itself.

Despite the numerous invocations of tradition and plentiful (re-) appraisals of individual political theorists, however, there has been a tacit division of labour for a long time: generally political theorists do not cover international affairs and IR theorists do not 'do' political theory. For revolutionary behavioural sciences theorists, this was actually a most explicit understanding. They did not want to have anything to do with political theory and essentially wanted to get rid of it. Martin Wight (1969) is also explicit as regards the distinction between political and international theory and claims provocatively, tongue in cheek like, that there can essentially be no international (political) theory. However, the inside–outside divide is much more pervasive than these explicit reflections suggest. When theorizing politics, many political theorists somehow automatically or instinctively stop at the border of national societies and avoid inclusion of the international dimensions in their political theory. This is so embedded in the tradition that many theorists do not even see or know about the problem. In an almost perfect reflection of this no-go area, many IR theorists are so happy to have identified a specific realm called 'the international' that they do not acknowledge the relevance of political theory. This said, most IR theorists accept that their theories have some kind of intellectual roots in political theory or philosophy before the 20th century, but at some point, somehow, somewhere and for some reason, a metamorphosis happened, making IR theory distinct from political theory.

This separation has not always characterized IR theory. In order to demonstrate this claim, a distinction between three phases of development neatly represents the genealogy of the IPT tradition:

- The early years
- The 40 years' detour
- The contemporary renaissance

During the early years, specialization between modes of theorizing was not very pronounced, and enquiries into international affairs were less stylized. Studies of international affairs frequently combined historical analysis, legal approaches, philosophical enquiry and normative concerns. Basically, this feature characterized reflections on international affairs during the first half of the 20th century.

All this changed during the second phase, that is, the 1950s and 1960s, not least in the United States, where interpretive and normative theory was pushed to the margins of the evolving discipline, and explanatory theory became the reigning norm in the social and political sciences. Donald Puchala (2003) has vividly described how department after department in the United States was conquered and subsequently shaped in the image of the scientific revolution. Significantly, this trend not only characterized the field of international relations. Political theory *per se* was exorcised from social and political science as well (Ball 1995). In the meantime, in the British Empire, the English School was founded, cultivating the traditional or classical version of International Relations, including, significantly in the present context, a dimension of political theory. In general, Great Britain did not follow American trends (Smith 1985), as demonstrated by the fact that instead of a political *science* association, there is a political *studies* association. Notable exceptions to the lack of interest in the new science of politics include Michael Nicholson and John Burton, the latter noting with approval that '[t]he study of International Relations is now moving out of the philosophical phase of the fifties into a period of consolidation. Terminology and clarity of concepts, tested against actual conditions, are the preoccupation of the sixties' (Burton 1968: xi; see also Nicholson 1996). In other parts of Europe and in the rest of the world, developments were quite similar to the British situation, characterized by a high degree of diversity in social scientific styles rather than a homogeneous monopolized unity. Though some scholars were inspired by the developments in the US, the major part remained for better or worse largely unimpressed and unaffected.

Whether or not the understanding and approval of cutting political theory and philosophy out of IR has been explicit or implicit, it has been increasingly questioned during the third phase – the last two decades. Whether intended or unintended, the negative consequences of dumping political theory have been increasingly acknowledged. Thus, according to Derek Drinkwater, '[t]wentieth-century international theory suffered by being cut adrift from the tradition of political theory' (Drinkwater 2005: 54). Based on a similar opinion, Steve Smith (1992) wrote a remarkable essay with the indicative title, 'The Forty Years' Detour: The Resurgence of Normative Theory in International Relations'. He argues that international relations theory suffers from a neglect of normative issues and that the behavioural revolution unfortunately has been successful in pushing political theory and philosophy out of mainstream theorizing. Furthermore, Chris Brown, describing normative theory as 'background theories', claims that the project of creating an international relations theory detached from political theory has been an outright failure:

> Mainstream international relations has tried to exist without the aid of these background theories. It is the thesis of this book that this

approach is mistaken, and that as a 'free-standing' academic discipline international relations has not proved able to provide an adequate account of how things hang together. (Brown 1992: 77)

Finally, Andrew Hurrell (2004) notes with disapproval that students are rarely introduced to the analytical and argumentative techniques required to conduct proper scholarly debates on normative issues. The unfortunate consequence is that such issues are often handled in a 'barefoot' manner, which hardly contributes to valuable knowledge or insight concerning international relations.

The publication and reception of John Rawls' seminal *A Theory of Justice* (1971) served as an early indication of the fact that political theory is back in business. The book is widely heralded as probably being the most important 20th-century political theory publication in the English-speaking world. The branch of political theory that cultivates the study of international issues is also back in business, to some extent directly triggered by *A Theory of Justice* (cf. Beitz 1979). The rise of this new IPT research community is perhaps not impressive in terms of numbers, but it has proved to be large enough to constitute a critical mass. The contours of a theoretical tradition have emerged on the horizon, characterized by most of the characteristics of an intellectual tradition. The emerging research community engages in reconstructing the IPT tradition, including reflections attempting to span the classical canon of political theorists and contemporary issues. Leading exponents of the tradition have imported important strands of thought – for example, cosmopolitanism, liberalism and communitarianism – from political theory, and they have considered their relevance and usefulness for our understanding of international relations. Furthermore, they engage in enquiries of contemporary issues in world politics, ranging from just war doctrines and humanitarian intervention to international order and justice.

Currents of thought

The seemingly straightforward task of introducing the main currents of thought within the IPT tradition in fact poses quite a challenge. This is partly because of IPT's complex dual identity as both a tradition in its own right and a field of study that focuses on the implicit or explicit normative dimensions of other theoretical traditions. But it also stems from the location of IPT at the intersection of political theory and international relations theory. Rather than glossing over the problem it is perhaps best to start by sketching four different views of IPT as it appears from four possible points of departure.

Figure 2.1   *Timeline: some key works in international political theory*

1515	Niccolò Machiavelli, *The Prince*
1625	Hugo Grotius, *On the Law of War and Peace*, three books
1660	Thomas Hobbes, *Leviathan*
1795	Immanuel Kant, *Perpetual Peace: A Philosophical Sketch*
1971	John Rawls, *A Theory of Justice*
1977	Michael Walzer, *Just and Unjust Wars: A Moral Argument with Historical Illustrations*
1983	Michael Doyle, 'Kant, Liberal Legacies and Foreign Affairs'
1983	Terry Nardin, *Law, Morality and the Relations of States*
1993	R. B. J. Walker, *Inside/Outside: International Relations as Political Theory*
1996	Mervyn Frost, *Ethics in International Relations*
1998	David Boucher, *Political Theories of International Relations*
1999	Nicholas Rengger, *International Relations, Political Theory and the Problem of Order: Beyond International Relations Theory?*
2002	Chris Brown, *Sovereignty, Rights and Justice*
2002	Chris Brown, Terry Nardin and Nicholas Rennger (eds), *International Relations in Political Thought*
2003	David Held, *Cosmopolitanism. A Defence*
2007	Furio Cerrutti, *Global Challenges for Leviathan: A Political Philosophy of Nuclear Weapons and Global Warming*

The first option is to take political theory as our starting point; then it is the currents of thought, configurations of debate and intellectual dynamics of this (sub-)discipline (for an overview, see Gaus and Kukanthas 2004; Heywood 2004) that provide the guidelines and structure our understandings. From this standpoint, for instance, cosmopolitan and communitarian currents of thought will figure prominently up-front, and configurations of political theory debates will shape scholarship within the IPT tradition. The IPT theorist will point out that cosmopolitanism includes a number of bedfellows – that appear rather strange in the eyes of the archetype IR theorist – for example, Kant, Marx and Bentham (and other utilitarians).

Nonetheless, Kant, Marx and others share basic cosmopolitan features. Similarly, the IPT theorist will highlight that communitarian theory also includes fairly different varieties, for example, Herder, Hegel, Mill and various nationalists (cf. Brown 1992: 23–81). Subsequently, it becomes possible to ask how these diverse yet internally coherent political theory currents of thought fit strands of IR theorizing, that is, which examples of cosmopolitan IR theory we can point to. A sample would include at least some liberal, some English School and some post-positivist theorists. In a similar fashion, Martin Griffiths (1992) explores what happens when the concepts 'realism' and 'idealism' – as understood within philosophy – are applied to IR theorists, such as Hans Morgenthau, Kenneth Waltz and Hedley Bull. What happens is that we realize that seemingly different IR theorists actually share some fundamental underpinnings, a fact that we remain unaware of exactly because political theory categories have rarely been systematically employed in International Relations scholarship. However, they are clearly applicable and more applications would greatly improve our understanding of the nature of existing and forthcoming IR theories. In summary, political theory as such has for centuries been characterized by its own intellectual dynamics. If we take these foundations and milestones as our starting point, they will inevitably inform IPT in ways that are difficult to achieve otherwise.

The second option is to begin with existing IR theory and then proceed to add a crucially important aspect, namely a consistent focus on the normative dimensions of IR theory. In this fashion, IPT is simply an analytical dimension that spans the IR theoretical traditions, implying in turn that IPT is far from being a small niche production at the margins of the discipline but rather a key dimension of theorizing international relations. Hence, it is possible to identify the political theories that are embedded in IR theoretical traditions, for example, liberalism, realism, the English School, international political economy and the post-positivist tradition (see Chapters 3 through 7). Some theorists acknowledge that the normative or ethical dimension plays a role in their theories and try to determine more precisely which role it plays. For instance, Yale Ferguson and Edward Mansbach (1988) have moved in this direction, but Nicholas Rengger (1990) basically argues that they do not go far enough. In other words, Rengger believes that Ferguson and Mansbach have erred both in terms of their diagnosis and the cure they recommend. Rengger argues that small 'add on' changes are insufficient if we want to fully understand the profound implications political theory perspectives have.

The third option has been the one chosen by a considerable segment of the IR community, namely neglecting political theory altogether or pushing it towards some remote corner, reserved for those with an interest in ethics and other, to self-acclaimed serious genuine IR theorists, marginal issues. The reasons for neglecting (international) political theory vary significantly. Some claim that only theory-informed empirical analysis counts as 'proper' or 'normal' science. They often have quantitative research in mind or disregard the empirical nature of a political theory-informed analysis of, for example, the UN principle 'Responsibility to Protect'. Others are consistently annoyed by the issues addressed by political theorists. Instead of asking so-called real questions about real issues, such as the balance of power in the contemporary international order, so the argument goes, political theorists ask, 'What is Machiavelli's conception of power?', or 'What is a balance?', or 'How have different theorists conceived of these notions at different times, not least in bygone worlds?' Within this perspective, currents of thought concern foremost different approaches to ethics, for example, ethics of responsibility and ethics of exclusion. No matter which reasons for neglecting or downplaying the importance or relevance of political theory to IR, the outcome is that IPT plays a marginal role as a grouping of scholars cultivating normative analysis.

The fourth option is to regard IPT as a freestanding tradition, that is, as neither IR nor political theory. In this case, theorists emphasize the specific and distinct questions that are raised and the issues that are addressed. Furthermore, the specialized debate and communication networks within IPT are highlighted. Finally, the connections of contemporary IPT to older traditions of IPT are underlined (see e.g. Brown, Nardin and Rengger 2002). In this fashion, a tradition with a clear *raison d'être* of its own has been created or is emerging. Not many theorists have explicitly opted for this solution but rather preferred to regard IPT as a hybrid tradition along the lines of the three options outlined above. Nonetheless, it happens that theorists, in the course of their analytical practice, conduct studies in a fashion suggesting that they implicitly regard IPT as a freestanding tradition. IPT conceived of as a freestanding tradition has not yet crystallized clearly identifiable currents of thought.

Kinds of theory

IPT is characterized by the employment of a range of different kinds of theorizing, just like any other theoretical tradition. As we saw in Chapter 1, we talk about 'kinds of theory' when we address issues of theoretical form. Some claim that the general aim behind the revival of IPT 'has been to theorize in the old way about new problems, for example international distributive justice or the morality of nuclear deterrence' (Brown 1992: 195). However, things seem slightly more complicated than that. Different commitments to social enquiry – for instance game theory, social constructivism, rational choice, behaviouralism and (post-)positivism – shape substantive theories differently and not always in 'the old way'. In the following, we will briefly examine four illustrative examples of what happens to IPT theories when they are shaped by different commitments to social enquiry.

First, game theory and political theory are not as mutually exclusive as intuitive thinking might suggest. When the latter is shaped by the former, 'ought' issues are typically translated into issues of 'choice'. When we suggest something that 'ought to be done', we often implicitly acknowledge a range of options and argue why we – given available alternatives – should choose one particular option. In any case, the outcome of the combination is called formal political theory or political game theory (Oudeshook 1995; McCarty and Meirowitz 2007). When it comes to analyzing international affairs, the combination of game theory and political theory is perhaps not particularly widespread. However, direct lines of thinking can be established between, for instance, Immanuel Kant's democratic peace argument and contemporary game theory-informed studies of war and peace (de Mesquita 2006). What has been described so far regarding game theory also applies to combinations of rational choice theory and political theory. That is, while some studies do exist, for instance, Brian Barry's *Theories of Justice* (1989), it is not a widely trodden path. Despite the examples of both game theory and rational choice-informed political theory, many IPT theorists do not accept any family resemblance between on the one hand game theory and rational choice theory and on the other hand IPT. On the contrary, they remain highly sceptical regarding the fruitfulness of such an endeavour.

Second, post-positivist commitments often imply interpretive analysis. In this context, it is important that IPT in many cases is no more and no less than conceptual analysis. Theorists choose one among many candidate concepts and explore, for example, the shifting meanings of sovereignty across time and space, the differences between community, international community and world community, or they analyze the extent to which it makes sense to regard the European Union as an international normative power. Beyond concepts and their often contested meanings, interpretive theory suggests several avenues for IPT. Where do we start? By asking relevant questions! What did Kant really say, and to what degree does Kant have something to tell (us) concerning contemporary issues of world politics? Does it make sense to translate Kant's seemingly peaceful 'republics' into 'democratic' states? Likewise, some refer to the Grotian tradition and/or Grotian theorists (Bull 1969; Haggard and Simmons 1987). For starters, what do such references imply? Who was Hugo Grotius, and why do some theorists find this 17th-century international lawyer of interest today? There is an abundance of such questions about political philosophers who seemingly have something to say in contemporary debates. In order to find out what they have to say, post-positivist commitments to interpretive strategies form IPT theories in ways that depend on the specific strategies in question.

Third, while game theory and political theory are compatible, the same does not apply to positivism/behaviouralism and political theory. As mentioned above, behaviouralists and positivists aimed at extinguishing (international) political theory, arguing it is not proper social science. Hence, this example of a distinct commitment to social enquiry does not result in any form at all. By contrast, it demonstrates that it is no coincidence that IPT has developed in parallel to the post-positivist tradition (see Chapter 7).

Fourth, the notion of normative theory refers to at least three different approaches to ethics. Andrew Hurrell has made a most helpful distinction between these three different approaches to normative enquiry:

> One can approach the subject of norms and ethics in IR from three distinct perspectives: the first considers the role that normative ideas play in the practice of politics ('How have ideas about what should be done influenced political behaviour?'); the second seeks to engage in rational moral debate as to the nature of ethical conduct ('What ought we to do?'); and the third examines the extent to which moral behaviour is heavily constrained by the dynamics of political life ('Given the realities of political life, what can be done?'). (Hurrell 2002: 137)

As the citation makes clear, some enquiries are normative in the sense that they examine norms. This can be done in a somewhat detached manner, that is, without being prescriptive. Other enquiries are normative in a different way. In that case, normative theory refers to theorists who not only theorize but also make normative pleas. They ask, for instance, what ought to be done? Some variants of international political theory are explicitly normative in this sense, which renders them distinctly different from most other traditions.

Finally, when considering kinds of theory, we have so far addressed issues of theoretical form. However, we should also pay some attention to issues of appearance (or style) and substance. The presentation of an argument is occasionally a question of style rather than an issue of substance. Let us briefly consider three examples of the role style can play. In the first place, pay attention to how Brown characterizes one of philosopher Richard Rorty's main publications: 'Rorty's major work, *Philosophy and the Mirror of Nature*, employs the rhetorical style of analytical philosophy to launch an all-out assault on "correspondence" theories of truth and the idea that a neutral framework of enquiry can be constructed' (1992: 207). The example demonstrates how the rhetorical style can be analytical philosophy while the substantive issue concerns correspondence theories of truth. In the second example, Craig N. Murphy and Douglas R. Nelson, observe that the journal *International Organization* has a 'rhetorical, if not substantive, attachment to the language of science. Thus, the language of theory, data and testing are widely deployed throughout the journal, even in the context of work that is essentially discursive' (Murphy and Nelson 2001: 404). In this fashion, the example demonstrates a relative separateness of style and substance. The third example is provided by Hedley Bull outlining his dramatic response to the behaviourists in the following way:

> The correct strategy, it appeared to me, was to sit at their feet, to study their position until one could state their own arguments better than they could and then – when they were least suspecting – to turn on them and slaughter them in an academic Massacre of Glencoe. (Bull 1991: xi)

In this way, Bull emphasizes the importance of knowing one's opponents and the value of perfect timing but he also emphasizes the importance of mastering certain styles of enquiry.

Main variants of theory

Before proceeding to the main variants of theory, it is helpful to consider three crucially important issues. The first issue concerns the relationship between currents of thought and concrete, specific theories. Commenting on the status of cosmopolitanism and communitarianism, Chris Brown emphasizes that each current 'is complex and contains within itself more than one theory of politics' (1992: 75). He continues by saying:

> What we are dealing with here are two frameworks within which theories can be sited rather than two theories as such. Or, perhaps, communitarianism and cosmopolitanism can best be seen as background theories which provide the assumptions upon which those theories which attempt to give a direct account of how the world works are based. (1992: 75)

Brown's argument supports the claim that it makes sense to draw a distinction between these two layers of theorizing. Conflating the two layers would be grossly misleading.

Second, within IPT the notion of theory is often fairly vague and unspecified. Terry Nardin, for instance, uses 'theory' interchangeably with 'discourse' and 'debate'. Within the context of discussing the possibility of building a general theory of international justice, he points out that:

> There is a discourse of justice in war ('just war theory') and a discourse of justice in relation to economic inequalities ... Each debate has gener-

ated a literature with its own characteristic questions and answers and its own conceptual vocabulary for expressing them. (Nardin 2006: 454)

Similarly, Chris Brown notably claims that 'international relations theory is not something separate from, running in tandem with, political theory: it *is* political theory, seen from a particular angle or through a particular filter' (1992: 8). However, he does not specify the characteristics of 'theory' in political theory in great detail. Instead, he refers to 'Grand theory' (10), 'the theory of nationalism' (71), the 'international theory of intervention and non-intervention' (114) and 'background theories' (cf. above).

Third, considering the stuff that political theory is made of – concepts such as justice, power, community, rules, norms, principles, obligations etc. – it is hardly surprising that conclusive answers are relatively rare in IPT and that most exceptions to the rule suffer from a considerable problem of trustworthiness. The stuff that goes into the making of political theory, that is, literally all concepts such as those just mentioned (and presumably with no exceptions) belong to the category Walter B. Gallie (1955) called 'essentially contested concepts', also labelled *The Terms of Political Discourse* by William Connolly (1984). While the point is that some concepts trigger different and contending meanings, the question is whether this produces problems for IPT. Brown tends to reject the problem, claiming that contested concepts first and foremost represent contested political values (1992: 234–5). Having thus sorted out a number of uncertainties as regards the employment of the term 'theory', we can proceed to a small sample of three theories meant to specify how (part of) the world hangs together and how it works. The just war theory holds a particularly strong position, and we will therefore visit this theory first.

Just war theory

Within just war theory, theorists attempt to maintain a prudent course in the difficult waters between pacifism and bellicism. Some cultivate the doctrine or principles of 'just war', arguing, for example, that by all means states should avoid war, but they should adhere to just war principles in the event that war cannot be avoided. In other words, war is not regarded as merely an exchange of 'naked' power but instead as a social institution embodying numerous rules, norms and principles. Within this strand of thought, we do not search for the causes of war but explore reasons or justifications for action; concretely the launch and conduct of war. Basically, just war theory deals with the justification of how and why wars are fought. Such justifications are necessarily concerned with the ethics of war. As most major international lawyers – Grotius, Pufendorf, Vattel and others – have written on just war, the theory has a very lengthy history. In the 20th century, political philosopher Michael Walzer's *Just and Unjust Wars* (1977) is among the most important studies. Theorists from the IPT tradition share their interest in just war theory with strong liberals, the English School and classical realists. For Hedley Bull (1977), of the English School, war is regarded as one of the fundamental institutions in international society, a means to secure or re-establish international order.

Theory of international justice

Terry Nardin (2006) points out that there is currently no theory of international justice but that such a theory could possibly be developed, and he outlines the process through which such a theory could be developed. In the short version, his reasoning is as follows. In John Rawl's theory of justice, the part on distributive justice was intended to be applicable only *within* states. Several critics were disappointed by the limitations and not satisfied with this solution, so they attempted to transfer a number of theoretical features from the domestic to the international sphere. In turn, this move causes considerable problems, not least because reflections on international justice have primarily concerned military issues, such as the just war tradition (see above), and not international distributive justice. Nardin's aim is to bridge these two discourses. In order to do so, he characterizes the two discourses along three parameters: their longevity, internal agreement and logical coherence. He finds that for a very long time, literally millennia, scholars have reflected on the issue of just war, whereas reflections on distributive justice constitute a much more recent phenomenon. Furthermore, he demonstrates that internal agreement is much stronger in the just war theory tradition than in the discourse on distributive justice. Finally, he points out that the two discourses have different foundations, for example, concerning the types and meanings of justice which can be both conduct- and possession-related. Despite these crucial differences, Nardin nevertheless wants to explore the option of bridging the two literatures and engages in lengthy reflection on humanitarian intervention and the duty to protect. The latter is especially important because, as Nardin explains, 'I have been exploring the hypothesis that at the centre of a unified and coherent theory of international justice is the idea of the duty to protect, a duty that is itself grounded in the Kantian principle of respect' (Nardin 2006: 464). This brings us back to the basic aim of Nardin's theorizing: 'The thought motivating the exploration of that hypothesis is that linking principles of international distributive justice to the idea of morally permissible coercion might bring focus, coherence and stability to the discussion of international distributive justice' (Nardin 2006: 464). Nardin's argument is clearly related to theories of general duty, obligation and responsibility (Bonanate 1995). Nardin's article is excellent, because it succinctly illustrates the value of international political theory, makes comments about the process of theorizing explicit, and contributes to the ongoing debate on international justice.

Theories of community

Theories of community are important in the context of international political theory because communities often are defined by their boundaries. The rights and duties of citizens as well as the very status as citizen have traditionally been granted to members of specific communities, implying that people just across the boundary may enjoy different conditions. The rights of national minorities have often become an international issue, not least when the minority in question belongs to an ethnic community enjoying a majority position in a neighbouring state. In such situations domestic and international issues become closely intertwined and normative concerns regarding justice, power and representation may become a source of vicious politics.

Among specific theories of community, Benedict Anderson (1991) has created a theory of nations as 'imagined communities', claiming that the community that bonds people together as a nation is imagined rather than foundational. In other words, nations are social constructions, invented at some historical point of time by means of social and political action. Most of Anderson's theory concerns political and cultural processes within the boundaries of nations. However, it takes little imagination to realize the significant consequences such a view has concerning the politics among nations, or international politics. Once again, we have an example of highly important inside–outside dynamics. The ramifications such dynamics have for theorizing can be considerable, whether we engage in political theory, international political theory or international relations theory.

Main intra-tradition debates

Given the dual nature of IPT – being both part of and exogenous to other traditions – it is somewhat misleading to make a clear and watertight distinction between intra- and inter-tradition debates. This said, it is indisputable that the following five debates have been crucially important for the development of IPT.

First, IPT theorists have engaged in debates with both international relations theorists and philosophers. Concerning the former grouping, IPT has, though revitalized, presumably a long way to go to persuade mainstream IR theorists regarding the necessity and qualitative features of IPT. Several international political theorists clearly feel a need to engage with 'naked' mainstream IR theorists, arguing in favour of IPT rather than just *doing* IPT (Beitz 1979; Frost 1996; Hutchings 1999). One can only speculate as to whether this feature will mainly characterize the relaunch phase of IPT and subsequently disappear with the future consolidation of IPT. There will presumably always be debates about the pros and cons of different ways of theorizing international relations. In any case, the relationship has been asymmetrical in the sense that IPT is the revisionist force that wants to change the current state of affairs, whereas IR theorists generally do not acknowledge the need to engage with IPT. As the relationship between the two camps will become less asymmetrical, it is likely that the debate will intensify between those who do IPT and those who do not. Concerning the latter grouping, that is, the philosophers, IPT will experience an equally uphill battle, because analytical philosophy – 'devoted to ever more detailed investigation of the meaning of words and sentences' (Brown 1992: 8) – has been cultivated at the expense of other forms of philosophy. Chris Brown (1992: 84–95) also explains that, within moral philosophy, meta-ethics has been playing centre court for decades while normative and applied theory has been playing on the less prominent courts.

Because international political theorists regard IR theory as political theory, they share a huge chunk of interest with political theorists, yet they also have a well-developed understanding of the limited or bounded perspectives that political theorists often have. Chris Brown provides an illustrative example, characterizing Charles Beitz's project:

> Beitz, having established that normative international relations theory is necessary and possible, proceeds by interrogating the subject matter of international relations from a political theory perspective, somewhat in the manner of an explorer conducting a well-equipped expedition to an unknown continent. (Brown 1992: 118)

Yet another illustrative example is David Held (1995), exploring the relationship between globalization and democracy. He clearly masters his theories of democracy, whereas his understanding of international relations is more limited. Held mainly focuses on formal institutional arrangements, for example, the UN Charter, and comes to conclusions regarding the dynamics of international relations on the basis of that focus. It would be tempting to interpret Held's position as being close to the utopian version of liberalism that E. H. Carr criticized as early as the late 1930s and which has since been abandoned by many contemporary liberal theorists (see Chapter 3).

Second, one of the major debates in political theory has been the liberal–communitarian debate. According to Andrew Heywood (2004), the communitarian side of the debate only established itself during the last decades of the 20th century. It was during this genesis that communitarians were bound to get involved in a major debate with liberal theorists. This is a debate characterized by many facets which should not distract us here. However, the key contested features concern the rights, duties and responsibilities of individuals, the role of society and the meaning of social institutions. Within political theory, the debate has been characterized by such key concerns, specific fault lines of theoretical debate and, generally, by its own dynamics. If we add 'international' to political theory, new themes and patterns of debate emerge. Theorists now discuss the rights of individuals – human rights – in international community vis-à-vis the specific rights of citizens within state boundaries. Furthermore, theorists discuss the rights versus the duties and responsibilities of states in international society. Finally, theorists discuss the value of value pluralism versus the common values of international society.

A third debate concerns the applicability of political theory categories. Conventional categories and classifications produce a rich yet predictable field of study. Within international relations, realism, liberalism and pluralism are examples of well-known categories. Some international political theorists make use of alternative categories and classifications and then explore the consequences. Hence, Chris Brown (1992) makes a plea for introducing the categories 'cosmopolitanism' and 'communitarianism' and subsequently explores the consequences. This approach enables an analysis of the trajectories of the discipline during the 20th century, including a strong case in favour of Brown's main thesis, namely that the discipline has been on the wrong track for decades and that the (re-)introduction of IPT will help get the discipline back on track. Similarly, Klaus-Gerd Giesen (2006) introduces the three categories encyclopaedism, historicism and positivism in order to better understand the intellectual currents within International Relations in the French-speaking part of the world. However, nothing suggests that these theoretical categories cannot also be employed in studies of intellectual traditions in other parts of the world. The two illustrative examples suggest that other well-developed classifications from political theory are capable of performing similar eye-opening services.

A fourth debate concerns international justice (Brown 1992: 155–92; Nardin 2006). As Nardin explains, theorists have primarily theorized international justice within the just war tradition. The question of how they have addressed the issue need not occupy us in the present context. What are more important here are the indications that there is an important debate on the likelihood or desirability of changes in the international justice tradition. Nardin (2006: 453) points out that, 'along with other debates about international affairs, the justice debate is shifting (for better or worse) from the society of states to a global society whose members are human beings, not states'. He characterizes the positions in the debate in the following manner:

Cosmopolitan theorists make the plea that a theory of international justice, must begin with the rights and duties of individuals, not only as citizens or as members of various religious, ethnic and other groups or associations, but also simply as persons. For internationalists as well as realists, global justice is a myth because it postulates that the unitary global society does not exist except as an ideal. (Nardin 2006: 453)

Hence, cosmopolitans aim at a theory of global justice, not merely a state-centric notion of international justice, whereas other theorists claim this endeavour would be a waste of time and highly misleading. Nicholas Rengger contributes to the debate with his claim that the just war tradition is characterized by increasingly serious problems. While acknowledging these problems, he concludes nevertheless that:

The just war tradition is a tradition of thought precisely because it has considered many different ways of understanding the relations between war and politics. Some have become dominant in the tradition, as it has developed, to be sure. But that leaves others to be recaptured if we so choose. And perhaps for this reason, above all, and notwithstanding all its problems, it seems to me that it would be a mistake to abandon the just war tradition. (Rengger 2006: 363)

Finally, there is a debate on interpretive strategies. In this context, Terence Ball (1995) emphasizes that interpretation is unavoidable. He continues by outlining some of the avenues of interpretation that are available. Such avenues are typically contested, because different theorists have different ideas about interpretation. Some are understandably keen to know what a given author really meant or what the author intended to say. Should the author be dead – which is often the case – we obviously do not have the option of asking. Hence, we are forced to make use of various techniques that can help us. Others prioritize the context in which concepts have been coined and intentions stated. In a sense, this issue is the agent–structure problem applied to political theory.

Research agenda

Since its revival, the international political theory tradition, characterized by its well-developed sense of conceptualization and theory building, has managed to produce a rich research agenda. First, realizing the relatively recent reappraisal of the tradition and the rather limited research community with an interest in IPT, international political theorists have engaged in consolidating and extending the ground seized. This priority is hardly surprising, and the agenda is broad enough to keep the representatives of the tradition occupied. Bridges to past traditions must be built, the consequences of adopting unconventional classifications must be explored, and the misleading interpretations of theorists or theories must be corrected. Terence Ball (1995) is a leading political theorist who has carried out excellent work on political meta-theory, addressing issues such as proper approaches to the inevitable task of interpretation, including appropriate or prudent balances between author intent, contextual factors and reader reception. Each option has its subscribers and its pros and cons. Hence, the introduction of international political theory allows us to tap into some of the key debates about how to work with or possibly build political theory. This important theme will be revisited in Chapter 9. Finally, old forms of theorizing need to be applied to new issues, and new forms of theorizing can possibly be developed. All these different consolidating activities make by necessity the tradition fairly incoherent and an archipelago of specialists. The following paragraphs outline five key concepts and how they have structured the research agenda.

Key concepts of political discourse are characterized by their ability to create entire research agendas and, thus, specialized literatures. One of the roles of political theory is to make sense of such concepts and keep track of their different and changing meanings. Box 2.1 shows how 'international' and 'world/global' can be added to key terms of national political discourse. The following paragraphs demonstrate how research agendas are founded on such concepts.

Concerning the two first concepts, we can take our point of departure in German sociologist Ferdinand Tönnies' distinction between society and community, arguing that society is the product of political architecture or engineering, whereas communities are the outcome of unplanned, 'organic' developments. In any case, whereas society is the object of an endless number of sociological theories, international society is the subject matter of an entire theoretical tradition, namely the international society tradition, also called the English School (cf. Chapter 5). The English School is distinct in its conception of international society and has explored this society more than any competing tradition. By contrast, it is hardly possible to refer to the scattered literature on world society as a tradition. Research on world society is simply too incoherent and diverse to deserve such a label. Something similar can be said about research addressing the international and world community. Such research comprises Andrew Linklater's (1998) analysis of the transformation of political community, Chris Brown's (1992) devastating criticism of the idea of world community, and various communitarians with an interest in the international dimension of community.

The study of politics comes in three versions, depending on the boundaries of political activity and the kind of actors who play key roles. Realist theorists were among the first to focus on the specific sphere of international

Box 2.1   National, state-centric and global key terms

National notions	State-centric notions	Global notions
Society	International society	World society
Community	International community	World community
Politics	International politics	World politics
Justice	International justice	Global justice
Order	International order	World order

politics, conceived of as politics among nations (i.e. states). Theorists who are less state-centric in their work often prefer to talk about world politics or global politics.

The pair of concepts – order and justice – has been the object of intense interest. Hedley Bull's seminal work, *The Anarchical Society* (1977), is first and foremost a study of international order, whereas English School solidarists tend to focus on and prioritize issues of justice (see Chapter 5). Most IPT theorists have included reflections on justice in their studies (for overviews, see Brown 1992; Nardin 2006; Rengger 2006). Nardin points out that the literature on just war is significantly more developed than the international distributive justice literature, though also that the latter is working to catch up. The five concepts have been chosen for their illustrative qualities. They are excellent for the objective of outlining the issues addressed by international political theorists, the questions they try to answer and the main ways of practising international political theory.

Finally, within the traditions of political theory and international political theory we find a more symmetrical balance between studies of theorists and of their theories. Hence, it is considered necessary to closely examine both author intent, context and text reception. In contrast, IR theorists are typically perceived as messenger boys or neutral catalysts who somehow manage to produce theories without any personal characteristics or qualities.

Conclusion

The employment of different notions of theory matters. Thus, the broad notion of theory introduced in Chapter 1 has cleared the path for the inclusion of the IPT tradition. Paradoxically, IPT is both the oldest and youngest tradition in the six-pack of traditions introduced in the present book. It is the oldest tradition in the sense that political theorists have always reflected on international affairs. Did Thucydides not analyze the Peloponnesian War? The classical canon of political theory is therefore an essential part of any serious or mature IPT, a fact that frequent references to Thucydides, Machiavelli, Hobbes, Grotius, Rousseau, Kant and Hegel demonstrate time and time again. IPT is the youngest tradition in the sense that IR theory and political theory have been strictly separated during most of the 20th century but are now in a process of being bridged. Contemporary IPT is an attempt to reactivate not a bygone tradition but a tradition that, for various reasons, has prematurely been declared dead.

The chapter has demonstrated that IPT has become a fairly well-established tradition, characterized by several main currents of thought. Given the relatively limited membership of this research community, this achievement is rather remarkable. The IPT theorists have nonetheless been able to demonstrate that IR theory has generally been on a long and winding detour and that a rapprochement between political theory and IR theory is a most fruitful endeavour; indeed that IR theory *is* political theory. The main currents of thought relate to older intellectual currents, a fact indicating that it truly makes sense to talk about a tradition. The tradition is characterized by a range of different kinds of theory, and the portfolio of concrete theories is considerable.

The chapter has also demonstrated that, in a certain sense, IPT can be seen as a branch of theorizing that is quite difficult to master. It takes considerable time and intellectual energy to enter and comprehend this special world of theorizing. It is conducted in its own keys and has its own mythologies, story-lines, main figures and structures of argument. In the widest sense of IPT, it spans political theory from Plato to Pogge, from Kant to Doyle and from Hegel to Frost. For newcomers to the field of study, this collection constitutes a somewhat deterring body of thought. When cultivated successfully, however, IPT contributes razor-sharp distinctions, crystal-clear arguments and eloquent jumps between abstract, general and theoretical reasoning to concrete, specific and practical application. These qualities are often most clearly highlighted when theorists engage in debates on substantive issues, such as international distributive justice.

Questions

- Is IPT a tradition in its own right or a normative dimension of IR theoretical traditions?
- Which currents of thought does IPT comprise?
- Which specific theories can be put under the roof of IPT?

- How does the classical canon of political theory play a role in contemporary IPT?
- Why do many IR theorists believe that IPT is of marginal importance for our endeavour to understand international relations?
- What are the main issues on the IPT research agenda? Please summarize the section on research agenda.
- What is a misreading? Which factors cause misreadings? Can they be avoided?

Further reading

Brown, C. (2002b) *Sovereignty, Rights and Justice: International Political Theory Today* (Oxford: Polity).
  A comprehensive introduction to contemporary international political theory.

Brown, C., Nardin, T. and Rengger, N. (eds) (2002) *International Relations in Political Thought: Texts from the Ancient Greeks to the First World War* (Cambridge: Cambridge University Press).
  An important introduction to older traditions of combining political thought and international affairs.

Buchanan, A. (2004) *Justice, Legitimacy and Self Determination: Moral Foundations for International Law* (Oxford: Oxford University Press).
  An eminent analysis of linkages between morality and law.

Caney, S. (2005) *Justice Beyond Borders: A Global Political Theory* (Oxford: Oxford University Press).
  A contemporary review of the feasibility of justice in international relations.

Frost, M. (1996) *Ethics in International Relations* (Cambridge: Cambridge University Press).
  One of Mervyn Frost's major works, making a plea for a new research agenda on the ethical dimension of politics.

Hurrell, A. (2002) 'Norms and Ethics in International Relations', in W. Carlsnaes, T. Risse and B. A. Simmons (eds), *Handbook of International Relations* (London: Sage).
  A concise review of literature on norms and ethics.

Hutchings, K. (1999) *International Political Theory. Rethinking Ethics in a Global Era* (London: Sage).
  A novel interpretation of political theory and normative dimensions of international relations.

Nardin, T. (1983) *Law, Morality and the Relations of States* (Princeton, NJ: Princeton University Press).
  A classic within international political theory.

Rengger, N. J. (1999) *International Relations, Political Theory and the Problem of Order: Beyond International Relations Theory?* (London: Routledge).
   Issues of order addressed by a leading contemporary political theorist.

Walker, R. B. J. (1993) *Inside/Outside: International Relations as Political Theory* (Cambridge: Cambridge University Press).
   An essential and pathbreaking study of IR as political theory.

Walzer, M. (1977) *Just and Unjust Wars: A Moral Argument with Historical Illustrations* (New York: Basic Books).
   A thorough analysis of just and unjust wars by a leading communitarian theorist.

Website for further information

www.international-political-theory.net/
   A major website addressing political theory issues.

Chapter 3

The Liberal International Theory Tradition

Liberal international theory contains a highly sophisticated – and by and large, accurate – description of the state of contemporary international relations. (Donald Puchala 2003: 211)

Liberalism is a many-headed creature. Stated differently, it is a multidimensional tradition dating back to the 17th and 18th centuries. To begin with, liberalism is a prominent political ideology and has also been heralded as perhaps the most important perspective within Western political philosophy. Thus, the liberal tradition is closely connected to the Enlightenment in Europe, and some simply identify liberalism with Western civilization. Furthermore, liberalism is often associated with strong commitments to individual liberties; at other times liberalism is presented as a doctrine cherishing free markets and pleading for minimizing political (state) intervention in the sphere of economics. Historically, the liberal tradition emerged as a critique of feudal political rule and the dominant foreign economic strategy at the time: so-called mercantilism (see Chapter 6). Finally, liberalism is a rich tradition of thought concerning international relations. The present chapter focuses on this latter dimension which, according to Donald Puchala (cf. above), essentially got it right and, according to critics, somehow got it wrong.

In general, the liberal tradition of international thought can be identified by means of five main characteristics. I begin this chapter by briefly outlining these five characteristics. First, liberal theorists have strong faith in human reason. The power of reason liberates humans from a life under the yoke of a foundational human nature and the restraints of revealed truth, whether ancient or theological. By the use of reason, we can understand and shape nature and society without depending on the assistance of a higher being. According to liberal theorists, human beings are capable of shaping their destiny, including shaping international relations and moulding the negative ramifications of the absence of a world government. Liberals lean towards assumptions of rationality and believe that humans are rational actors. This characteristic can be traced back to the political philosopher John Locke (1632–1704).

Second, theorists within the tradition believe in the possibility of historical *progress* or, stated differently, they believe that it is both possible and desirable to *reform* international relations. At the same time, they are keen to emphasize that 'being possible' obviously does not imply that it necessarily will be easy. When encountering the distinction between cyclical and linear perspectives on historical development, liberals firmly cultivate linear and sometimes unidirectional conceptions of history. They do so because human reason and processes of social learning render progress possible. Accordingly, we are not doomed to live in a state of perpetual conflict.

Third, liberal theorists focus on state–society linkages and claim the existence of a close connection between on the one hand domestic institutions and politics and on the other hand international politics. These two spheres of political and social action do not exist separately and should not be analyzed separately. Ever since German philosopher Immanuel Kant (1724–1804) published *The Perpetual Peace* (1795), many liberal theorists have been convinced that there is a causal link between domestic regime form and the probability of war. Specifically, Kant claimed that 'republican' (i.e. democratic) states are more peaceful, at least vis-à-vis one another. In a contemporary context, this idea is the intellectual origin of the so-called republican strand of liberal thought and the theory of democratic peace.

Fourth, some liberal theorists claim that increasing economic interdependence among states reduces the likelihood of conflict and war. During feudal times, conventional wisdom regarded mercantilist goals and war as perfectly compatible. In contrast, liberals argue that free trade is preferable to mercantilism, because trade produces wealth without war. In this context, David Ricardo (1772–1823) and his theory of comparative advantages of trade played an important role. Richard Cobden (1804–1865) went further, arguing that trade and economic interdependence would reduce the occurrence of military conflict between states. During the 20th century, the claimed causal impact of interdependence has played a key role in numerous liberal studies and formed the basis of an entire current of thinking: interdependence liberalism. This is also where the liberal tradition and international political economy partly overlap (see Chapter 6).

Fifth, liberal theorists can be identified by their arguments about the positive effect of processes of institutionalizing international relations. Institutionalization can be accomplished by different means. Some emphasize the positive impact of an ever-denser network of international organizations and point to the significant growth in international organization since the first international governmental organization – the International Telegraph Union – was founded in 1865. After World War I, the creation of the League of Nations was put on the international political agenda, because many analysts and policy-makers believed that a global international organization could prevent war better than the alternatives, including traditional balance of power politics. Others emphasize the importance of international agreements (regimes) or 'negotiated orders' (Young 1983). Still others point to the option of legalizing international politics. International law can be regarded as the oldest international institution regulating relations among states. In general, liberals believe that anarchy can be moulded. Hence, it makes sense to think in terms of a spectrum ranging from raw to mature anarchy. The German expression '*Weltinnenpolitik*' (world politics assuming domestic politics characteristics) captures the liberal enterprise perfectly.

In the context of international relations, these five characteristics constitute a formidable rupture with the past and more traditional conceptions of means and ends in world politics. In addition, the liberal approach creates a window of opportunity in terms of rendering political action possible and potentially worthwhile. Human reason counters fatalism and makes progress possible. Domestic institutions can be reformed and democratized and, in turn, contribute to an expansion of the international zones of peace. The conditions of interdependence reduce temptations to engage in foreign adventures, particularly because such adventures are likely to harm the adventurous state. The process of international institutionalization can be actively cultivated by means of opting for multilateral foreign policy strategies. Finally, because human beings are capable of understanding and influencing their environment, it makes sense to teach international relations. By means of better understanding world politics, students enhance their capacity to influence the world of their making. Combined we have a powerful package of theoretical and practical reasoning. How this package has evolved over time is the topic of the next section, focusing on liberalism's genealogy.

Genealogy

Liberalism plays a unique role in the history of International Relations. In the early 20th century, liberal-minded thinkers introduced some of the early liberal key arguments, for instance, that war does not benefit anybody and should therefore be avoided (Norman Angell) or they coined key concepts, such as international anarchy (G. L. Dickinson). Furthermore, part of the liberal project was the establishment of an academic discipline addressing international relations, specifically in order to improve our understanding of such relations and, in turn, to improve or reform the relations. In short, the discipline International Relations was originally *conceived of* and *founded by* liberal thinkers and therefore unsurprisingly created in the image of key liberal ideas. However, the 20th century was not kind to liberalism, marked as it was by the shadow of three systemic wars: World War I and World War II (1914–1918 and 1939–1945) and some 45 years of

Cold War, beginning in the late 1940s. Liberal thinkers were prominent at the time in diagnosing a number of prime causes of World War I (fatal misperceptions among political elites, secret diplomacy and lack of democracy, war-prone military establishments, lack of international institutions) and designing a political programme to address these issues in the inter-war years. In doing so, they put a significant mark on the dominant foreign policies of the day. Within a few years, the world had witnessed the creation of the League of Nations (the first global international governmental organization [IGO] for the promotion of international peace and co-operation), also one of the first major instances of liberal institutionalism in practice. Second, new constitutive rules were introduced implying, for instance, that international treaties would no longer be considered part of international law if they were concluded secretly, in other words, they should be made public. Third, several specialized institutes and university chairs were created, specifically designed for research and teaching related to international affairs. During the 1920s, such institutes were established in Berlin, Hamburg, London, New York and Toronto. At the same time, university chairs designated to teaching international relations were established in Aberystwyth and Geneva. The value of knowledge was clearly cherished: if we understand international affairs better, we will be better able to avoid war. Fourth, traditional national security institutions were complemented by a collective security system under the auspices of the League of Nations. Early 20th-century liberalism regarded *collective security* as the correct substitute for old-fashioned balance of power politics, claiming that historical experience had demonstrated that balance of power politics is a very difficult statecraft to conduct prudently; it often fails, in turn causing war.

If successful in terms of influencing policy-making, however, the liberal programme failed fatally in terms of reaching stated objectives, that is, avoiding conflict and war. The seemingly bright future of post-World War I soon turned into what has been referred to as the 20 years' crisis (Carr 1939) and subsequently World War II. The emergence of communism, fascism and Nazism on the European continent and beyond proved to be very hard soil for liberal ideas and strategies to grow in. The collective security system fatally failed, just like most other features introduced as ingredients in the liberal recipe for cooperation and peace. These failures led to World War II and, subsequently, to experiments with more advanced forms of international institutions, including the United Nations and the European Community. Several decades after the war, liberals were still shaken by real-world developments and their theory-turned-practice failures during the first half of the century. Nevertheless, even in this shadow of failure they managed to build new theories and achieve a significant share in the research agenda of International Relations.

An early indication of the liberal come-back is provided by David Mitrany, writing one of the most remarkable books emerging from within the liberal tradition in London during World War II: *A Working Peace System* (1943). This book is important for several reasons. In the present context, one should note that liberalism has a distinct notion of politics. Indeed, according to one of its critics, 'liberals have shown a strong desire to get politics out of politics' (Waltz 2000: 8). Waltz claims that only international politics is genuine politics. By contrast, a liberal critic of neorealism, Friedrich Kratochwil, claims that neorealism is the science of *Realpolitik without politics* (cf. Kratochwil 1993). The idea is that neorealism is so 'clinical' in its calculations that politics has been left out of consideration. This 'exchange of views' demonstrates how different notions of the key term 'politics' lead to fundamentally different conceptions of international politics and sharply contrasting conclusions about its nature. In other words, the notion of politics constitutes one of the core axes on which every possible international theory hinges and Mitrany's book illustrates what happens when politics is replaced by functionalism and technocratic rule.

Probably the most extreme version of this strong desire is presented in Mitrany's book in which he proposes the transfer of the functions of politics to a High Authority, commissioned to decision-making based on functional or technical rationales. During the 1930s, Mitrany travelled widely in the United States. He was highly impressed by what he saw. He took a special interest in the Tennessee Valley Dam project, particularly the novel High Authority substituting local political entities and boundaries. Basically, he elevated the institutional design of the Tennessee Valley Authority to the global level. In other words, he makes a plea to move from *divisive* politics (i.e. international politics, conflict and war) to *integrative* non-political technical problem-solving, thereby allowing the value of peace to trump the value of democracy (in the sense of political participation). This solution leads to the third reason why this book is important as a trendsetter. Mitrany's proposed strategy has largely been the strategy followed by governments creating international organizations (cf. the term *functional* UN agencies) or the creation of a polity such as the European Union (the forerunner of the European Commission was tellingly named the 'High Authority').

After World War II and during the Cold War, liberal perspectives on world politics generally had a hard time. Nonetheless, liberals attempted to regain their previous, prominent role. Though colonial wars and the Cold War characterized the period, there were also instances of hope and progress. In the first place, liberals could find some encouragement in the reintroduction of part of the liberal political programme: the League of Nations had been replaced by the United Nations, and the United States promoted multilateral solutions to international problems, particularly in their relations with

Europe. Furthermore, the process of European integration was launched during the 1950s and promised to be one of several instances of global processes of regional integration. Liberal analysts also pointed out that the security dilemma somehow could be moulded and complemented by the creation of security communities (Deutsch 1957; Adler and Barnett 1999). During the last three decades of the 20th century, the liberal tradition was thoroughly reinvigorated and started to flourish in terms of novel theoretical reflections on transnational relations, patterns of interdependence, international institutions, logics of democratic peace, regional integration and global governance.

Just like other theoretical traditions, the liberal tradition comprises several distinct currents of thought. The following section is devoted to introducing the three major strands of thought.

Currents of liberal thought

The following presentation of liberal currents of thought emphasizes the development of three strands of thought over the course of the 20th century. Each current has developed through a number of phases, ranging from early to contemporary versions.

Interdependence liberalism

As mentioned above, the idea of interdependence dates back to the 19th century. During the 20th century, the idea continued to play a very important role in liberal thinking. Theorists believe that processes of modernization produce an increasingly modern world and that states in this modern world increasingly depend on each other. Liberal thinkers often focus on economic interdependence and consider the ever-more interwoven global markets to be a feature supporting their argument. Interdependence liberals emphasize the importance of both state actors and transnational actors. They tend to focus on non-military aspects of world politics, including global welfare politics. Increases in interdependence make states more sensitive towards each other, thereby increasing the costs of conflict, in turn making conflict less tempting or beneficial. During the first decades of the 20th century, interdependence theories were first and foremost sets of linked ideas, represented by a fairly diverse group of theorists (de Wilde 1991).

New versions of interdependence liberalism began to be formulated in the early 1970s and developed further during the 1970s and early 1980s. Keohane and Nye pioneered the new trend by thoroughly criticizing the state-centric model of international relations (cf. Keohane and Nye 1971). The authors chided the state-centric approach (traditionally conceived of as

Figure 3.1   *Timeline: some key works in the liberal tradition*

1913	Norman Angell, *The Great Illusion*
1916	Goldsworthy Lowes Dickinson, *The European Anarchy*
1936	Alfred Zimmern, *The League of Nations and the Rule of Law*
1943	David Mitrany, *A Working Peace System*
1957	Karl Deutsch *et al. Political Community and the North Atlantic Area*
1958	Ernst Haas, *The Uniting of Europe: Political, Social and Economic Forces*
1968	John W. Burton, *Systems, States, Diplomacy and Rules*
1971	Keohane and Nye, *Transnational Relations and World Politics*
1977	Keohane and Nye, *Power and Interdependence: World Politics in Transition*
1984	Robert Keohane, *After Hegemony*
1986	Michael Doyle, 'Liberalism and World Politics'
1990	Robert Axelrod, *Cooperation Under Anarchy*
1992	Francis Fukuyama, *The End of History and the Last Man*
1995	Thomas Risse-Kappen, *Bringing Transnational Relations Back In*
1998	Andrew Moravcsik, *The Choice for Europe*
1999	Alexander Wendt, *Social Theory of International Politics*

a key characteristic of e.g. realism and English School thinking) for neglecting the growing importance of transgovernmental and transnational actors in world politics since World War II. Subsequently, they published *Power and Interdependence* (1977) in which they attempted to synthesize realism and liberalism. While they recognized that realism was a useful model in situations in which states were engaged in intensive military competition, they argued that these situations were increasingly the exception rather than the norm. In order to synthesize the insights of realism and liberalism, Keohane and Nye outlined the basic assumptions and ramifications of two extreme positions: the ideal types of pure power politics and complex interdependence. Having established the endpoints on the continuum, they argued that many – if not most – bilateral relationships (e.g. France and Germany or

Japan and Russia) fall between these two extremes. They labelled the centre of the continuum the realm of 'interdependence'. Rather than attempting to refute realist or liberal theories, they wanted to 'explore the *conditions* under which each model will be most likely to produce accurate predictions and satisfactory explanations ... one model cannot explain all situations' (1977: 4, emphasis in original; see also Keohane and Nye 1987). In Europe, liberal interdependence theorists include, for example, Francois Duchêne who coined the notion of civilian power Europe, arguing that Europe should not aim at becoming a traditional military great power.

Republican liberalism

This strand of liberal thought originates in the writings of the German philosopher Immanuel Kant, especially outlined in a pamphlet entitled *Perpetual Peace* (1795/1983). In this book, Kant speculates on the nature of relations among the kind of states he calls 'republican states', hence the label 'republican liberalism'. Kant's reflections can be boiled down to three claims: i) domestic governance structures and domestic political cultures have an impact on the nature of international relations. More specifically, republican or democratic modes of governance make a strong independent variable in our search for the causes of war and conditions of peace; ii) Kant coined the term 'pacific union' in order to describe the role of individual freedoms and common moral values; iii) he coined the term 'spirit of commerce' for the idea that trade is mutually beneficial, causes interdependence which, in turn, promotes peace. This latter claim is the forerunner of the interdependence liberalism introduced above.

Ever since Kant theorized in this fashion, liberal-minded scholars have been attracted to this current of thinking, although different theorists have emphasized the three elements differently. The most recent revival of republican liberalism can be traced back to the 1980s, when a different group of scholars rediscovered Kant's thinking on international affairs (Doyle 1983a, 1983b). Republican liberalism has been able to produce theories of democratic peace that are underpinned by both rationalist and constructivist formats. After the end of the Cold War, a significant number of states became democratic, especially in East and Central Europe and in Latin America. Republican liberalists pay close attention to this historical change because it promises a marked extension of the international zones of peace.

Neoliberal institutionalism

Robert Keohane is among the leading representatives of neoliberal institutionalism. One should note that this liberal theoretical perspective belongs to the liberal tradition because some of the basic liberal assumptions remain in place. Thus, Keohane professes that 'I am a child of the Enlightenment – a chastened child, to be sure, but nevertheless a believer in the *possibility* of progress, though by no means in its inevitability' (1989: 21). The background for this theoretical perspective is that for some time in the early 1980s, Keohane flirted with game theory and formal models, though ultimately concluding that 'it was unlikely that greater formalization derived from game theory would provide a clear structure for precise and insightful investigation of world politics' (1989: 29). Instead, he created neoliberal institutionalism; a perspective on world politics, but *not* a theory as such. The perspective focuses partly on international institutions and their functions and partly on state interests. According to Keohane:

> Neoliberal institutionalism is not a single logically connected deductive theory, any more than is liberalism or neorealism; each is a school of thought that provides a perspective on world politics. Each perspective incorporates a set of distinctive questions and assumptions about the basic units and forces in world politics. Neoliberal institutionalism asks questions about the impact of institutions on state action and about the causes of institutional change; it assumes that states are key actors and examines both the material forces of world politics and the subjective self-understanding of human beings. (Keohane 1989: 2)

In this fashion, Keohane combines material and ideational dimensions of world politics, specifies differences between theoretical perspectives and specific theories – and outlines basic assumptions.

Importantly, neoliberal institutionalism is a theoretical perspective operating at the systemic level of analysis. It does not raise questions about the possible impact of a given international institution on a specific state. Rather, it has an interest in the degree to which the international system is institutionalized, including factors capable of explaining the process of institutionalization. Keohane's view on cooperation is important for understanding his theoretical perspective. In concrete terms, his version of liberalism does not depend on many of the factors characterizing other strands of liberalism:

> International cooperation does not necessarily depend on altruism, idealism, personal honor, common purposes, internalized norms, or a shared belief in a set of values embedded in a culture. At various times and places any of these features of human motivation may indeed play an important role in processes of international cooperation; but cooperation can be understood without reference to any of them. (1989: 159)

The quotation also illustrates the impact the previous debate on cooperation under anarchy has on Keohane's thinking. He has simply been persuaded by some of the critiques and acknowledged that other liberal currents are based on unnecessarily weak foundations.

Kinds of liberal theory

As mentioned in the introductory chapter, theorists make use of several different kinds of theory. In the following, we will see how different ways of mixing form and substance have produced five different versions of liberal theory. It should be added that the presentation is far from exhaustive, intended instead to illustrate how liberal perspectives have been shaped by their theoretical form.

First, like other traditions, the liberal tradition is underpinned by normative engagement. Phenomena such as democracy, development, modernization, interdependence, integration and international institutions are considered progressive threads in the social fabric of international affairs – and hold great promise for a more peaceful future. Similarly, multilateralism is viewed as an important form of international cooperation. Hence, there are good liberal reasons to suggest 'Two Cheers for Multilateralism' (Keohane and Nye 1985). However, normative underpinnings are not to be equated with normative theory, because such theory is shaped by the stylized conventions of political theory. Norman Angell is among the leading early 20th-century liberals. He cultivated normative theory rather than explanatory theory, and in this fashion pioneered normative liberal theory. Similarly, democratic peace theory has a dual nature in the sense that it is based on the normative position that democracy ought to be preferred to non-democratic forms of governance. However, most of the theory is explanatory in the sense that a causal link is established between the nature of state polity and likely behaviour.

Second, in their attempt to reclaim intellectual legitimacy and authority, leading American liberals in particular became heavily involved in the behavioural revolution and claimed scientific status for their own perspectives, accusing realism and other perspectives of traditionalism of being inferior. They fundamentally changed their discourse of theory, effectively abandoning more traditional languages of social enquiry. David Singer and Bruce Russett were among the principal figures of this movement, whereas Karl Deutsch, a leading representative of the liberal transnational strand of theorizing, was strongly influenced by cybernetics. In Europe, some liberal peace researchers joined forces with their American peers (cf. John Burton and Johan Galtung). It took theorists within the realist tradition more than a decade to respond to this liberal challenge effectively which, in effect, triggered the emergence of neorealism (see Chapter 4).

Third, in the early 1980s some theorists engaged in marrying liberal thinking and game theory. Robert Axelrod published his path-breaking study, *The Evolution of Cooperation* (1984), which inspired a new generation of scholars. In this fashion, Axelrod managed to set a significant part of the liberal research agenda for years to come. Robert Keohane's *After Hegemony: Cooperation and Discord in the International Political Economy* (1984) discusses the substantive issue of the role of hegemonic states. In the present context, however, it is significant that the approach and analysis are heavily influenced by game theory. Some years later, Keohane abandoned game theory as a promising analytical tool (cf. paragraph below). However, other liberal scholars soldiered on within the form of enquiry provided by game theory. Significantly, some theorists from other theoretical traditions also draw on game theory, thus demonstrating that game theory ought to be seen as a neutral analytical device that can be coloured by a range of substantive claims and propositions, including those belonging to the liberal tradition.

Fourth, Keohane (1989; see also Keohane, Nye and Hoffmann 1993) replaced game theory with rational institutionalism, a somewhat broader and less formal theoretical perspective. Basically, it is a version of rational choice theory designed to help us conduct research addressing international institutions. Andrew Moravcsik's liberal intergovernmentalist theoretical framework (1998) offers another example of using rationalist formats (see also section below). Major parts of contemporary scholarship are characterized by such rationalist underpinnings.

Finally, Alexander Wendt is an important example of a theorist who combines constructivist meta-theory and liberal substantive theory. During the 1990s, he systematically explored the potentials of constructivism, famously claiming that 'anarchy is what states make of it'. In his landmark study, *Social Theory of International Politics* (1999), Wendt proceeds one step further and outlines a constructivist liberal theory of international cooperation. In other words, he explores a classic liberal issue – international cooperation – yet draws systematically on the insights of constructivism. In the words of Hidemi Suganami (2001b), 'when all its theoretical décor is stripped, the architectural substance of his *Social Theory of International Politics* turns out to be a structurationist/symbolic interactionist answer to Robert Axelrod's earlier path-breaking work (1984/1990) on the evolution of cooperation'. However, Wendt is far from alone in this attempt to marry constructivism and liberal substantive theory.

Each of the five examples demonstrates how substance and form can be combined and how the outcome of such blending represents different kinds of theory.

Main variants of theories

As mentioned above, the liberal tradition is a rich tradition, especially in terms of having produced a broad range of specific, applicable theories. In this section, four such theories will be introduced: democratic peace theory, transnationalist theory, a theory of cooperation and liberal intergovernmentalism.

Democratic peace theory

The classic issues in International Relations concern war and peace. What are the causes of war and the conditions of peace? The democratic peace theory addresses this issue head-on. According to democratic peace theory, democracies do not fight wars among themselves. They possibly wage war against non-democracies, but never democracies. Immanuel Kant introduced this idea in the 18th century – though he focused on republican states – and it has proved to be a most sustainable idea. Basically, contemporary republican liberals claim that Kant was right (Doyle 1983a, 1983b, 1986). Furthermore, the proposition that domestic forms of governance *do* have effects on international relations tends to be verified empirically. Rigorous empirical studies demonstrate that democracies actually engage in war with one another extremely rarely. Though methods and research procedures can be discussed – and have been – the conclusion is nothing but significant and intriguing (Russett 1989). We may ask whether or not republican liberals have identified one of the few empirically valid general laws of the social sciences.

During a lengthy historical process, peaceful democracies have generated a zone of peace, and democratic peace theorists base their optimism on the extension of this zone of peace. Though setbacks surely occur, the zone has generally been extended significantly since the end of the Cold War. Hence, liberals share Andrew Linklater's criticism of neorealism for overlooking this: 'the foremost macropolitical trend in contemporary world politics: the expansion of the liberal zone of peace' (Linklater 1993: 29). Francis Fukuyama's *The End of History and the Last Man* (1992) has become one of the best-known works within democratic peace theory. Fukuyama argues that, since the end of the Cold War, liberalism has become the only, largely uncontested, political paradigm in world politics. Democracy is spreading throughout the world. Hence, there are reasons to be very optimistic if not downright triumphant. Fukuyama's general view is archetypal liberal: progressive, linear and directional. His timing was almost perfect in launching his triumphant book a few years after the end of the Cold War and the signature article 'The End of History' almost in parallel to the fall of the Berlin Wall. If the same book had been published a decade later, it would probably have disappeared in the reverberations of the fallen World Trade Center.

The logical follow-up argument to the democratic peace theory is that if democracies do not fight each other, then we had better promote democracy worldwide. However, the principles for doing so vary. Some democratic states believe in the power of playing role model and that, at the end of the day, the processes of state socialization will do their work and have their effect. In other words, less successful states will adapt to or copy the strategies of successful states. Other states engage in missionary-like activities; actively promoting democracy, so to speak. Strategies of persuasion are applied; promotion programmes are launched; and linkage policies are introduced. In this scenario, development aid or macroeconomic packages will be given, provided that principles of good governance are introduced. Still other states engage in crusades, directing their aggressive energies towards non-democracies. In fact, some liberals are so fond of democracy and individual freedom and rights that they are ready to promote such values by almost any means. Therefore it is not entirely unjust to talk about liberal interventionism; even the label 'B52 liberals' has been employed. In this context, it is significant that US neoconservatives are former liberals who have maintained their former beliefs in axioms of democratic peace theory.

Transnationalist theory

During the 1950s and 1960s, liberalism regained some ground from other traditions. Theories of European integration, neofunctionalism in particular, represent liberal attempts to understand contemporary politics in regional settings (Haas 1958; Nye 1970). However, some neofunctionalists changed their focus from regional sub-systems to the international system, thus contributing to the development of transnationalism. Karl Kaiser (1969) was among the first to point out the limits of state-centric perspectives, but Robert Keohane and Joseph Nye's *Transnational Relations and World Politics* (1971) is widely considered to be the prime work of this strain of liberalism. Among other transnationalists, we find James Rosenau (1980, 1990), Karl Deutsch *et al.* (1957) and John Burton (1972). The label 'transnationalism' signifies that theorists cultivating this approach look beyond state–state relations and argue that society–society relations are equally – if not more – important for world politics. Burton illustrates this more complex set of relations in his cobweb model. Similarly, the term 'world politics' is preferred to 'international politics' or 'international relations', because it connotes a broader notion of politics. According to the theory, we witness an increasingly transnational world – cf. ongoing processes of globalization – and world politics will likely become more peaceful than during previous eras. If transnationalism somehow lost some of its momentum at some point, Thomas Risse-Kappen has made a plea for *Bringing Transnational Relations Back In* (1995). Such a title is indicative of the fact that theoretical perspectives often first gain momentum followed by a decline or waning interest, only to be brought 'back in' by someone who continues to find them inspiring or puzzling.

A constructivist liberal theory of cooperation

Alexander Wendt (1999) has created a fourth liberal theory. In his main work, *Social Theory of International Politics*, he outlines a constructivist liberal theory of international cooperation. It is telling that the title of the book is strikingly similar to Kenneth Waltz's main work, *Theory of International Politics* (1979). This similarity signifies that Wendt's theoretical ambition is to build a systemic theory, yet emphasizing social rather than material structures. Furthermore, Wendt's theory is 'robust' in the sense that it can deal with a significant number of key questions. Nevertheless, such a theory does not please the more 'purist' schools of thought. Why then categorize Wendt within the liberal tradition? Primarily because he emphasizes a process-perspective, which in fact somewhat dilutes his state-centrism. In his view, constructivists and strong liberals share a lot:

> With respect to the substance of international relations ... both modern and postmodern constructivists are interested in how knowledgeable practices constitute subjects, which is not far from the strong liberal interest in how institutions transform interests. They share a cognitive or intersubjective conception of process in which identities and interests are endogenous to interaction, rather than a rationalist behavioral one in which they are exogenous. (1992a)

Essentially, he criticizes his fellow strong liberals for not working with social theories matching their interest in the substance of social ontology. His notions of identity and interest mixed with social and ideational factors promise to feed one of the most sophisticated liberal theories. The liberal tradition has produced several more similar theories, for example, constructivist theories of socialization (Checkel 1998).

Liberal intergovernmentalism

Theories of international cooperation and integration have been among the most important contributions of the liberal tradition. Theories of integration were launched in the 1950s and 1960s (Haas 1958), whereas theories of international cooperation and negotiation followed later (e.g. Putnam 1988; Evans, Jacobson and Putnam 1993; Patterson 1997). More recently, these theoretical endeavours have come together in liberal intergovernmentalist theory. In order to enhance our understanding of European integration,

Andrew Moravcsik (1998) created liberal intergovernmentalism, which basically is a theoretical framework synthesizing theories of domestic preference formation, strategic bargaining and institutional design. Moravcsik's framework focuses in particular on the history-making decisions in the context of intergovernmental conferences on treaty reform. The liberal component is most clearly at play in the strong emphasis on domestic processes of preference formation, whereas governmental behaviour and institutional design is less archetypal liberal thinking; these two elements, however, also have been put on a solid rationalist foundation. Similarly to Keohane's neoliberal institutionalism, Moravcsik creates his theoretical framework on a rationalist, material platform, thereby defining the role of social and cultural factors out of his research agenda.

Main intra-tradition debates

The liberal tradition is characterized by several important internal theoretical debates among theorists. Liberal currents of thought are based on significantly different conceptions of human nature, politics, the state and the international system and, therefore, likely to trigger wide-ranging intra-tradition debates. Moreover, as a long, rich and diverse tradition, liberals share some understandings, yet profoundly disagree about a considerable range of key features. In the following, three of the most important debates will be reviewed. First, it is significant that Robert Keohane deliberately and explicitly distances himself from two other liberal schools of thought:

> my arguments diverge from those of much liberal international political theory. Liberalism in international relations is often thought of exclusively in terms of what I have elsewhere called *republican* and *commercial* liberalism. Republican liberalism argues that republics are more peacefully inclined than despotisms. In its naive version, commercial liberalism argues that commerce leads necessarily to peace. (1989: 11, emphasis in original)

In other words, Keohane subscribes neither to the liberal democratic peace argument nor to the 'naive' versions of commercial liberalism. In turn, his position, the neoliberal institutional perspective on world politics, has triggered contending liberal views. Many liberal theorists have been wholeheartedly dissatisfied with the almost complete sell-out of liberal ideas by neoliberal institutionalists. They are unimpressed by the so-called 'neo-neo' synthesis and argue that the price for accommodating neorealism has been too high. Others do not find the strong structural-systemic focus of neoliberal institutionalism particularly appealing, pointing out that liberal approaches always have emphasized the important role of domestic factors. Still others point to the lack of process variables or the limited impact of international institutions on state identities.

The second debate has been about the merits and vices of idealism. On the one hand, idealism has been the target of criticism during the 20th century from both liberal theorists and those belonging to other theoretical traditions. Nonetheless, explicit reappraisals of idealism keep popping up (Long and Wilson 1995; Kegley 1993). Several adherents of democratic peace theory reject the option of being mere observers of world politics and therefore engage in promoting democracy worldwide. Given that liberal scholars are inclined to believe in the possibility of progress, they are bound to encounter idealist challenges and lures.

The third important debate is the liberal version of the contemporary rationalism–constructivism debate. Both of these meta-theoretical and epistemological positions clearly have liberal subscribers, and many liberal theories can therefore be found in both constructivist and rationalist versions. This applies to theories of democratic peace, theories of cooperation and theories of integration. In the latter case, liberal intergovernmentalism (Moravcsik 1998) is explicitly situated within a rationalist framework for analysis, whereas generic theories of identity, socialization and norms are based on constructivist underpinnings (Christiansen, Jørgensen and Wiener 2001). The important thing to notice is that substantive liberal arguments and orientations can be given different theoretical forms and that these differences in turn trigger theoretical contestations and debates about their relative merits.

Research agenda

Is the liberal tradition up to providing important insights about contemporary world politics? Donald Puchala (2003) provides a fairly upbeat answer: '[L]iberal international theory contains a highly sophisticated – and by and large, accurate – description of *the state of contemporary international relations*' (2003: 211, emphasis in original). Subsequently, he points out issues of cooperation, international governance, zones of democratic peace and complex interdependence as key features of contemporary world politics. Finally, he concludes that '[a]ll of these happenings, liberal international theory, and *only* liberal international theory, alerts us to look for and challenges us to understand' (2003: 211, emphasis in original). If true – and it seems to be – this is no negligible accomplishment. The follow-up question is how liberal scholars explore these important aspects of contemporary world politics.

In this context, it is significant that most liberals, unlike neoliberal institutionalists, do not begin by accepting most of the basic realist assumptions.

This implies that most liberals do not accept neorealism's causal logic of anarchy, state-centric world view or the idea that states are like units. According to Wendt, many liberals do not adopt an approach exclusively focused on behaviour, that is, an approach according to which 'process and institutions may change behaviour but not identities and interests' (Wendt 1992a). In other words, identity and interest are not assumed to be etched in stone. They may change, and process and institutions possibly play a role in triggering such change. Furthermore, most liberals do not assume states to necessarily be the dominant actors in the international system and, finally, they do not define security exclusively in, 'self-interested terms'. Many liberals want more. The 'more' they want differs considerably, meaning that their research agenda is very wide. Liberal scholars work on some of the key issues of contemporary world politics: war and peace, cooperation among states and transnational relations. In the following, six major issues addressed by liberal scholars will be presented.

One of the most important issues on the liberal research agenda concerns the role of international institutions (Kratochwil and Ruggie 1986; Kratochwil and Mansfield 1994). Several scholars contribute to the trend. Robert Keohane (1989: 13, 1990) has made a well-argued plea for research on international organizations and Ernest Haas (1990) has, by using the force of example, argued for attention to be paid to the relationship between international organizations and institutional learning. A consensus 'to bring international organizations back in' has emerged, clearly helped by the new, extended role of many international institutions in the post-Cold War world. However, the important question of how to analyze these institutions remains inexorably unsettled. In a book written by Margaret Karns and Karen Mingst (1990), the creation of a linkage between system-level theories of regimes and national-level processes and behaviour is among the main objectives. The existence of a two-way flow of influence is explicitly assumed. One flow of influence comes from the states: how do they use international organizations (IOs) instrumentally? The other flow of influence comes from the international organizations: how do they influence the behaviour of states? In order to analyze this two-way flow of influence, four questions are asked: (i) How has the use of IOs as instruments of US policy changed over time? (ii) How have the constraints and influence of IOs on the United States changed over time? (iii) Why have these changes occurred? (iv) What are the policy implications of these patterns of changing influence for the USA? (Karns and Mingst 1990: 2–3). Such questions are also relevant to ask as regards other major international players, including Russia, Japan, China and the European Union.

The second issue on the agenda, multilateralism, is related to research on international organizations but has a broader focus. In a book edited by John Ruggie, multilateralism is analyzed as an institutional form characterizing international society. In this way, the book leaves the analysis of other institutional forms such as bilateralism and imperialism for another time. In the introductory chapter, Ruggie presents a formal definition of multilateralism followed by a conceptual explication and a series of working hypotheses. Multilateralism is defined as:

> an institutional form which coordinates relations among three or more states on the basis of generalized principles of conduct: that is, principles which specify appropriate conduct for a class of actions, without regard to the particularistic interests of the parties or the exigencies that may exist in any specific occurrence. (Ruggie 1993: 11)

It is emphasized that merely counting, one-two-'multilateral', is insufficient. Numbers matter, but so do the qualitative aspects. Ruggie specifically refers to such qualitative aspects as generalized principles, appropriateness and non-strategic exigencies. He elaborates this approach with two sets of protagonists in mind. First, the neorealists for whom institutions do not matter, and, second, neoliberal institutionalists for whom institutions – but not the institutional form – matter. Finally, Ruggie emphasizes that no theory has been advanced, vindicated or tested in his article. His approach has nonetheless triggered a very extensive research agenda on multilateral institutions. Apart from advancing a research agenda on multilateralism, Ruggie's article also demonstrates the benefits of careful conceptual analysis – indeed, provides a model example of it.

Third, the democratic peace theory has notably triggered a range of highly topical questions about contemporary world politics. Recent democratization processes have altered the political landscape of Europe entirely, implying that the identity of Europe is changing rapidly. Similarly, the imposition of democratization processes has been attempted on the Middle East. But is the Middle East resilient to change and will democratic advances in Latin America prove to be sustainable? In an age said to be characterized by terror, we have hardly noticed that a previously dominant feature of international politics has withered away. Thus, Mueller (1990) points out that inter-state war has become quite a rarity. Analysts of democratization processes contemplate whether this strikingly new feature of international politics has something to do with the extension of the zones of peace.

The fourth issue concerns international cooperation yet focuses specifically on international regimes. Stephen Krasner's classic definition of regimes includes 'sets of implicit or explicit principles' understood as 'beliefs of fact, causation and rectitude' (Krasner 1983). In general, Krasner's definition brings principles together with norms, rules and procedures. In the present context, there is no reason to go into regime analysis as such. What is important, however, is to understand that in drawing the analytical consequences of this definition, we find one of the sources of 'the great divide' between constructivist and rationalist approaches and between different liberal approaches (Kratochwil and Ruggie 1986; Keohane 1989; Hasenclever, Meyers and Rittberger 1997). Contemporary research on multilateralism, cf. the section above, is closely related to these debates. The significant interest in processes and informal institutions is bound to lead to new research analyzing the role of international institutions and global governance in the 21st century. At the same time, new actors emerge on the horizon, cf. the changed configuration of interests within the WTO, where both the EU and the G21 play significant roles.

Fifth, the transnationalist perspective currently appears to merge with studies on globalization, and new and old issues will therefore be approached in a novel fashion. In this way, studies of economic and political processes of globalization seem to be versions two, three or four of previous transnationalist studies. Analysts often examine political responses to economic processes of globalization, emphasizing the role of a complex web of different actors (states, international institutions, social forces and transnational companies). Other analysts focus on the uneven process of globalization and some explore the role of regionalism, that is, the cooperative and integrative processes we find at the level of world regions.

Finally, liberal scholars – like all theorists – are engaged in intense theoretical dialogues with their critics. These critics can be fellow liberals who have abandoned previous liberal assumptions, or they can be theorists belonging to other theoretical traditions and other currents of thought.

Conclusion

In this chapter we have learned that liberalism is a very rich tradition of thought, drawing on a wide range of philosophical and political ideas. During the 20th century, liberalists were capable of establishing the academic discipline, International Relations, and placed the tradition squarely as one of the most important traditions in international relations theory. We have also seen that the liberal tradition comprises three major strands of thinking, each with their own distinct nature and features: neoliberal institutionalism, republican liberalism and interdependence liberalism. Each of these currents of thought comprises a wealth of specific theories and approaches. Liberal theorists have a multifaceted and complex understanding of international affairs. Though some liberal theories are strongly state-centric, liberals generally insist that states are involved in complex relations with other sovereign states and with actors in civil society. The changing interests of states originate in these civil societies, meaning that, according to liberals, no perpetual national interests exist. The chapter emphasizes that, during the 20th century, liberalism has experienced its ups and downs. In terms of meta-theoretical commitments liberalism has sometimes developed alongside – at other times merged with – meta-theoretical *Zeitgeists* such as positivism, behaviouralism, formal theory and constructivism.

Questions

- How has the liberal tradition evolved during the 20th century? Identify different phases and characterize each phase.
- What currents of thought comprise the liberal tradition?
- What can we use specific substantive theories for?
- How would you categorize neoliberal institutionalism by means of the levels-of-analysis model?
- How has Alexander Wendt combined constructivism and liberal ideas?
- Which kinds of theory have been cultivated by liberal theorists?

Further reading

Burton, J. (1972) *World Society* (Cambridge: Cambridge University Press).
    One of the first systematic arguments in favour of focusing on world society.

Doyle, M. W. (1986) 'Liberalism and World Politics', *American Political Science Review*, 80,(): 1151–69.
    A brief yet eminent analysis of the liberal tradition.

Keohane, R. O. (1989) *International Institutions and State Power: Essays in International Relations Theory* (Boulder, San Francisco and London: Westview).
    A collection of essays outlining the position of neoliberal institutionalism.

Keohane, R. O. and Nye, J. S. (1987) 'Power and Interdependence Revisited', *International Organization*, 41, 725–53.
    An article by two leading liberal theorists, looking back, ten years after, on one of their most famous publications.

Keohane, R. O. and Nye, J. S. (2000[1977]) *Power and Interdependence: World Politics in Transition*, 3rd edn (New York: Addison Wesley Longman).
    A classic within the liberal tradition, exploring linkages between power and interdependence.

Mitrany, D. (1998[1943]) 'A Working Peace System', in B. F. Nielsen and A. C.-G. Stubb (eds), *The European Union: Readings on the Theory and Practice of European Integration* (Basingstoke: Palgrave Macmillan): 93–114.
    One of the main pleas to redefine political issues as technical issues for which technical solutions might be identified. Represents a functional approach to politics.

Moravcsik, A. (1998) *The Choice for Europe: Social Purpose and State Power from Messina to Maastricht* (London: UCL Press).
    An eminent analysis of the dynamics of European integration.

Zacher, M. W. and Matthew, R. A. (1995) 'Liberal International Theory: Common Threads Divergent Strands', in C. W. Kegley, *Controversies in International Relations: Realism and the Neoliberal Challenge* (New York: St Martin's Press).
    A very useful overview of liberal currents of thought.

Websites for further information

www.mtholyoke.edu/acad/intrel/kant/kant1.htm
    Perpetual Peace by Immanuel Kant.

www.nobel.se/peace/laureates/1933/angell-bio.html
    Biography for Norman Angell.

www.lib.byu.edu/~rdh/wwi/1914m/illusion.html
    Extract from *The Great Illusion* by Norman Angell.

europa.eu
    The official European Union website.

www.un.org
    The official United Nations website.

www.osce.org
    The official OSCE website.

www.riia.org and www.chathamhouse.org.uk
    The website of the Royal Institute of International Affairs.

europa.ciia.org
    The website of the Canadian International Council.

www.cfr.org
    The website of the Council on Foreign Relations.

www.cefr.org
    The website of the Council on European Foreign Relations.

Chapter 4

The Realist Tradition

Man's aspiration for power is not an accident of history; it is not a temporary deviation from a natural state of freedom; it is an all-permeating fact which is of the very essence of human existence.
(Hans J. Morgenthau 1948: 312)

Structures never tell us all that we want to know. Instead they tell us a small number of big and important things.
(Kenneth Waltz 1979: 72)

As the citations above show, realist perspectives span Hans Morgenthau's strong emphasis on human nature and Kenneth Waltz's focus on systemic structures explaining the behaviour of great powers. Despite the broad scope, realism is a well-established and very rich theoretical tradition that has produced some of the finest studies within the discipline. Theorizing within the realist tradition of thought is characterized by six main features. In the first place, realism is a tradition that essentially claims a monopoly on really understanding the realities of international politics. In this context, it is telling that the category of antonyms for realism includes notions such as idealism, utopianism, illusions, wishful thinking, symbolism and rhetoric. Second, realism is characterized by a strong sense of tragedy or, stated differently, a considerable degree of pessimism as regards the prospects of a more peaceful world. The tragedy is that we can know our fate without being able to do much about it. Hence, we are doomed to live with conflict and war. Third, most theorists within the tradition have an almost exclusive focus on 'the political' (as opposed to e.g. economics, culture or religion). In addition, they employ a distinct conception of politics, defined as the kind of social action through which all human beings and states seek to exercise or maximize power. Fourth, the tradition is characterized by a clear-cut distinction between domestic and international politics, and almost exclusive priority is given to the latter sphere of politics. Fifth, the theories within the tradition are all theories of conflict. If cooperation is considered at all, it is typically in the form of military alliances, or cooperation is seen as a reflection of the balance of power. Finally, the tradition tends to cultivate a cyclical view of history, that is, power politics is considered to be an endless, repetitive form of social action to which there is no enduring solution. In the following, we will see how these features have been combined in different configurations, yet always give realists a distinct take on international politics.

Genealogy

Though realists often invoke intellectual classic predecessors such as Thucydides, Machiavelli, Rousseau or Hobbes, this chapter will focus on the realist tradition and the currents of thought it has produced since the beginning of the 20th century.

Realism was born and raised in Europe and essentially reflects 19th-century European *Realpolitik*, yet the tradition grew up in the United States, where it has been among the dominant traditions for a very long time. To a considerable degree, European academic émigrés were instrumental in transferring the tradition from Europe to the United States. In other parts of the world, realism has been less prominent and far from being a dominant tradition. After World War II, Europe did not completely forget its realist tradition, though studies within the tradition tend to be meta-studies or the application of theory rather than innovative theory building (cf. Guzzini 1998; Williams 2005). In China, the reception of, for example, hegemonic stability theory has been characterized more by criticism than by applause, yet the tradition seems to be increasingly attractive (Feng and Ruizhuong 2006). Elsewhere, realism has been a more or less implicit framework for thinking about international affairs, sometimes mixed with the dogma of old-fashioned geopolitics.

During the 20th century, the realist tradition has generated three main currents of thought: classical realism, neorealism and post-neorealism. Each of these currents will first be briefly described in this section and then described in further detail in the following sections.

Classical realism took off during the 1930s, established itself during the 1950s, and managed to maintain its prominent position until the 1980s, that is, until neorealism gradually began to be seen to represent the tradition. Under the label of post-neorealism, however, there has been a realist life after neorealism – less coherent perhaps, yet nonetheless very much 'alive and kicking' and therefore having an important impact on the contemporary research agenda. For this reason, it is important not to stop the account of the tradition some 30 years ago, when the most important neorealist work was published (Waltz 1979). The currents have since developed in parallel, thus demonstrating that they – despite their labels – are more than just different phases but have existed parallel to or alongside one another. In this fashion, the realist tradition is 'a many-mansioned tradition of thought' (Spegele 1987: 189). It is a highly diverse tradition implying that attempts at squeezing diversity into a uniform conception are potentially misleading.

The realist tradition can thus be said to be similar to other traditions, predominantly unified when considered in relation to other traditions of thought.

During the most recent phases of development, realism has become more heterogeneous. On the one hand the increasing pluralism can be seen as a sign of strength, because a tradition that is capable of generating an increasing number of theoretical perspectives indicates that the tradition is alive and kicking, that is, innovative and progressive (Donnelly 2000). On the other hand the increasing pluralism of perspectives can also be understood as a sign of weakness, because realism might have lost its sense of direction and appears to be able to generate an abundant number of perspectives and *ad hoc* refinements (cf. Legro and Moravcsik 1999).

Currents of realist thought

As mentioned in the previous section, it has become common to draw a distinction between three main currents of realist thought: classical realism, neorealism and post-neorealism. In the following sections, we will examine these currents in further detail.

Classical realism

The first realist current has been called political realism and retrospectively labelled classical realism. Its origins are often traced to E. H. Carr (1939) and Hans Morgenthau's (1946) critique of the liberal tradition (see Chapters 3 and 8). In order to properly understand the significance of classical realism, however, we ought to pay attention to the fact that the 1930s and 1940s were characterized by a range of realist publications, including Martin Wight (1946/1977) and Georg Schwarzenberger (1941) in Europe. In the United States, Reinhold Niebuhr (1932) and Frederick Schuman (1937) represented classical realism. Carr's criticism of what he labelled 'utopian liberalism' does not constitute a realist theory as such. Rather, his book highlights a number of realist characteristics and perfectly demonstrates how such features can be employed in a devastating critique of other traditions, particularly aspects of early 20th-century liberal thinking, such as the false promises of the League of Nations. Moreover, Morgenthau's first publication was also a critique of another tradition. In Morgenthau's own words:

> I tried to confront what I considered to be the existential, political, and social problems with the ways in which the American tradition attempted to come to terms with them. This tradition assumes that all problems are susceptible of a rational solution and that if they seem to

Figure 4.1 **Some key works in the realist tradition**

1929	Hans Morgenthau, *The Nature and Limits of Judicial Function in International Law* (doctoral dissertation)
1939	E. H. Carr, *The Twenty Years Crisis, 1919–1939: An Introduction to the Study of International Relations*
1941	Georg Schwarzenberger, *Power Politics: An Introduction to the Study of International Relations and Post-war Planning*
1946	Hans Morgenthau, *Scientific Man vs Power Politics*
1946	Martin Wight, *Power Politics*
1951	John Herz, *Political Realism and Political Idealism*
1959	Kenneth Waltz, *Man, the State and War*
1962	Inis Claude, *Power and International Relations*
1979	Kenneth Waltz, *Theory of International Politics*
1981	Robert Gilpin, *War and Change in World Politics*
1987	Stephen Walt, *The Origins of Alliances*
1991	Jack Snyder, *Myths of Empire: Domestic Politics and International Ambition*
1993	Barry Buzan, Charles A. Jones and Richard Little, *The Logic of Anarchy: Neorealism to Structural Realism*
1997	Glenn H. Snyder, *Alliance Politics*
2003	John Mearsheimer, *The Tragedy of Great Power Politics*

resist such a solution, if you only spend more energy, more time, more manpower, and more money on them, they are bound to be solved. (Morgenthau 1984: 379)

He adds the following significant words: 'I tried to show the tragic character of political and social problems which escape a clear-cut solution but which must be lived with and manipulated, problems which cannot be exorcised by some technological, social, or, political contrivance' (Morgenthau 1984: 379). In this fashion, he critically characterized the American liberal tradition and emphasized the unavoidable role of tragedy.

Classical realism did not suddenly emerge out of nowhere. Rather, classical realists drew on a number of intellectual sources. Morgenthau had a profound and sustained interest in the notion of politics and was inspired by one of the prime thinkers on politics of the day, German lawyer Carl Schmitt, with politics defined in terms of friend and foe. Furthermore, Morgenthau was very familiar with the German *Machtschule*, including the work of Max Weber, and its focus on the role of power. Finally, theories of conflict represent a continuation of established intellectual traditions that include a very diverse set of theorists, ranging from Charles Darwin to Karl Marx. Concerning Frederick Schuman, the story is somewhat different. He had been trained at the University of Chicago by the promoters of the – at the time – new science of politics, that is, political science, and attempted to introduce the new social science to the study of international relations. Hence, he consciously downplayed the role of law and formal institutionalism and upgraded the role of politics and power. Due to this preoccupation with power and politics many books were simply entitled 'power politics'. The classical realists insisted on describing the world *as it is*, not as it *should be* according to international law or formal rules of covenants. In a certain sense, the classical realists drew upon a Rankean conception of historiography, aiming at describing events and developments *wie es eigenlich gewesen*, that is, as a non-distorted, unbiased, true representation of reality 'as is'. In short, the classical realists did not invent the analytical tools they employed, but they were among the first to fairly systematically apply these tools in academic studies of international politics.

Classical realism comprises a large number of theorists and can only be described as a rich current, particularly thriving before newer social science techniques were developed. Classical realism is first and foremost a blend of political theory, IR theory and historical analysis. The classical realists contributed significantly to the development of the discipline. John Herz (1950) coined the term 'security dilemma', and Henry Kissinger analyzed – before he became US Secretary of State – the classical 19th-century European multipolar order in *A World Restored* (1957). Raymond Aron (1967), though a contested realist, was among the main figures attempting to theorize international relations and explain the causes of war. In the following, three illustrative examples – on Hans J. Morgenthau, Inis Claude and George Kennan – provide further detail regarding important aspects of classical realists (on classical realism, see Guzzini 1998; Donnelly 2000; Williams 2005).

Morgenthau's strong emphasis on politics, power and the national interest is unsurprising, particularly if one considers that he was deeply influenced by Carl Schmitt's conception of politics and that he wrote a PhD thesis in 1929 at the University of Munich on the limits of international law vis-à-vis international politics. Similar to Michel Foucault, Morgenthau thinks power is ubiquitous, implying it is naive – at times dangerously naive – to believe in 'power-free' zones. Furthermore, there is a direct link between power and politics; indeed, power is regarded as the essence of politics. Finally, by means of foreign policy instruments, states (and their representatives) will always do their utmost to further what is perceived to be in the national interest. Thus far, everything described is set for creating contradictions like interests vs ethics; or realists vs normative theorists (cf. Chapter 2). However, even a superficial reading of *Truth and Tragedy* (Thompson and Myers 1984) or the annual *Ethics and International Affairs* suggests that such contradictions are false.

Classical realism also addresses the role of principles in international politics. One example is Inis Claude, according to whom the master proposition is that 'states do not, but certainly should, consistently engage in principled behaviour in the international setting' (Claude 1993: 215). He points out that calls for (more) principled behaviour flow from three sources: from moral disapproval of states unguided by principles; from alarm about the consequences of such behaviour; and from moral aspiration for a better world order. Furthermore, he outlines the historical tradition of appealing to adherence to principles, ranging from the launch of international law in the 16th century to the 'turn to international institutions' in the early 20th century. In Claude's words, international law and organization constitute the reform movement in international relations. The purpose of his article, however, is not to join these appeals and this movement but to make a plea for pragmatism, that is, flexible adherence to principles. According to Claude, the prime reason for making flexibility a virtue is the very diverse nature of states and the lack of uniformity in the international system. He rejects the view that pragmatists are necessarily immoral actors, writing instead about the moral value of adapting policy to fit special circumstances. Jack Donnelly reaches a similar conclusion: 'There need be no real inconsistency in treating similar violations differently ... A blind demand that violation x produces response y is simplistic and silly' (cited in Smith 2001: 198). Other scholars have similar perspectives on the tension between principle and pragmatism (cf. Ruggie 1991; Thompson 1993).

A second example of principles at work in realist scholarship is George Kennan who provides a particularly apt definition. According to Kennan, 'a principle is a general rule of conduct by which a given country chooses to abide in the conduct of its relations with other countries' (1995). He also connects principles and self-images in an interesting fashion that shows that at least some realists are no strangers to the role of identity:

> a country, too, can have a predominant collective sense of itself – what sort of a country it conceives itself or would like itself to be – and what sort of behaviour would fit that concept. The place where this self-image

finds its most natural reflection is in the principles that a country chooses to adopt and, to the extent possible, to follow. (1995)

Finally, several classical realists had a very close relationship to religion. Martin Wight was a conscientious objector during World War II (Molloy 2003: 86; Drinkwater 2005: 15). It is often claimed that it is impossible to understand Hans Morgenthau's realism without taking his deep religious beliefs into account. Reinhold Niebuhr was a classical realist, yet also a Protestant theologian. They all share the feature of having developed strong linkages between religion, politics and realism. It is thus hardly surprising that they share a profound interest in morality, human nature, ethics, values and principles. This fact raises an important yet almost unexplored issue about the relationship between religious conviction and classical realists.

The neorealist current

The 'neo' in neorealism does not indicate that it is merely a continuation of classical realism, perhaps characterized by some additional or novel features. Rather, neorealists take classical realism as their point of departure but then engage in essentially abandoning the current, thus representing a significant rupture within the realist tradition. Neorealism is mainly associated with the writings of Kenneth Waltz, who is influenced by a specific philosophy of science and models of microeconomics. In many ways, *Theory of International Politics* (1979) is among the finest products to be based on rationalist assumptions.

Neorealists characterize actors *a priori* and therefore deliberately ignore real actor characteristics, identify a few prime players in the international system (great powers) and, on this basis, constitute the structure of the international system. Subsequently, they deduct the likely behaviour of these prime players in changing structural settings, conceptualized as varying polarities. Finally, neorealists are content to explain a few but important things and are happy to leave untouched what they regard as the nitty-gritty analysis of other issues in international politics. In short, Kenneth Waltz reinvented the realist tradition in a new image and based on new philosophical underpinnings. The key features of the new image comprise an ontology that is similar – if not identical – to microeconomics, a distinct philosophy of science combined with a distinct conception of theory, and a structural explanation of behaviour that exclusively focuses on the systemic level of analysis.

Kenneth Waltz's neorealism has three layers of explanatory factors that contribute to explain state behaviour: i) anarchy (self-help system), ii) functional differentiation of units and iii) changing distribution of power capabilities, that is, changing configurations of polarity (one, two or more great powers). However, anarchy has been a constant ever since the emergence of the international system during the 17th century and polarity change happens relatively seldom, leaving balance of power the predominant factor when explaining changing great power behaviour. Other scholars have somewhat different emphases, and while broadly remaining within the confines of Waltz's model, they tried to shape neorealism slightly differently. Thus, Barry Buzan (1993) engaged in reconstructing neorealism by means of introducing more variables (process variables and interaction capacity). Steve Smith engaged in a comprehensive conversation with the philosopher Martin Hollis (Hollis and Smith 1990), and he reflected on key issues of ontology and epistemology from a neorealist position. Glenn Snyder (1984, 1997) has built a specific theory of alliance politics that is based on an essentially neorealist foundation.

A systemic, material theoretical current of thought such as neorealism, insisting on not being a theory of foreign policy (Waltz 1979, 1996), seems to have little to offer the study of foreign policy. However, neorealism may have more to offer than intuition suggests. First, though Waltz has insisted on neorealism not being a theory of foreign policy, the aim of his systemic theory is to explain state behaviour (Fearon 1998). Thus, neorealism explains different kinds of state behaviour, including balancing, bandwagoning and seeking relative or absolute gains. No matter which kind of behaviour, it will always be explained by systemic structural factors, that is, strategically by changing polarities and, tactically or operationally, by balance of power theory.

Though the impact of neorealism has been profound both within and beyond the realist tradition, neorealism does not represent the end game of realism. This leads us to the post-neorealist current of realist thinking.

The post-neorealist current

As mentioned above, the realist tradition did not stop with the publication of Waltz's *Theory of International Politics* (1979); while some continued as 'refiners' or 'appliers' of neorealism, others took alternative paths. Thus, the realist theorists behind the somewhat vaguely defined post-neorealism current entered the scene, mainly during the 1990s and the first decade of the 21st century. If neorealism was a clear-cut break with classical realism, post-neorealism represents a much less radical rupture and should perhaps first and foremost be seen as a continuation of neorealism, although with slightly new emphases and various additives.

One such emphasis is the preoccupation with the encounter between theoretically deducted state strategies and the actual foreign policies of states in general and American foreign policy in particular. On the one hand post-neorealist scholars aim at preserving their point of departure in systemic characteristics, yet unlike neorealists, they aim also at explaining foreign policy. A second emphasis within post-neorealism concerns the difference between offensive and defensive realism. This emphasis is directly related to the encounter between theory and practice. This theme has also been present in other realist currents of thought, but it is only with the rise of post-neorealism that it has become a defining feature. Both camps take their point of departure in state security. Offensive realists such as John Mearsheimer argue that states seek to maximize their power relative to other states, especially because they, in an anarchic environment, are bound to be insecure. By contrast, defensive realists such as Michael Mastanduno argue that states seek to minimize power losses relative to their adversaries. In this perspective, states assess the threats they face and subsequently aim at building an adequate amount of power.

Somewhat unfairly, it has been claimed that post-neorealists have been engaged in shuffling and reshuffling a limited number of rather traditional variables. A heated debate between defensive and offensive realists may have triggered refined theoretical claims but not innovative theoretical advances. This meagre outcome is possibly because normative factors are regarded as less important, thus continuing the tradition from neorealism; possibly because post-neorealists remain steeped in the parameters of material theories or feel uncomfortable dealing with the kind of theory that would be adequate to apply when handling issues of morality, ethics or identity.

Important exceptions to this largely negative, broad-brush painting of post-neorealism ought to be noted. Stephen Walt (1987) coined the balance of threat concept – and it is difficult to conceive of balances of threats without some kind of role for perceptions, perhaps particularly perceptions of others but also self-perceptions. Walt is generally less materially minded than Waltz, and he has modified neorealism significantly by incorporating social factors. Furthermore, some have cultivated a pronounced interest in various intervening variables, operating between international structures and the conduct of foreign policy. As a result of this interest, they have engaged in studies of foreign policy, focusing on both non-material and domestic factors (Snyder 1991; Elman 1996). Samuel Huntington (1993) and Henry Nau (2002) have demonstrated that realism and the 'cultural' factor are far from antithetical, and both Walt and Snyder have demonstrated that political elites risk being caught by their own political rhetoric. However, while the post-neorealists have engaged in analyzing dimensions of social reality they have not done so systematically. Further steps could be to take realist key notions such as 'interest' and 'power' and relate them to 'morality', 'ethics' and 'identity'. Reconsiderations along this line would probably result in a kind of realism similar to Hans J. Morgenthau's classical realism. The key question as to whether post-neorealism is best regarded as a degeneration of the realist paradigm (Vasquez 1997, 1998) or as the potentially innovative dynamics of a tradition (Wivel 2003) remains an essentially open question.

Kinds of realist theory

Classical realists did not display much interest in which kind of theory they cultivated, probably because differentiation among different kinds of theory was not considered that important. Morgenthau's *Politics Among Nations* (1948) is famous for its six principles of political realism (see Box 4.1).

The nature of principles implies that they function as broad guidelines summarizing more detailed ideas. Hence, Morgenthau's six principles make a realist cocktail consisting of the following ingredients: morality, politics, power, interests, human nature and objective laws. In order to understand the precise meaning of these key terms, we are bound to engage in interpretation (cf. Chapter 2). In the first place, it is significant to note that these principles were introduced only in the second edition of his textbook. It seems as though something happened that prompted Morgenthau to revise his first text, and revise it in a certain direction. Furthermore, we may ask ourselves why the principles contradict the other parts of Morgenthau's book to the extent that they do. One of the leading contemporary realists, Robert Gilpin, is of great help in this context. He explains that when Morgenthau:

Box 4.1　Morgenthau's six principles of political realism

1. Political realism believes that politics, like society in general, is governed by objective laws that have their roots in human nature ...
2. The main signpost that helps political realism to find its way through the landscape of international politics is the concept of interest defined in terms of power ...
3. Power and interest are variable in content across space and time ...
4. Realism maintains that universal moral principles cannot be applied to the action of states ...
5. Political realism refuses to identify the moral aspirations of a particular nation with the moral laws that govern the universe ...
6. The difference, then, between political realism and other schools of thought is real and it is profound ... Intellectually, the political realism maintains the autonomy of the political sphere.

(Source: Hans J. Morgenthau, *Politics Among Nations*, 2nd edn, 1954, pp. 4–10)

---

went to Chicago ... he found it dominated by the social science fashion of the time; he apparently realized that if he were to make an impact, he had to learn and write social science. He decided that international politics had to aim at becoming an objective science. (Gilpin 2005: 365)

In other words, the image of Morgenthau's realist theory being built on positivist premises is at best misleading (see also Williams 2005; Guzzini 1998). Concerning Morgenthau's theory, it remains unclear whether his theoretical reflections were normative, analytical, or prescriptive – or everything in one go. Similarly, we can explore his distinction between realism and idealism, including the normative underpinnings of the distinction. Finally, we can ask whether it is possible to reconcile Morgenthau's concept of rationality and his perceptions of human nature as fundamentally evil, aggressive and unpredictable. Basically, Morgenthau theorized international politics by means of a mixture of explanatory, interpretive and normative theory. In general, classical realists did not expend much energy on explicating their notion of theory.

The behavioural revolutionaries of all trades did not find much value added in such a mixture. Behaviouralists concentrated their energy on explanatory theory and causal analysis. Furthermore, they introduced a distinction between empirical and normative theory and argued that only the former was of value for genuine scientific enquiry worthy of the title. Hence, normative theory was not their game; if it were to disappear altogether, so much the better. Most contemporary realist theories are still based on these premises and are consequently thoroughly framed as explanatory theory. They follow the standard procedures of no-nonsense causal analysis, and the language of independent, intervening and dependent variables provides the basic structure of contemporary realist theorizing. Given the particular prominence of the realist tradition in North America, it has been fundamentally marked by the area's dominant and specific conceptions of social science, political science and philosophy of science.

Critics have raised some serious doubt about the preponderant explanatory shape of realism. Let us briefly revisit the definitions of interpretive and normative theory (see Chapters 1 and 2). Interpretive theory is concerned with making sense of events or developments. Normative theory tells us what our attitude to phenomena x, y and z should be. For instance, is it our duty to risk our lives to defend our country? Should states remain focused on balance of power issues and thus avoid becoming engaged in humanitarian interventions or in adventurous military engagements aiming at regime change or the promotion of democracy and human rights? With these definitions and functions in mind, let us now reconsider the kinds of theory that are cultivated within the realist tradition. Realist theorists appear to be endlessly engaged in making sense of key terms, such as power, sovereignty, morality, interests, anarchy, hierarchy and states. Furthermore, it seems as though realists take normative positions on key issues in world politics. Realists concede that they disagree on the issue of whether multipolarity or bipolarity produces the most stable international order. Morgenthau assumes the former position whereas Waltz (1964) takes the latter. While the difference is significant in its own right, what matters in the present context is that they agree that stability is preferable to instability. In other words, even if they make no explicit reference to ethics, their subtext is profoundly normative. Most recently, even constructivist realism has emerged (Nau 2002; Barkin 2003), suggesting that the previously heralded 'realism versus constructivism' contradiction has been grossly misleading.

In summary, then, realist theorists employ all major kinds of theory. However, they are very explicit concerning explanatory theory and argue that they want to avoid hair-splitting exercises regarding the different meanings of key terms, such as states, power and anarchy. These notions of course have the meaning that we, the realists, have chosen to give them. Given the implicit presence of the interpretive and normative theory in the realist tradition, some reconstruction of the theories is required to recognize these underpinnings.

Main variants of theories

No matter which tradition we explore, we can rest assured that we will know innovative living traditions by their ability to produce a rich portfolio of concrete, applicable theories. The realist tradition is no exception to this rule. Three such concrete theories will be introduced in the following: balance of power theory, alliance theory and power transition theory. Each illustrates how realists theorize international relations.

Balance of power theory

Kenneth Waltz has famously stated that '[i]f there is any distinctively political theory on international politics, balance-of-power theory is it' (1979: 11). In a similar vein, Morgenthau devoted almost half his seminal *Politics Among Nations* (1948) to balance of power issues. Balance of power theory employs several of the key terms in the realist vocabulary, including anarchy, security dilemma, hegemony, alliances, polarity, balancing and bandwagoning. The points of departure are the notions of anarchy, self-help and security dilemma. In the words of Kenneth Waltz:

> Because any state may at any time use force, all states must constantly be ready either to counter force with force, or to pay the cost of weak-

ness. The requirements of state action are, in this view, imposed by the circumstances in which all states exist. (Waltz 1959: 160)

According to this view, anarchy is for states clearly not merely a problem to be solved or avoided but simply an essential condition of life.

Concerning the security dilemma, John Herz was among the first to coin the term. He defines the dilemma as:

> a structural notion in which the self-help attempts of states to look after their security needs tend regardless of intention to lead to rising insecurity for others as each interprets its own measures as defensive and the measures of others as potentially threatening. (Herz 1950: 157)

Since the introduction, the notion has become part of the realist standard conceptual repertoire and a significant building block in balance of power theory. In this context, some may wonder about the difference between an international balance of power and a domestic configuration of checks and balances. Waltz explains that:

> [t]he opportunity and at times the necessity of using force distinguishes the balance of power in international politics from the balances of power that form inside the state ... The balance of power among states becomes a balance of all the capabilities, including physical force, that states choose to use in pursuing their goals. (Waltz 1959: 205)

In this context, capabilities should be understood broadly as '[p]opulation and size of territory, resources, economic strength, military capability, political stability and competence' (Waltz 1979: 131). Thus, in order to survive in an anarchic environment, states may seek to balance against other states by forming alliances or coalitions with others. Bandwagoning offers an alternative option, that is, aligning with the stronger power rather than opposing it.

As we have seen, realists typically claim that states tend to balance power *per se* more than their ideological opponents. This is not the image one receives when reading newspapers or listening to speeches delivered by politicians. However, consider the following examples of changing relationships and balances of power. In the 1920s, the Soviet Union started off as an ideological enemy of the Western great powers, including the United Kingdom, France and the United States. Subsequently, the country became an ally during World War II, only to become, once again, an opponent during the Cold War. During this latter phase, the Soviet Union can be viewed as an ideological opponent that should be contained or, in balance of power terms, a state whose power should be balanced, no matter the domestic features of the state. From the perspective of the Soviet elite in

Moscow, however, it was American power that was on the rise and had to be balanced. Mutual balancing ultimately triggered and almost guaranteed the arms race that so profoundly characterized the Cold War. A second example of non-ideological 'clinical' power balancing includes Saddam Hussein's Iraq, treated by the West as a partner during the 1980s, at a time when the objective of Western foreign policy was to balance Iranian influence in the Middle East region. Subsequently, Iraq was treated as a threat to international peace and security during the 1990s and invaded by the United States in 2003. A final example, on a more grand scale, is the case of China. Communist China was long perceived to be a threatening enemy of the United States. Then, in the early 1970s, a new US foreign policy was suddenly adopted, and China was promoted as a new member of the UN and even a permanent member of the UN Security Council. The new US policy ensured a split within the communist bloc, and the Soviet Union began to feel contained, if not encircled.

Some take balance of power theory in a slightly different direction. Stephen Walt (1987) has developed a theory of balance of threat, arguing that it is not power *per se* but rather threats that states tend to balance. Assessments of power are therefore combined with perceptions of threat. It is only when the power of a state is perceived to be threatening that balancing behaviour is triggered. In contrast, Randall Schweller (1994) remains focused on power, yet argues that states actually tend to bandwagon rather than balance power. Critiques of balance of power theory abound. Both Inis L. Claude (1962) and Ernest Haas (1953) pointed out that the trouble with the balance of power is not that it has no meaning, but that it has too many meanings. As we shall see in Chapter 5, also the international society tradition employs a notion of balance of power, albeit understanding it differently. Whenever one discusses the nature or problems of balance of power, the specification of meaning is therefore a precondition for a purposeful debate.

Realist theories of alliances

Most theoretical traditions pay some attention to alliances. Neoliberal institutionalists, for instance, regard alliances as a kind of international institution (Keohane 1989: 15; see also Chapter 3). However, no tradition has conceptualized and theorized alliances in a richer manner than the realist. Given that the take on alliances differs significantly between classical realists and neorealists, the distinction between the two strands of thought once again shows its usefulness.

On the one hand classical realists have explored historical examples of alliances, their characteristics as well as contemporary alliances. They have pointed out the limited usefulness of alliances in the sense that they are formed to counter a specific threat and the alliance is usually dissolved once this threat has disappeared. Furthermore, it is claimed that membership of alliances is based on utility calculations of costs and benefits rather than ideational commitments. Yet such commitments may enforce alliance cohesion. Significantly, alliances play an important part in making or preserving balances of power.

On the other hand neorealist alliance theory takes its point of departure in the structure of the international system. Accordingly, it matters whether we look at alliances in unipolar, bipolar or multipolar systems. When outlining alliance theory in a neorealist first-cut fashion, Glenn Snyder begins by pointing out the specific domain of alliance politics (as related to other domains). 'It is analytically useful to postulate separate alliance and adversary games, despite their entanglement in reality. Each of these games is played on three policy levels: armament, action, and declarations' (1990: 106). He proceeds by describing the following causal connections:

> Systemic anarchy is one stimulus to ally, although not always a sufficient one. Structural polarity – how military power and potential are distributed among major states – has important effects on the nature of alliances and alliance politics. Alliances are substantially different in multipolar and bipolar systems. (Snyder 1990: 107)

Different polarities – bipolarity, unipolarity or multipolarity – cause different logics for patterns of alliance formation, alliance politics and possible alternatives to a given alliance. The beauty of neorealist alliance theory is to be found in the parsimonious point of departure but also in the conceptualization of alliances that make it possible to avoid the crude deductions that neorealists often feel forced to make. Claims and predictions concerning the behaviour of states in and among alliances become less abstract, more concrete.

Among the key words in neorealist theory of alliances, we find the notion of 'free-riding', an almost inevitable term given that alliance politics is collective action, which brings with it the option or temptation to free-ride, or pass the burden to alliance partners. Key words also include chain-ganging, connoting something similar to a chain reaction. States are chain-ganged into war by alliance partners, because alliance commitments force states into war even if they have no special interest in the war in question. The most oft-cited example of chain-ganging is found in World War I. In contrast, buck-passing refers to a pronounced reluctance to counter a given threat while hoping that other states will do something about it. A good example of such behaviour is the prelude to World War II. Given the rise of Nazi Germany, the policy-makers in the relevant great power capitals – London, Paris, Moscow and Washington – were asking, 'Who is going to confront Hitler?' while thinking to themselves, 'Let's hope someone else will'. The final important key words are defection and realignment. According to the theory, states constantly calculate the costs and benefits of a given alliance. Hence, states are constantly insecure about what their allies are up to. Are some of their allies considering defecting from the alliance, abandoning their former allies by aligning themselves instead with a competing alliance? Finally, Snyder defines entrapment in the following:

> Entrapment means being dragged into a conflict over an ally's interests that one does not share, or shares only partially ... Entrapment occurs when one values the preservation of the alliance more than the costs of fighting for the ally's interest. (Snyder 1984: 467)

During the Cold War, the fears of potential defection and entrapment were a constant in NATO. The very definition of what should be considered within NATO's domain and out-of-area, respectively, is an example of entrapment fears at play. Thus, the United States feared being dragged into European colonial wars and NATO's boundary was therefore defined as the Tropic of Cancer. Early on, tension was also triggered when an invitation to join the alliance was extended in the mid-1950s to West Germany, the former enemy. Here, bipolar alliance logics overruled strong remnants of enmity. Later came doubts as to whether West Germany would defect, that is, leave NATO, if the Soviet Union offered reunification on the condition of neutrality. Ultimately, France was the state that defected from NATO's integrated military command, forcing NATO to move its headquarters from Paris to Brussels. Such examples of insecurity abound in alliance politics worldwide.

Power transition theory

Power transition theory was introduced by A. F. K. Organski and originally presented as part of his textbook, *World Politics* (1958). The theory was further refined by Organski and Jack Kugler (1980), who examine the behaviour of great powers and theorize the causes of war. Reflecting on the stability of the international order and the causes of war is a conventional realist preoccupation. However, power transition theory is distinctly different from much of realist theory. In Margit Bussmann and John R. Oneal's succinct formulation, power transition theory 'is constructed on three fundamental claims: the internal growth of nations influences international politics, world politics is characterized by hierarchy rather than anarchy, and relative power and evaluations of the international status quo are important determinants of interstate wars' (Bussmann and Oneal 2007: 90). In contrast to balance of power theory, power transition theory claims that instability is most likely when relative parity characterizes the relations among potential competitors. The set-up of power transition theory is a pyramid of power, with a dominant power on top and other great powers, among them a potentially future challenger, lower in the pyramid. Stability is secured if the satisfied great powers align themselves with the dominant power. Instability is likely if a dissatisfied challenger great power reaches rough parity with the dominant power. Like all concrete theories, power transition theory can be applied or tested. In the first place, the logic of power transition theory has been illustrated by historical examples. The emergence of Germany as a great power at the beginning of the 20th century and the emergence of the USSR as a superpower after World War II are two oft-cited examples. More recently, the rise of China has also been analyzed (Tammen and Kugler 2007). The US doctrine of prohibiting the emergence of any challenger seems to emphasize the continued relevance of power transition theory. Finally, power transition theory has been tested in a number of studies with mixed results, depending on the specific aspects that were tested.

Main intra-tradition debates

The realist tradition has evolved over the course of the 20th century through four major intra-tradition debates, or debates among realists. The first major debate took place between the classical realists and neorealists. As seen above, classical realism is a very rich intellectual current characterized by a bundle of different conceptions and numerous theorists. However, Kenneth Waltz (1979, 1990) challenged this tradition head-on in the 1970s, arguing that the tradition might be rich in terms of realist thought but at the same time is exceptionally weak in terms of theory. Though Kenneth Waltz's *Theory on International Politics* is effectively one long criticism of classical realism, Waltz's criticism of classical realism is most clearly presented by a rather brief article from 1990. The article is tellingly entitled 'Realist Thought and Neorealist Theory', thus emphasizing that Waltz does not regard classical realism as proper theory. Waltz's argument eminently illustrates how a specific conception of theory can be employed in fierce criticism and contributes to the abandonment of conventional realist wisdom.

Given the prominence of neorealism, it is hardly surprising that the second major debate within the realist tradition takes its point of departure from neorealism. As we have seen above, neorealism has three layers contributing to explain state behaviour: (i) anarchy (self-help system), (ii) functional differentiation of units and (iii) changing distribution of capabilities – the dimension of polarity issues. In a historical perspective, however, anarchy came into being at the same time as the modern state system, that is, during the 17th century. Hence, it has been a constant for more than four centuries. The same can be said about the second level: like units. Configurations of polarity change slightly more often, and we have witnessed two such changes in the 20th century: from multipolarity to bipolarity in the 1940s and from bipolarity to unipolarity or multipolarity during the 1990s. Hence, two of three layers are essentially constants across centuries or decades, and the balance of power alone provides a source of explanation that is alive and kicking. Several realist theorists, who otherwise found neorealism attractive, are discontent with this state of affairs. They found it unsatisfactory that state behaviour could only be explained by means of the balance of power variable and concluded that the parsimony of neorealism was analytically counterproductive. In their view, the challenge was to relax some of the strictness of neorealism without sliding back into classical realism. Barry Buzan (1993) suggested a 'reconstructed' neorealism in which Waltz's three layers of explanation were extended to five layers. The two new layers, process variables and interaction capacity, contribute to a richer understanding of structure and, in turn, to a richer explanatory set-up. Glenn Snyder's ambition (1997) is quite similar to Barry Buzan's work in the sense of remaining with neorealism yet reconstructing and slightly extending it. In concrete terms, Snyder aims at explaining alliance politics, a purpose that forces Snyder to begin with but then move beyond the systemic focus characterizing neorealism. In order to move beyond the systemic focus, Snyder makes use of concepts such as entrapment and abandonment. In summary, the second debate was a debate within the broad confines of structural neorealism. Buzan and Snyder diagnosed Waltz's neorealism in a manner similar to – and perhaps inspired by – John Ruggie's criticism (1983). Yet, where Ruggie operates within the liberal tradition, Buzan and Snyder sought to identify solutions within the realist tradition in general and within the confines of structural neorealism in particular.

The third major debate has been between neorealists and post-neorealists. The latter grouping comprises theorists who prefer to relax Waltz's parsimony and scientism in various ways. In this fashion, neorealism has been succeeded or complemented by a range of realist theories, all of which share the feature of relaxing some of the strict dimensions of neorealism. Individual theorists engage in this kind of revision, each in their own way. The first major indicator of the interest in leaving parts of neorealism behind is Stephen Walt's (1987) study of alliances in the Middle East. Walt argues that rather than a balance of *power*, there is talk of a balance of *threat*. Walt's conceptual change of focus from power to threats may appear limited, but it has wide-ranging analytical consequences. One such consequence is that the exclusively structural mode of explanation is abandoned, because the assessment of threats inevitably includes assessments of intentions. A second consequence of replacing power with threat is that perceptions (and misperceptions) are bound to enter the analytical set-up. Combined, the exclusively structural and material basis of neorealism has been undermined and replaced by a richer ontology. The second indicator is Joseph Grieco's (1990) interest in the independent role of international institutions. Whereas neorealists typically consider international institutions to be arenas for power politics or reflections of the distribution of power in the international system, Grieco accepted that international institutions matter:

> [R]ealist theory would agree – perhaps to the surprise of some neoliberals – that international institutions do matter for states as they attempt to cooperate. Indeed realists would argue that the problem with neoliberal institutionalism is not that it stresses the importance of institutions but that it understates the range of functions that institutions must perform to help states work together. Realists would agree that international institutions are important because they reduce cheating; yet, realists would also argue, they must do much more than that if cooperation is to be achieved. (Grieco 1990: 234)

Charles L. Glaser (1995) joins this acknowledgement of the role of international institutions, suggesting that they can reduce or minimize the security dilemma, for example, when they assume the form of alliances or arms control regimes. Randall Schweller and David Priess (1997) have also attempted to expand the realist research agenda on international institutions. Finally, whereas neorealism is defined by its strict focus on third image dynamics, Randall Schweller (1994, 1996, 2003) relaxes this area of concentration and explores second image features as they unfold in the making of foreign policy; *American* foreign policy, that is. Combined, all of these openings, refinements or reconstructions have produced a heterogeneous and multifaceted contemporary realism. On the one hand it is a type of realism that is more sensitive towards real-world phenomena and practical policy problems; on the other hand it is also a realism that is open to charges of inconsistency and incoherence, that is, a degenerated theoretical position that has lost its intellectual core and survives by means of 'ad-hockery' and add-on hypotheses (Legro and Moravcsik 1999; see also Chapter 8).

The fourth intra-tradition debate concerns the relationship between realism and economics. In many cases, political realists have turned a blind eye to economics. Book titles such as *Power Politics* and *Politics Among Nations* suggest the focal point. Similarly, Kenneth Waltz's main work is tellingly entitled *Theory of International Politics*, and economic factors only enter his analytical design through the backdoor; economic assets are acknowledged as a source of the capability of states, thus contributing to the package referred to as power. Other realists have a fundamentally different take on the role of economics, acknowledging connections between economics and politics (see also Chapter 6).

Research agenda

The core of the realist research agenda remains studies of world politics, seen as balance of power politics, including research on polarity change and contending perspectives on the predominance of balancing or bandwagoning strategies. Kenneth Waltz (1993) discusses shifts in polarity, arguing that a multipolar international order is in the cards. Others discuss the case of the rise of China, drawing on offensive realism (Mearsheimer 2003) or power transition theory (Tammen and Kugler 2007), or they study the case of the EU's foreign policy (Posen 2004).

Realists typically argue that the leaders of great powers should be concerned about the balance of power and little else. For this reason, realists have often been ardent critics of American foreign policy. According to Morgenthau, the US violated one of the basic principles of political realism when engaging in the Vietnam War. 'Never put yourself in a position from which you cannot advance without loss of face and from which you cannot advance without undue risk' (Morgenthau 1984: 382). According to Mearsheimer and Walt (2003), the attempt to extend democracy to the Middle East by means of invading Iraq was not based on balance of power concerns and is best seen as an idealist adventurous foreign policy.

Contemporary realism is exceptionally US-biased. Most realists live and work in the United States, implying in turn that most of the intra-tradition debate has been among American realists. Some of them, such as Mearsheimer (2006), reject the very existence of realists outside the US. Most post-neorealists are preoccupied with the analysis of American foreign policy. Perhaps it is significant that some of the finest work *on* realism has been produced by scholars – Stefano Guzzini, Michael Williams and Martin Griffiths – living and working outside the US. By means of a comprehensive analysis of Machiavelli, Hobbes and Morgenthau, Michael Williams (2005) emphasizes that realism should first and foremost be seen as a doctrine of restraint. It is equally interesting to note that Chinese scholars have also started to engage in the debate regarding the merits of defensive and offensive realism (Feng and Ruizhuang 2006). Both defensive and offensive realism have practical implications in terms of policy prescription. Once bipolarity has been left behind and the superpowers have withdrawn from Europe, John Mearsheimer (1990) expects that Europe will slide back to the future, that is, be characterized by the instability and power politics that characterized the multipolar 19th-century Europe. Similarly, Mearsheimer is an ardent critic of American foreign (economic) policy towards China. Why? Because by increasingly including China in the international system by means of trade, membership of international institutions and foreign direct investment in China, the United States inevitably helps China to significantly maximize its power relative to the US.

The rise of the EU as a power is a theme that has been markedly down-played by realists. They have employed different strategies vis-à-vis European integration. Some have attempted to explain (away) the significance of European integration and governance. One example is Mearsheimer, arguing that the Cold War 'was principally responsible for transforming a historically violent region into a very peaceful place' (Mearsheimer 2003: 187). Others refer the issue to a hypothetical unlikely future situation (Waltz 1979) or argue that traditional state power lurks behind the European multilateral institutions, implying that the traditional realist analytical repertoire can still be employed. Still others argue that the key functions of states will never be transferred to collective policy-making (Grieco 1997). Such arguments have often been overtaken by developments within a decade, and sometimes faster. In general, realists have systematically underestimated the dynamics of European integration and governance. Stated differently, very few realists have acknowledged that realism has a consistent problem with understanding the politics and economics of a key region in world politics and have attempted to do something about it (Wivel 2003).

Realism is widely perceived as having nothing to offer concerning ethics or identity; indeed, realism is often presented as antithetical to such issues. In contrast, Chris Brown (2001) and others claim that this image of the realist tradition is 'pop-realism' in the sense that it is both widespread *and* largely unfounded. Crucially, he points out that pop-realism is on the whole unfounded in both theory and state practice. Brown adds that 'the notion that action can only be described as ethical if motives are absolutely pure and untainted by self-interest is bizarre, and, as suggested above, unsupported by any plausible moral philosophy' (Brown 2002a: 182). Brown's analysis corresponds well with Friedrich Kratochwil's (1982) explication of the notion of interest. Only in extreme cases are states not at all other-regarding, that is, states rarely cultivate a very narrow, purely egoistic, short-term conception of national interest.

Many share the view that the creation of more specific theories is needed. According to Donnelly:

> [r]ather than *Theory of International Politics*, we need *theories* of international politics, realist and non-realist alike, that together give us a chance to begin to come to terms with the multiple human purposes and complex practices and processes that make up world politics. (Donnelly 2000: 198)

In this perspective, there are three main challenges for theorists working within the tradition. Rather than merely reproducing the ontology of the realist tradition, they are challenged to produce more specific theories and demonstrate the value of these theories by means of theory-informed empirical studies. Rather than stubbornly sticking to purely explanatory theory, theorists could helpfully broaden their agenda by means of producing different kinds of theory and cultivating different meta-theoretical commitments. Because phenomena as diverse as ideational, social and cultural factors qualify as non-material, long-term engagement will be required to sort out precisely how one can square realism and non-material factors. Finally, realists should apply their theories to a range of different counter-intuitive actors, processes and structures – for instance, asking which insights offensive realism or power transition theory has to offer the political leadership in China, the EU or Russia.

Conclusion

In this chapter, we have examined theorizing within the realist tradition, a tradition that continues to be highly relevant for our understanding of contemporary international politics. Issues of power, conflict, war, interests and security appear to be here to stay. States continue to be among the main actors in the international system. Perhaps the security dilemma can be moulded, yet is unlikely to disappear.

Although realism enjoys continued relevance, it seems as if the tradition has lost its role as a hegemonic tradition. Jack Donnelly explicitly rejects the image of realism as a kind of master tradition to which all other traditions should demonstrate their added value. Instead, Donnelly insists that realism is only one tradition among several. In his words, '[r]ealism should not be ignored. But it should not be allowed to shape the study and practice of international relations, as it has for so much of the past half-century' (Donnelly 2000: 5). In addition to being an argument that has inspired the design of this book, it is important to emphasize that Donnelly's verdict is particularly relevant for the state of affairs in the United States, the prime contemporary bastion of realism. In Europe, research has primarily consisted of meta-studies rather than realist studies as such. However, this might change with the emergence of the EU as a major global player that encounters the harsh reality of international politics. Similar changes might occur in other emerging powers, including China, India, Japan or Brazil. Indeed, power transition theory predicts that future shifts in global power configurations might produce systemic instability.

Questions

- How does the tragic dimension inform the realist tradition?
- Which three strands of thought does realism comprise, and which key features characterize each current of thought?
- What major differences and similarities do you see between the three main realist currents of thought?
- Given that power is so important to realist theorists, how do they measure power?
- How would you describe the relationship between normative, interpretive and explanatory theory in the realist tradition?
- How would you describe linkages between, on the one hand, ontology and epistemology and, on the other hand, the realist tradition and discrete applicable theories?
- Why has realism become a primarily American theoretical tradition?
- What is pop-realism?

Further reading

Buzan, B. (1993) 'From International System to International Society: Structural Realism and Regime Theory Meet the English School', *International Organization*, 47, 3, 327–52.
> An article discussing what we might learn from comparing different theoretical traditions and currents of thought.

Donnelly, J. (2000) *Realism and International Relations* (Cambridge: Cambridge University Press).
> An excellent critical introduction to realism, written by a non-realist author.

Guzzini, S. (1998) *Realism in International Relations and International Political Economy: The Continuing Story of a Death Foretold* (London: Routledge).
> A major reappraisal of realist arguments.

Morgenthau, H. J. (1984) 'Fragment of an Intellectual Autobiography: 1904–1932', in K. Thompson and R. J. Myers (eds), *Truth and Tragedy. A Tribute to Hans J. Morgenthau* (New Brunswick and London: Transaction).
> An intellectual autobiography by the famous classical realist, Morgenthau, focusing on the challenges, concerns and coincidences of scholarly work.

Smith, M. J. (1986) *Realist Thought from Weber to Kissinger* (Baton Rouge, LA: Louisiana State University Press).
> Outlines the trajectories of the classical tradition throughout the 20th century.

Snyder, G. (1997) *Alliance Politics* (Ithaca, NY: Cornell University Press).
> Written by a leading realist scholar, this book is simply the best introduction to understanding alliance politics.

Tammen, R. L. (2000) *Power Transitions: Strategies for the 21st Century* (New York: Chatham House).

> This book represents power transition theory and outlines policy implications.

Waltz, K. (1990) 'Realist Thought and Neorealist Theory', *Journal of International Affairs*, 44, 1, 21–37.

> In this brief but excellent article, the leading neorealist compares classical realism to neorealism.

Williams, M. (2005) *The Realist Tradition and the Limits of International Relations* (Cambridge: Cambridge University Press).

> A major reappraisal of the realist tradition.

Websites for further information

www.ssrc.org/features/view/back-to-the-future-of-political-realism/

> An interview on the persisting role of political realism.

www.iht.com/articles/2005/05/11/opinion/edkissinger.php

> The former US Secretary of State, Henry Kissinger, discusses in a contemporary context the (ir)relevance of terms such as realism and idealism.

Chapter 5

The International Society Tradition

The English School as an approach to international relations (IR) is ripe for reconsideration.   (Barry Buzan 2001: 471)

The international society tradition is a distinct major tradition of thought, mainly cultivated in Europe, yet increasingly popular worldwide, and defined by five key features. In the first place, the distinctiveness of the tradition rests on its holistic conception of international society; an anarchical society, but a society nonetheless. This anarchical state society is constituted by common values, rules and institutions. Second, theorists within the tradition refuse the relevance of the so-called domestic analogy – that is, order conditioned by hierarchical authority – pointing out the possibility and existence of a non-hierarchical international order. Third, the tradition represents an institutional approach to the study of world politics, although the so-called 'fundamental' institutions include a number of fairly unusual institutions, including diplomacy, balance of power, international law, great powers and war. Fourth, though the tradition is somewhat split between more or less state-centric conceptions of international society; it is a question of degree rather than kind. Finally, the tradition represents a *via media* perspective on international relations, that is, a middle-of-the-road perspective. Somehow, situated between realism and liberalism, it can be characterized as a splinter grouping which used to be at home either in the realist tradition (see Chapter 4) or in various internationalist perspectives (Knudsen 2000). Being a *via media* tradition, it is always forced to argue for its distinct nature – being more than just a blend or a diluted version of the traditions we find along the roadside. Indeed, some critics claim that the break-away from realism was merely a half-hearted farewell to (English) realism.

Genealogy

The international society tradition, also called the English School, represents a tradition of thought reaching back to the philosopher Hugo Grotius (Bull

1966b; Wight 1991). Just like any other intellectual tradition, the international society tradition is characterized by a mixture of continuity (and therefore a tradition) and discontinuity (and therefore a dynamic tradition). Centuries of thought on international society include common focal points, key concepts and understanding of the nature of international society, yet also ruptures and progress. While various thinkers have analyzed individual attributes of international society, for instance diplomacy, they have not seen this and other similar institutions as fundamental institutions that contribute to a degree of order. Significantly, those working within the tradition were for decades not aware of the fact that they constituted a tradition. Though some early signs of a distinct school can be traced back to the 1950s, the English School only emerged as a fairly coherent tradition in the 1960s. The School was first explicitly *recognized* as a school in the early 1980s (Jones 1981; Dunne 1998; Jørgensen and Knudsen 2006). The founders of the tradition include Charles Manning, Martin Wight, Hedley Bull and John Vincent.

The English School has been almost exclusively cultivated within British – or rather British Commonwealth – academic institutions and traditions. Launched in the UK in the late 1950s and cultivated during the 1960s and 1970s, its first generations of scholars developed a rich research agenda contributing to what they believed was a better and more nuanced understanding of world politics. For better or worse, the nature of the English School has always been interdisciplinary and aimed at systematizing practical knowledge.

Birthmarks from older, well-established academic traditions such as (diplomatic) History, (International) Law, Sociology and Philosophy – but not Economics – are pronounced in the *oeuvre* of the English School. Some sceptics would therefore be inclined to ask: what is the English School if not Realism plus Sociology minus Economics? In any case, these disciplinary traditions merged at a certain juncture and produced, in an American context, social (and political) science, including International Relations (Hoffmann 1977; Schmidt 1998), whereas the older disciplinary traditions in Britain have produced what? Yes indeed; a distinct school of thinking about 'the international', called the English School and also sometimes institutionalized in the form of independent departments of international politics. These two parallel yet different genealogies of the discipline probably explain the consistent British fascination with 'the little difference' between British and American International Relations (see Smith 1985).

Even if some of its founders died relatively young, the School managed to publish several important studies during the last two decades of the 20th century. Several scholars identified with the School and publications continued to come out carrying the School's signature yet in most introductory textbooks the School remained unrecognized. At the end of the 1990s, attempts were made to 'reconvene' or relaunch the School on a global scale (Buzan 2001; Little 2000; Buzan 2004; Linklater and Suganami 2006). These calls to reconvene the School have been successful in terms of genuinely reactivating the School and attract new up-coming theorists; thus, it has (again) become a major theoretical tradition in its own right.

Currents of thought

The international society tradition is characterized by its distinctiveness vis-à-vis other traditions and by two major currents of theorizing: pluralism and solidarism. Each current has its own distinct understanding of international society, actors and processes. The policy prescriptions flowing from these currents are often contradictory, as representatives recommend fundamentally different political action. In the following, the distinctive features of the School will be introduced; subsequently, each of the two currents will be introduced.

The founders of the School did not find the simplistic binary distinction between idealism and realism particularly attractive or adequate. In their view, the distinction ruled out nuance and neglected a centuries-old perspective on international politics. In order to situate the School in the wider theoretical landscape, it is most helpful to use Martin Wight's (1991) image of international relations theory divided into three traditions. Paraphrasing Tocqueville, he writes:

> If one surveys the most illustrious writers who have treated of international theory since Machiavelli, and the principal ideas in this field which have been in circulation, it is strikingly plain that they fall into three groups, and the ideas into three traditions: Let them be called Rationalists, Realists and Revolutionist: these names do not sacrifice accuracy in any degree to the charms of alliteration. (Wight 1991: 7)

Let us briefly examine how he specifies the characteristics of each tradition:

- 'The rationalists are those who concentrate on, and believe in the value of, the element of international intercourse in a condition predominantly of international anarchy. They believe that man, although manifestly a sinful and bloodthirsty creature, is also rational' (Wight 1991: 13). According to rationalists, an international society has been created; not always by design, but also by custom and practice-led.
- 'The revolutionists can be defined more precisely as those who believe so passionately in the moral unity of the society of states or international society, that they identify themselves with it, and therefore they both claim

Figure 5.1   *Timeline: some key works in the international society tradition*

1962	Charles Manning, *The Nature of International Relations*
1966	Herbert Butterfield and Martin Wight (eds), *Diplomatic Investigations. Essays in the Theory of International Politics*
1974	John Vincent, *Non-Intervention and International Order*
1977	Hedley Bull, *The Anarchical Society*
1986	John Vincent, *Human Rights and International Relations* Alan M. James, *Sovereign Statehood: The Basis of International Society*
1989	Hidemi Suganami, *The Domestic Analogy and World Order Proposals*
1991	Martin Wight, *International Theory. The Three Traditions*
1992	Hedley Bull, Benedict Kingsbury and Adam Roberts (eds), *Hugo Grotius and International Relations*
1992	Adam Watson, *The Evolution of International Society*
1998	Tim Dunne, *Inventing International Society. A History of the English School*
2000	Nicholas Wheeler, *Saving Stranger: Humanitarian Intervention in International Society*
2000	Robert Jackson, *The Global Covenant: Human Conduct in a World of States*
2004	Barry Buzan, *From International to World Society? English School Theory and the Social Structure of Globalization*
2005	Alex J. Bellamy, *International Society and its Critics*
2006	Andrew Linklater and Hidemi Suganami, *The English School of International Relations. A Contemporary Reassessment*

to speak in the name of this unity, and experience an overriding obligation to give effect to it, as the first aim in international policies. For them, the whole of international society transcends its parts; they are cosmopolitan rather than "internationalists", and their international theory and policy has "a missionary character"' (Wight 1991: 8). The moral unity of the society of states is often referred to as world society by other theorists.
- 'The realists are those who emphasize in international relations the element of anarchy, of power politics and of warfare' (Wight 1991: 15).

According to realists, the units of the system, that is, states, constitute an international system. There is no such thing as an international society.

Though it is a broad-brush way of describing the traditions of international thought, Wight's distinction has been a source of inspiration for generations of theorists, and a range of different conceptions has been proposed, cf. Table 5.1. Stated differently, the charms of alliteration have been considerable.

In Table 5.1, the first row shows Wight's (1991) conception of the three traditions. Based on the three traditions, Richard Little (2000) makes a distinction between system and society and between two different versions of society. Claire Cutler (1991) points out that each tradition has its own philosopher as a kind of key intellectual root. Finally, Andrew Linklater (1998) claims that each tradition also subscribes to different epistemologies.

The fact that the School rejects realism can serve as a suitable starting point. After all, some of its founding members came from realism, with Herbert Butterfield and Martin Wight as the most prominent (compare Wight 1946 to Wight 1977; see also Molloy 2003). Even if some of the members of the School rejected realism, however, it is worth noting that others soldiered on within the realist tradition (e.g. Michael Howard and Herbert Butterfield), and still others have been ready to draw on realism whenever suitable (Little 2000; Molloy 2003). In the ontology of the English School, international phenomena such as war and the balance of power play a significant role (cf. Hedley Bull's *The Anarchical Society*). As such, they share vocabulary with realism but not always the meaning of such key concepts. Despite this somewhat ambiguous identity, the English School is generally considered a *via media* school. Being a *via media* theoretical orientation, the School not only rejects realism, but also idealism. Bull was equipped with a highly developed penetrating sense for harsh criticism and enthusiastically engaged in conversations with idealist scholarly opponents such as Richard Falk.

The very starting point of the English School is (European) international society. Indeed, one of the most important characteristics is its notion of international society, which can be said to be nothing less than *the* defining feature of the School. The notion of international society implies the avoidance of making order dependent upon hierarchy. In other words, international society is regarded as anarchical, yet this does not exclude order. The

Table 5.1 *A triptych of conceptions of the English School and two other traditions*

realism	rationalism	revolutionism	(Wight)
international system	international society	world society	(Little)
Hobbes	Grotius	Kant	(Cutler)
positivism	hermeneutics	critical theory	(Linklater)

definition of international society should be seen in relation to the definition of international system.

- 'A system of states (or international system) is formed when two or more states have sufficient contact between them, and have sufficient impact on one another's decisions, to cause them to behave – at least in some measure – as parts of a whole' (Bull 1977: 9–10)
- 'A society of states (or international society) exists when a group of states, conscious of certain common interests and common values, form a society in the sense that they conceive themselves to be bound by a common set of rules in their relations with one another, and share in the working of common institutions' (Bull 1977: 13)

Bull adds that an 'international society in this sense presupposes an international system, but an international system may exist that is not an international society' (Bull 1977: 13). According to Wight, the definition should be slightly different:

> International society is, prima facie, a political and a social fact, attested by the diplomatic system, diplomatic society, the acceptance of international law and writings of international lawyers, and also, by a certain instinct of sociability, one whose effects are widely diffused among almost all individuals, from tourist curiosity to a deep sense of kinship with all mankind. (Wight 1991: 30)

In this fashion, Wight's conception overlaps with that of Charles Manning, the first English School theorist to comprehensively examine the nature of international society. No matter the nuances and emphases, the three theorists share a common core.

Critics of the image of three traditions point out that it is vague or unclear and fails to identify the identity of the English School. Steve Smith (1995: 12–13) has three specific points of criticism: First, he claims that there are other ways of dividing international political theory. Second, he emphasizes that the conception creates more clarity than is actually warranted. In other words, many theorists do not fit easily into the individual traditions; nonetheless, if they are squeezed into traditions, the outcome is potentially misleading. The third point, which is probably the most serious or difficult, addresses the problem of determining whether the debates among the traditions can be resolved; and if yes, on the basis of which criteria. In Smith's words:

> there is no basis for deciding between the traditions that is external to each but not external to all. By this I mean that each tradition had its

own, and distinct, evaluative criteria, with no criteria being agreed on by the three traditions. (Smith 1995: 13)

According to Table 5.1, the English School is to be found at the centre part of the triptych. However, two distinct currents have developed within the School, each with its own characteristics, distinct emphases and conventional leanings. These two currents are introduced in the following sections.

Pluralism

Scholars adhering to this strand of thought strongly emphasize the pluralist nature of international society, hence its name. The 'pluralist' label is suitable, because each state cultivates its own conception of the 'good life'; in other words, international society consists of qualitatively different states. Some are dictatorships – for example, the conditions in contemporary Belarus, Myanmar, North Korea or China – and others are based on religious values – for example, Iran. Still others are failed states – for example, Zaire, Yugoslavia, Sudan, Czechoslovakia, or Somalia, while others yet are democracies (e.g. India, the United States, Denmark). All of these different states co-exist in international society. Co-existence is thus based on a *minimum* of common rules and norms; indeed pluralists assume that states cannot agree on matters beyond certain minimum purposes of mutual interest. All this indicates that pluralists have a relatively *thin* conception of international society. According to pluralists, the appropriate role of international law is to confirm the area of agreement among states by spelling out authoritative principles, leading to a reduced ambiguity concerning the scope and implications of society (Knudsen 1999). Nonetheless, international society *is* a society, not a mere international system. This concept constitutes a key difference between pluralists and realists. Among the leading pluralist members of the English School, we find Hedley Bull and Robert Jackson.

Pluralists do not necessarily value order more than justice, but they argue that order is a more basic value than justice. In their view, it would make little sense to pursue justice in a non-orderly society of states. To the degree order has been achieved, they argue, we eventually could begin contemplating the inclusion of the issue of justice on the agenda, provided that order is not put at risk. According to Hedley Bull (1966b), a dual system of rights and duties for both states *and* individuals would involve a threat to international order. First, because only states have rights and duties in international law, and human rights would be at odds with the pluralist preference for the principle of sovereignty and states' reliance on the loyalty of citizens. Second, as long as there is no international agreement concerning the substance of human rights and on individual justice more generally, there is a risk that human rights become a source of international conflict and disorder in itself. Rather than endorsing the further growth of human rights, then, pluralists point out the foundational principle of non-intervention. The essence of pluralism is that each individual state can decide for itself what the 'good life' is. For better or worse, this axiom places the destiny of individuals in the hands of the state (Vincent 1986).

Given the fact that, in political practice, human rights have been granted a more prominent role in international society during the 20th century, Hedley Bull points out that both the UN Charter and various Conventions and declarations have first and foremost been declaratory politics without much guidance concerning their implementation. The contemporary pluralist conception of international society thus leaves some room for a declaratory set of human rights (Knudsen 1999). However, there is not much support for a right of enforcement of human rights, since this would endanger the principle of non-intervention and, thus, international order. Humanitarian interventions can be accepted by pluralists, provided they are supported or authorized by an overwhelming majority of state members of international society and implemented collectively. The principles protecting individuals do not defend international order in the pluralist sense, but are rather an instance of international justice that involves a potential threat to the sacred position of the state. Accordingly, these principles ought to be enforced in a manner that maintains the maximum authority of states and involves a minimum of risk for great-power confrontation, for example, through great powers' collective authorization and implementation. If this cannot be secured, there should be no enforcement of human rights or international law (Jackson 2000: 249–93).

Thus, the pluralist project should be seen as an attempt to derive the law of nations from international treaties and custom. It is here we find the rules and principles to which the members of international society have given their consent. This pluralist position is also evident in the contemporary debates concerning the legality of intervention and coercive diplomacy, for example, the bombing of Yugoslavia in the spring of 1999 as a means of bringing an end to the persecution of the Albanian population of Kosovo. Since no general right of humanitarian intervention is included in the UN Charter or elsewhere in international law, and since the UN Security Council could not agree to authorize any intervention based on its new practice of linking massive violations of human rights with the defence of the peace under Chapter VII of the Charter, the question is whether legal grounds for the humanitarian intervention in Kosovo can and should be found in a broader interpretation of international law, for example, by reference to the preamble of the UN Charter, evolving UN practice in the area of humanitarian intervention and the Genocide Convention. The pluralists tend to say 'no', whereas the solidarists are inclined to respond affirmatively.

Robert Jackson's *The Global Covenant* (2000) is among the most prominent pluralist studies of world politics. It eminently restates the pluralist conception of international society. It deals with the world of states and states-people, as well as how we can or should be studying this world. Nonetheless, Jackson also argues in favour of taking values and principles seriously. He claims that they matter; indeed are highly important. The book constitutes one long argument in favour of the crucial importance of the normative superstructure of international society, a fabric weaved by threads such as norms, doctrines, rules, principles and values. Jackson exemplifies values by pointing out the values of the equal sovereignty of states, territorial integrity and non-intervention (2000: 178), and to personal as well as national security (2000: 185–8).

Furthermore, he elaborates on the notion of value pluralism, explaining that it refers to diversity and plurality of states: each state cultivates and is free to cultivate its own set of domestic values. 'There are many groups in world politics, each with different values, or different versions of the same value, which are distinctive to themselves' (2000: 179). Finally, he insists that we, as academics, should be sceptical of not only 'prevailing values' but also of 'reforming values', for example, overly ambitious ideas about reforming international society (2000: 81). Tellingly, in a chapter on democracy and international community, he includes a section on 'The Hubris of the West?' In other words, he argues that despite the value of democracy, states should not be missionary or crusading in their conduct of foreign policy. All this said, one should not forget that the entire book has been written to argue that diplomacy and foreign policy cannot be conceived of without taking the role of values into account. This is the primary reason for his criticism of Kenneth Waltz and Thomas Schelling, who do not recognize the role of values, including the values and normative structure that are present in their work.

In summary, the pluralist view on such issues as the sources of international law, human rights, the collective enforcement of international law, the use of war, sovereignty, international organizations and global governance hardly amounts to an ambitious conception of international society. In other words, when pluralists talk about international society, they have a minimalist society in mind.

Solidarism

The name of this current of thought, solidarism, is derived from the notion of solidarity, specifically solidarity among states concerning the security and welfare of individuals. In this fashion, solidarists cultivate a *thick* notion of international society contrasting, as we saw above, the pluralist thin notion. A key feature of solidarism is that individual human beings are regarded as direct members of international society, even though states are the stronger and more dominating members (Bull 1966b). This attitude to the position of the individual in international society follows logically from the premier solidarist principle, namely that despite the dominance of states in international life, international society is a society of mankind. Furthermore, it also reflects the strong belief that the individual is the ultimate member of international society. Accordingly, individuals have rights and duties in their own right, and domestic as well as international law should observe these rights. Consequently, individual rights may become the object of international enforcement, either by one state or by a collective of states, just like the international rights of states (Knudsen 1999: 56). As we shall see below, this conception leads solidarists to strongly endorse the doctrine of humanitarian intervention. The thick notion of international society also shows when it comes to the enforcement of international law (Bull 1966b; Wheeler 1992, 2000; Knudsen 1999). According to solidarists, states have a common responsibility to the institution of international law and are, in turn, obliged to offer diplomatic or military support to any state whose international rights have been violated.

In general, the solidarist current of thought has been less widespread than pluralism (Wheeler and Dunne 1996). For some time it was mainly represented by John Vincent (1986). However, solidarism has gained ground during the 1990s in both foreign policy practice and in theoretical reflection on practice. Among contemporary solidarists, we find Nicholas Wheeler, Tonny Brems Knudsen, Timothy Dunne and Thomas Weiss.

By means of returning to its original sources of inspiration, that is, to Hugo Grotius and neo-Grotian champion, Hersch Lauterpacht, the solidarist project began with issues related to the enforcement of international law (Bull 1966b; Knudsen 1999). Due to the lack of a global law enforcement authority, responsibility concerning enforcement would necessarily rest with states. A key question therefore becomes the degree to which they will enforce law. Thus far in the line of argument, the solidarists are in line with pluralists. At the next turning point of the argument, however, they depart from pluralism. How solidarist would states behave? How *should* solidarist states behave? When addressing the issue, solidarists consistently expect more rather than less.

A second and related issue has also been addressed. In the words of Wheeler, '[t]his conception of international society recognizes that individuals have rights and duties in international law, but it also acknowledges that individuals can have these rights enforced only by states' (2000: 11). This second issue takes its point of departure from the close relationship between the enforcement of law by states and the rights of individuals. The latter aspect is important, because it leads to considerations on the principle of non-intervention. Contemporary solidarists have primarily worked with this second issue in general and with humanitarian intervention in particular. The clear conclusion is that there is – or ought to be – exceptions to the principle that intervention is illegitimate. In cases of gross violations of human rights, it ought to be possible to relax the principle of non-intervention, particularly if intervention is conducted collectively and preferably authorized by the United Nations Security Council. In short, in certain circumstances and with certain provisos, humanitarian intervention should be considered legitimate. Solidarists claim that states have a right to humanitarian intervention (Wheeler 2000: 49). The argument is that states have a right to protect the human rights of individuals, even if doing so is at odds with the principle of non-intervention or with the basic ordering principle of state sovereignty.

During the Cold War, the notion of humanitarian intervention did not have a prominent position, except among a group of international law experts. Nevertheless, in practice and theory alike, it has experienced a renaissance after the Cold War. Wheeler's main interest is with humanitarian intervention, the principle of non-intervention and the value of human rights; he has an interest in a foreign policy practice which, since the end of the Cold War, has been fairly high on the agenda of world politics. His solidarist theory of legitimate humanitarian interventions attempts to identify the criteria or requirements compulsory for intervention to be deemed legitimate. In other words, he lists the foreign policy principles that are applicable within the field of practice we call humanitarian intervention, which is somewhat similar to Inis Claude's reflections on the relations between principle and pragmatism. Principles should not be regarded as etched in stone. The difference is that both Wheeler (2000) and Knudsen (2000) find it necessary or desirable to have explicit operational principles for the exceptions to the rule. The *raison d'être* of such criteria is that they contribute to reducing the risk of abusing the right to intervention; they provide legitimacy, shape common expectations, and enable collective action.

The issue of a right to humanitarian intervention is closely related to international deontological ethics, that is, to issues concerning not only the rights but also the *duties* of states in international society. Though there has been a tradition of thought on such issues since Grotius, it has recently experienced a renaissance, cf. writings by Michael Walzer (1977) and Luigi Bonanate (1995; for a brief introduction to deontology, see Hardin 1995 and Donaldson 1995). Within the English School, primarily John Vincent (1986) and Wheeler (2000) have examined issues of duty.

According to the solidarist doctrine, international solidarity is not confined to the relationships between states, and this is professed to be true as a matter of both legal principle and state practice. First, individuals also have rights and duties under international law, and the enforcement of these rights and duties may be a legitimate concern for international society as a whole under some circumstances, either on behalf of the individual or groups of individuals, for example, an ethic minority in need of protection. Second, states are obliged to defend the interest of all mankind by imposing upon themselves an element of self-restraint in matters of global relevance and by preventing crimes against humanity as a whole (Knudsen 1999).

Solidarists agree with pluralists that war ought to be viewed as a social institution (Bull 1977). As mentioned above, they believe that international law and human rights can be enforced collectively. Hence, war is seen as a social institution. However, war must only be used in defence of international order and the basic rules, values and rights in international society, which implies in turn that solidarists endorse the distinction between just and unjust wars. Consequently, this position regards the first Gulf War as a just war (i.e. the defence of international order). Similarly, NATO defending the Albanian population in Kosovo in 1999 by coercing the Serbian authorities to end attacks on Albanians also counts as a just war, whereas very few if any solidarists will consider the US-led invasion of Iraq in 2003 as legally or morally just (Dunne 2003). This attitude demonstrates that solidarists have a basis for examining different reasons for the use of force, namely the principles and purposes of international law, just war theory and solidarist conceptions in general.

Some might ask whether there is any deeper foundation of the solidarist position on human rights and principles of justice. Garrett Gong (1984) has claimed that 'human rights' and 'development' indicate a modern standard of civilization, that is, a global value hierarchy contradicting the pluralist conception of international society in which we find nothing but value pluralism. In this fashion, Gong connects current solidarist research to the otherwise bygone notion of civilization. In a sense, the English School has come full circle here because, among its many sources of inspiration, historians of civilization play a particularly important role, cf. the influence of Arnold Toynbee and other historians. In the context of Buzan's invitation to apply the English School in research on the European Union, Gong's notion of a modern standard of civilization could potentially play an important role, not least if the *acquis communautaire* and the Copenhagen criteria are interpreted as the current standard of European civilization.

Hedley Bull (1966b: 73) famously concluded his examination of the Grotian tradition by stating that the solidarist conception of international society has proved 'premature'. What is his argument? First, it has been difficult for him to find much evidence supporting the solidarist conception of an international society, that is, an enhanced commitment to justice. Second, he did not like what he found. Basically, he questions whether the consequences of well-intended solidarist action are counterproductive for the maintenance of international order. Whether or not this fruitless search is due to one of the few examples in which personal values have influenced Bull's analysis, it is a matter of fact that he devoted most of his energy to the pluralist conception of international society. Most of his classic work, *The Anarchical Society* (1977), applies pluralist conceptions, and the title of the book clearly connotes this leaning. He has serious doubts regarding the collective enforcement of international law, argues against the conception of any right of individual states to humanitarian intervention, and finds limited space for individual human beings in the international society of states. On the other hand, Bull later offered a more favourable interpretation of the feasibility of the solidarist position, indeed much of Nicholas Wheeler's work can be seen as a continuation of Hedley Bull and John Vincent's later reflections on solidarism.

Kinds of theory

Pluralists and solidarists agree that the English School cultivates and should cultivate a non-explanatory kind of theory. They argue that their type of theory is somewhat similar to (international) political theory, cf. Wight's (1969) argument in a famous essay entitled, 'Why is There No International Theory?' Hence, they regard the English School as an example of political theory that has strong affinities with both interpretive and normative theory (see Chapters 1 and 2) rather than with explanatory theory. Scholars in search of explanatory theory in English School writings will therefore be disappointed most of the time. This take on theory has wide consequences for which analytical game English School theorists see themselves being involved in. Jackson (2000) strongly emphasizes that English School theory ought to be seen as a political theory about international affairs, a conception that obviously has consequences for the nature of enquiry, which is considered to be essentially normative. Furthermore, he insists that International Relations is a craft discipline and rejects excessive scientist pretentions. In general, English School scholars analyze the norms and common understandings that guide states in their foreign policy and general behaviour. Obviously such an analytical endeavour does not necessarily entail prescribing desirable policy but theoretical reflections on the normative basis for action make it possible to understand and interpret the action of states as well as the nature of international society.

To the degree the English School is meta-study embedded, it has been informed by studies such as E. H. Carr's *What is History?* (1961) rather than by the Vienna Circle émigrés to America, Rudolph Carnap, Carl Hempel and Ernest Nagel, and their impact on creating a positivism-informed social and political science. Similarly, the English School rejected implicitly (Martin Wight) or explicitly (Bull 1966a) the predominantly American behavioural revolution, which otherwise almost succeeded in cleansing International Relations of Philosophy and History (on the dimension of history, see Puchala 2003). From this follows that historical and comparative methods have been employed in research practice. Hence, in order to better under-stand the present state system, several English School representatives have been engaged in diachronic comparisons of state systems (see Wight 1977; Buzan and Little 2000).

How can the School know about all of these things; what is its take on epistemology? The short answer is that interpretations differ. One reading is provided by 'monists' who homogenize the imbroglio of English School epis-temologies to just one homogeneous epistemology and, in turn, explore the potentials and limits of that preferred path. In contrast, Richard Little (2000) argues for a strategy of multiple paths. On the one hand he suggests that the English School is characterized by multiple epistemological positions. On the other hand he risks falling into the trap Bull once described as eclecticism masquerading as tolerance. Parts of the English School have always been informed by the position now labelled constructivism (Dunne 1995; Suganami 2001a, b; Linklater and Suganami 2006).

English School theorists generally claim to make use of the so-called clas-sical approach (Bull 1966a; Jackson 2000) and employ interpretative research strategies similar to those used by some sociologists, historians and international lawyers. According to Hedley Bull, the international society approach can be summarized as deriving from 'philosophy, history and law' and 'characterized above all by explicit reliance upon the exercise of judge-ment' (Bull 1969: 20). This is probably as far from an explicit methodology as one can possibly get. The lack of reflection concerning method has tradi-tionally been the School's Achilles' heel.

Main variants of theory

In this section we will review the main variants of English School theory. However, we will begin the section with a discussion of three more general English School-related issues. We have seen above that the English School is an intellectual tradition, comparable to other traditions such as realism, liberalism and IPT. Like other such traditions of thought, the English School primarily deals in general theories, that is, it provides a key to the main entrance of a building but not necessarily to the individual rooms of the building. Drawing on Joseph Lepgold's (1998) distinction between, 'four major groups of literatures and professional activities in the field: general theory, issue-oriented puzzles, case-oriented explanations and policy-making', it is fair to say that the members of the English School have been active in all four areas but primarily contributed to general theory. From Charles Manning onwards, the English School has theorized international society and international order; in the case of international society, this work has been more thorough and advanced than any competing tradition.

We have also seen that the international society tradition contains two major currents of thinking: pluralism and solidarism. But currents of thought do not constitute the kind of partial, specific theories we review in this section. For instance solidarism might well have a distinguished conception of international society but that does not amount to theory. Furthermore, solidarists may have cultivated their distinct understandings of key concepts, including sovereignty, non-intervention, responsibility and war. Similarly, they may have arguments concerning the relations between individuals, states and international society. But again, does that amount to a theory? Is it more than a conceptual framework? And in this context, where is the exact boundary between detached analytical enquiry and personal normative preferences? The question concerns solidarism specifically but suggests that English School theorists have generally been unable or unwilling to specify or explicate their conception of theory or meta-theoretical underpinnings. They have been vocal in their criticism of other theoretical orientations but significantly less vocal in stating in detail their understanding of theory (Bull 1966a; Jackson 2000).

Finally, it is important to understand that the issue, whether it is possible or desirable to develop English School-informed partial theories, is a most contested one. On the one hand we have Robert Jackson (2000: 77–96), who strongly emphasizes that the English School should be seen as a craft discipline, a perspective within the Humanities as opposed to the social sciences. The enterprise of building first-order (i.e. substantive) theories informed by the English School runs counter to Jackson's understandings of the School and what it can or should be. On the other hand strong criticism has been directed towards the English School. Martha Finnemore (2001) has formulated a brief yet caustic criticism of the School in which she points out that it is a challenge to many non-English School scholars 'simply figuring out what its methods *are*. There is remarkably little discussion of research methods anywhere in the English School canon' (2001: 509). Furthermore, and more important in the present context, she claims that a second source of puzzlement 'involves the theoretical ambitions of much English School work. What, exactly, are its advocates offering? What, exactly, are they claiming theoretically?' (2001: 510).

The answer to Finnemore's pointed question is quite simple. We have seen in the section on 'kinds of theory' that English School theorists consistently avoid explanatory theory and consistently engage in interpretive theory and sometimes address normative issues. Three specific theories stand out as particularly prominent.

A theory of international society

Hedley Bull (1977) has developed a highly original theory of international society, including its fundamental institutions. The theory makes the following core claims: (i) the international system includes an element of society; (ii) states are the principal members of this international society; (iii) the society in question is constituted by common rules and institutions, the latter including international law, diplomacy, great powers, balance of power and war; (iv) the international society has existed over centuries, yet is dynamic and characterized by metamorphoses; (v) the international society is what states make of it. As the claims make clear, the theory has scope conditions. While the theory does not deny that the international system to some degree (also) is characterized by a Hobbesian state of war or a Kantian world society, it concerns specifically one of the elements of the international system. The theory is state-centric but only to a point: the theory focuses on states yet it readily points out that states shape international society and are shaped by it. Thus, we are witnessing a process of mutual constitution. The theory emphasizes the role of fundamental institutions, causing a certain degree of order. In this context it is telling that the subtitle of Bull's book is *A Study of Order in World Politics*. Similarly, it is telling that Bull devotes an entire chapter to each of the five fundamental institutions, thereby emphasizing their importance. The theory's claim about the historical endurance of international society underlines the importance of this element of the international system and it provides the theory with a certain degree of sensitivity towards historical change. The fifth claim underscores how the theory is based on constructivist underpinnings: the international society is dependent upon its members continuously cultivating it. If they do not engage in reproducing it, it declines and other elements of the international system will play a relatively bigger role.

A theory of humanitarian intervention

While solidarism first and foremost is a current of thought, contemporary solidarists realize that solidarism lacks a theory of humanitarian intervention. In his book entitled *Saving Strangers: Humanitarian Intervention in International Society*, Nicholas Wheeler (2000: 33–52) provides such a theory. Being a solidarist interpretive theory, it explicates in some detail the meaning of humanitarian intervention. Wheeler begins by emphasizing that not all interventions are humanitarian and readily acknowledges that the subject is bound to be controversial. Is it, for instance, possible to establish criteria for legitimate humanitarian interventions? If yes, how many of these criteria should be fulfilled in order to make an intervention legitimate? Wheeler then specifies four threshold requirements, all derived from the just war tradition (see Chapter 2):

- There should be a just cause (what Wheeler prefers to call a supreme humanitarian emergency)

- Use of force should be a last resort
- A principle of proportionality should be adhered to
- There should be a high probability of a positive humanitarian outcome

Wheeler examines each of these criteria in detail and then continues to review four potential criteria above the threshold. He first dismisses the relevance of a 'humanitarian motives' criterion on the ground that solidarists care about the victims of a humanitarian emergency, not the motives of intervening states. Subsequently, he reviews the 'reasons for action' criterion, that is, the justifications states give in favour of their interventions. This issue is linked to potential abuse. Finally, he addresses the issue whether humanitarian interventions need be lawful and the potential problem of selection bias – the problem that states only intervene in some and not in other cases of supreme humanitarian emergency. Concerning each of the eight criteria, whether below or above the threshold, Wheeler carefully examines the criterion and makes a reasoned argument in favour of his choices. In this fashion, Wheeler builds a solidarist interpretive theory of humanitarian intervention. The theory is subsequently applied in order to assess the humanitarian characteristics of the cases of intervention analyzed in the book.

Towards a theory of hegemony

Ian Clark (2009) has built an English School theory of hegemony or, rather, he has outlined a kind of pre-theory which could, in turn, be transformed into a fully fledged theory. Clark's starting point is that without a theory of hegemony, the English School has next to nothing to say about unipolar modes of order. Thus acknowledging the absence of such a theory, Clark's theory-building procedure is to 'excavate' a theory from various writings of English School theorists, essentially claiming that hegemony is a potential institution of international society. Hence, the English School theory of hegemony should be seen as an extension or an aspect of the broader theory of international society, particularly elements stressing the role of international institutions. In this context, 'excavation' means exploring and interpreting what English School theorists have previously said about hegemony and, subsequently, welding these bits and pieces into a coherent theoretical position. The core claims are that hegemony requires material power but material power is insufficient. This is an example of reasoning by means of analogy: also great powers require material power but their order-producing managerial roles need to be socially recognized.

Each of the three theories demonstrate that the English School is fully capable of generating specific or partial theories that can help us understand important aspects of international or world politics.

Main intra-tradition debates

We have seen that the English School occupies a contested position some-where between idealism/liberalism and realism; furthermore, it comprises two distinct currents of thought. Whenever there are contending currents of thought there are theoretical debates and the English School is no exception. In the following, three important issues will be addressed.

First, recalling Robert Jackson's claim that world politics cannot be understood without exploring the normative superstructure, it is hardly surprising that he explicates the notion of 'norm'. In this context, he makes an important distinction between two different vocabularies: on basic procedural norms and basic prudential norms, respectively. The former refers to 'a vocabulary of international procedure which is part of a larger ethics of principle'. Basic prudential norms concern the ethics of statecraft. It is here worth remembering that Jackson regards International Relations as a craft discipline, that is, not as a scientific enterprise. Statecraft is like an art, and our role as scholars is similar to the role played by art or literature critics. In his discussion of the responsibilities in independent statecraft, Jackson draws a distinction between national, international and humanitarian responsibility, and he does not attempt to conceal the fact that he considers national responsibility to be the primary (Jackson 2000: 169–78). He is very keen on the importance of the situational ethics of independent statecraft, that is, the outcome of meetings between actor, circumstance and standards of conduct. Realists tend to emphasize circumstance and denigrate standards of conduct, whereas idealists tend do the opposite. The members of the English School 'exercise judgement' based on endogenous standards. Jackson strongly insists that imposing exogenous standards is as irrelevant and misleading as it possibly can be. On balance, Robert Jackson's contribution to the international society tradition is both distinct and comprehensive. He has much to say about international society and considerably less about foreign policy. Consequently, because he focuses on the important role of prudent judgement by statesmen, his IR theory has greater relevance for foreign policy analysis than most other general IR theories.

Second, we have seen above that pluralists highly value the principles of sovereignty and non-intervention which, in turn, inevitably leads to criticism of the increasingly widespread practice of humanitarian intervention. Hence, Robert Jackson is predictably highly critical of the NATO campaign in Kosovo in 1999 (Jackson 2000). A second target of the pluralist criticism of contemporary trends in world politics is the notion of human security (Jackson 2000). In general, pluralists sceptically observe the spread of human rights and democracy after the end of the Cold War – cf. Robert Jackson's cautious endorsement of humanitarian intervention to prevent genocide provided it is under the authority of the UN. Ken Booth (1995), observing the pluralist distaste for humanitarian intervention, argues that they sacrifice human beings on the altar of the sovereign state. Returning the compliment, some argue that solidarists potentially sacrifice the value of order in order to prioritize the value of human rights. This is a serious and classical criticism, because these critics add that there can be no justice without order. Without order, promoting justice is an illusive quest. Solidarists may counter that the pluralist stance implies that justice will never be placed on the global political agenda. Why? Because, in the absence of order, order is what is sought. When there is order, nothing should be allowed to put that order at risk. Hence, pluralism is an inherently conservative position and solidarists want more.

Third, let us briefly revisit Hedley Bull's definition of international society:

> A society of states (or international society) exists when a group of states, conscious of certain common interests and common values, form a society in the sense that they conceive themselves to be bound by a common set of rules in their relations with one another, and share in the working of common institutions. (Bull 1977/1995: 13)

On the one hand pluralists are keen to emphasize the importance of 'independence, self-determination, self-government, co-existence, non-intervention, and reciprocity' (Jackson 2005a: 652), that is, all of the features that go into the genesis of sovereign statehood. But if these features concern the constitution of units (i.e. states), where then is the dimension of society? On this issue, Jackson points out that 'mutual recognition and regard of states, along with their affirmation and ratification of shared norms, is the metaphorical glue that helps to keep pluralist international society from deteriorating into a mere international system' (Jackson 2005a: 652). However, this is a very thin layer of society on top of strongly self-centred states. In comparison to Bull's definition, the common interest and values have disappeared along with common institutions.

Some argue that solidarism is best seen as a (political) vision and not as a significant dimension of contemporary international society. Thus, Robert Jackson (2005b) points out in a slightly harsh summary, that solidarism:

> is about prospects and possibilities rather than actualities, the future more than 'here and now'. That is owing to the fact that international solidarism confronts realities of the nation-state and national interest. It also confronts realities of the world population by culture, history, language, religion, civilization etc. and it confronts difficulties of providing international public goods beyond the nation-state or the pluralist society of states. (Jackson 2005b: 767)

Solidarists possibly respond that major parts of the global normative superstructure actually possess the status of actualities rather than prospects and possibilities. Conventions on human rights, genocide and more have been in place for decades. The ban on landmines was introduced due to concerns for the security of individuals, not state security. Human security is on the agenda of global politics. Furthermore, particularly after the end of the Cold War, a veritable change of practice has occurred concerning the doctrine of humanitarian intervention (Knudsen 1999; Wheeler 2000). Finally, despite opposition coming from a group of like-minded states, the International Criminal Court has been inaugurated and the first rulings have been made.

In the context of the reconvention of the English School, the debate between pluralists and solidarists is of crucial importance to securing momentum and theoretical-analytical progress. Their competition to interpret current international affairs is promising as regards the future directions of the English School. To the degree that pluralists and solidarists engage in debate with non-English School traditions or currents, they are also in a position to influence the development of the discipline.

Research agenda

According to one English School critic, Dale Copeland (2003), the English School has primarily been engaged in excessive critical self-centred navel-gazing. Copeland points out that many English School-informed studies:

> seem more interested in establishing the history of the School (how it developed, who is 'in' or 'out'), in discussing different ways of conceiving the core concepts (for example, international society vs international system), or in providing exegetical points on the founding fathers (what did Wight or Bull really say?). Such efforts may be important ground-clearing exercises for the development of theory, but they are not theory themselves. (2003: 431)

What are we to make of this kind of criticism? On the one hand Copeland points out a clear meta-tendency in English School scholarship, an approach that cannot continue in the long run if the attempt to launch the English School as a major source of inspiration for studies of world politics is to have any clout. On the other hand Copeland seems to suggest that English School theorists alone engage in interpreting – political theory-like – what the founding fathers really said. Furthermore, for a tradition that is in the process of being 'reconvened', it makes considerable sense to explore such issues. Finally, English School theorists have produced a wide range of conceptually informed empirical studies, thereby demonstrating how the tradition and its currents of thought can be applied in empirical interventions in world politics. As we have seen, the English School is capable of delivering concepts – even very refined concepts – conceptual distinctions and taxonomies. Actually, the English School seems obsessed with categorizing and conceptualizing state practice. Such a research agenda may serve as a helpful starting point. However, a research tradition primarily capable of delivering concepts is an insufficient source of inspiration. The English School may be able to add to the ontology of international politics. However, ontology is a point of departure, but there should also be arrivals. Otherwise, there is the risk that the exercise turns sterile and becomes a non-progressive intellectual project.

Second, the systemic focus is very clear in a major part of the research agenda. Thus, when Bull (1986) analyzes interventions, he focuses on interventions in world politics. And when Bull or Wight analyze international institutions, they focus on the fundamental institutions of international society and reduce international organizations to the status of pseudo-institutions (Bull 1977: xiv). Many issues in world politics only belong in one of the rooms in the main building, that is, these issues have their place at a sub-systemic level, and the main key provided by the English School does not always fit well in the research on these sub-systemic phenomena. From time to time, the founders of the English School did leave the systemic level behind in order to analyze phenomena at less general levels. Their findings are not particularly different from the findings produced by other perspectives, however, meaning that the value added from taking an English School perspective seems to be limited. This is not to argue that general conceptual constructs are unhelpful in research on sub-systemic phenomena; only that some sort of 'translation' is necessary in order to arrive at fruitful interfaces between the level of general theory and more specific and applicable theories; between general conceptual constructs and less abstract concepts; and between 'grand' ontological narratives and concrete research questions. Indeed, general theories may function as the cement that joins over-specified explanations together within a comprehensive framework of understanding. Barry Buzan has attempted to transcend the English School's focus on systemic dynamics. In the first place, he extends the analysis of international society (interstate) with an analysis of world society (transnational). Furthermore, under the umbrella of a global international and world society, he opens the possibility of the existence of regional international and/or world societies (2004). Finally, he explores what the English School has to offer in terms of understanding the Middle East (Buzan and Gonzales-Palaez 2009). These contributions contribute to significantly broaden the research agenda of the English School.

Third, Barry Buzan and Maria Gonzales' (2005) point of departure is that a significant part of John Vincent's theory has been neglected, namely his reflections on the right to subsistence, particularly the right to food. Vincent claims that the elimination of starvation should be the minimum standard for the society of states to achieve legitimacy. Buzan and Gonzales assess the normative and practical viability of that enterprise as a project of solidarism in international society. In principle, their investigation could be extended to health, poverty, environmental safety and related matters. Similarly, Richard Shapcott (2001) focuses on shifts in the practices of global governance and the solidarist turn in international society. He claims that they force us to rethink the constitutive norms of international society. He is particularly interested in exploring the means whereby consensus and consent for the practices of global governance and a solidarist international society may be achieved and points out specific forms of communicative action. Given that pluralism involves difficult moral choices, pluralists are bound to reflect on linkages between theoretical orientation, power, prudence and morality. This not only applies to pluralists – witness how realists tackle the issue – but pluralists have to do it their way due to their distinct theoretical orientation. Robert Jackson (2005a: 653) points out that the main normative challenge to pluralism concerns the issue of how to deal with the obvious facts of the abuse of state power and failed states. He considers a number of solutions to this problem but then concludes that 'abusive governments or failed states may be a price pluralists have to pay for an international society that upholds local liberty across the world via the doctrine of non-intervention' (2005a: 653). This solution is most likely not sustainable, and the issue will therefore remain on the pluralist agenda.

Fourth, given the solidarist conception of international law, they find it natural to revisit the boundary zone between international law and politics, which is not just any boundary. On the contrary, this boundary has been used to argue in favour of a distinct sphere of politics, namely international politics, thus providing a rationale for the establishment of the discipline of International Relations (Knudsen 2005). Some solidarists have taken up the classic theme of considering the potentials of world society (Vincent and Wilson 1993). They argue that the principles of sovereignty and non-intervention have become less absolute. Significant changes in the status of human rights have caused this development, and they consider new foundations of international legitimacy. Solidarists are generally not reluctant to push for justice in international society; indeed, they do not accept the state-centric approach of their pluralist opponents. Instead, solidarists cultivate the notion of a world society constituted by individuals, each entitled to enjoy human rights. The suppressors of human rights should not be able to hide behind state borders. It is the responsibility – for some solidarists even a duty – of individuals and states to protect and promote human rights, also beyond state borders. Furthermore, solidarists strongly believe in the potential of collective enforcement of international law (including legal principles), and collective management of international order and international affairs more generally (global governance). Finally, according to the solidarist conception, sovereignty is qualified in the sense that sovereignty can be nullified if rulers do not adhere to the principles of human rights.

Barry Buzan (2001) claims that the EU is the most solidarist international society that has ever existed. In this fashion, he has sought to bring together the EU, EU studies and solidarism. Given that the English School has largely ignored European integration and governance, Buzan's initiative promises to open a new chapter in the *oeuvre* of not only solidarism but also the English School in general (see Diez and Whitman 2002). In many ways, the English School has been made by men (and a few women) of the British Commonwealth, not of Europe. They focus on major international relations issues rather than on European specifics. Thus, Bull did research on superpower politics and arms control, not on European Community specifics, such as procedures for the making of foreign policy. Consequently, post-war Europe has been a predominantly blank spot on the map. Most of the few references to European integration actually have a quasi-realist nature. The pronounced blindness towards economic factors of all sorts ensures that the CAP, the Single European Market, European trade policies and globalization are all no-go areas. The pronounced blindness towards economic factors is probably because the English School was created by specialists in (diplomatic) history, international law and sociology. Furthermore, if European states fully integrate, it is really no big deal. Sure, the new Euro-state will be a new international player, but it will not change the nature of international society. When considering potentially fruitful encounters between the English School and EU studies, it is worth noting that the English School contributes valuable reflections regarding the kind of world in which the EU has been raised and is currently growing up in (see Diez and Whitman 2002). Furthermore, the expansion of international society is intimately linked to de-colonization and the globalization of the European model of sovereign statehood (Bull and Watson 1984). There is an interest in quasi-states (Jackson 2000: 294–315), but not specifically in EC–ACP relations; there is an interest in the UN (Roberts and Kingsbury 1988) but not specifically in EU policies vis-à-vis the UN. Finally, the classic debate between the liberally minded Francois Dûchene (1972) and Hedley Bull (1982) has by now been transcended by reflections on what has been called 'normative power Europe' (Manners 2002).

In summary, the English School generally offers a helpful point of departure for research on issues such as contemporary (unipolar) international society, the promotion of human rights and democracy, humanitarian intervention, and war crimes tribunals. Given that contemporary international affairs are characterized by the absence of a balance of power, significant breaches of international law and critical problems for the UN, the anarchi-

> ### Box 5.1   The English School between idealism and realism
>
> 'Idealists: Life, internationally, is nasty and brutish, but there is a way out. Let us repeat what we have done domestically. Let us, this time, create a greater Leviathan (or its negative surrogate).
>
> Realists: Life, internationally, is nasty and brutish, and ideally, a greater Leviathan would be the right solution. But there is little we can do to create it. So let us think of how to survive in this miserable condition.
>
> English School: Life, internationally, is not that bad. What a surprise. Let us work out why.'
>
> (Hidemi Suganami 1983: 2369)

cal society seems to be under attack (Dunne 2003). The new interest in English School ways of thinking about the international society has resulted in a significant extension of the tradition's research agenda. Whereas it used to focus on the dynamics of international society, international order and human rights issues, several major issues have been added since the relaunch.

Conclusion

The English School is a distinct theoretical tradition originating in the British Commonwealth. In the context of Wight's three traditions of international relations theory, the English School represents rationalism, thus occupying a central position. In contrast to the liberal tradition, the English School has a relatively strongly developed agnosticism when it comes to progress and utilitarianism. In contrast to realism, the English School emphasizes the international society, including common institutions and norms.

The key concept 'international society' – along with a pronounced interest in the history of international society – probably renders the English School capable of delivering the deepest insight into the European state system available, including its history and the 'secession' of international society from the European state system. The English School is characterized by a pronounced tension between two clearly discernable currents of thought: pluralist and solidarist conceptions of international society (Bull 1966b). The term 'international society' is among the School's key terms, but other terms such as 'balance of power', 'international institutions' and the 'sociology of international relations' contribute to the distinct nature of this School, not least because their meaning is distinctly different from other theoretical orientations.

The English School pursues an extensive research agenda and addresses several topical issues of the 21st century, including humanitarian intervention, European integration and governance, and international organizations. The School has been critically reappraised; it has engaged in self-referential reflection. Many have reflected on the theoretical promise of the English School, ranging from Roy Jones's (1981) famous article to the contemporary increasing interest in the School (Dunne 1998; Little 2000; Buzan 2001a; Linklater and Suganami 2006). The School is often met by a severe criticism of lack of methodological and theoretical ambition and clarity. In recent years, attempts have been made to reconvene or relaunch the English School as a major theoretical tradition. The School is thus experiencing this relaunch, demonstrating that new and older generations of scholars continue to find the School inspiring and worth examining.

Questions

- What are the basic characteristics of the English School?
- Which theoretical orientation did English School theorists leave behind? Why?
- Which major currents of thought are represented within the English School?
- What is the purpose of reconvening the English School?
- What are the basic characteristics of the solidarist orientation?
- Which contending views do solidarists have vis-à-vis pluralists?
- How do solidarism, humanitarian intervention and social justice proceed?
- Does solidarism share any features with strong liberalism?
- What are the basic characteristics of the pluralist conception of international society?
- What makes international society a society?
- Which consequences concerning policy-making flow from pluralism?
- What are the main differences between pluralism and classical realism?

Further reading

Bellamy, A. J. (ed.) (2005) *International Society and its Critics* (Oxford: Oxford University Press).
    A very informative critical reappraisal of the deeds and vices of the English School.

Bull, H. (1996 [1977]) *The Anarchical Society. A Study of Order in World Politics* (Basingstoke: Palgrave Macmillan and New York: Columbia).
> Perhaps the most famous book to come out of the international society tradition.

Buzan, B. (2001) 'The English School: An Underexploited Resource in IR', *Review of International Studies*, 27: 471–88.
> An important article in which Barry Buzan invites theorists to reconvene under the 'auspices' of the English School.

Dunne, T. (1998) *Inventing International Society: A History of the English School* (Basingstoke: Palgrave Macmillan).
> In this book, Timothy Dunne explores the historiography of the English School and its main founders.

Jackson, R. (2000) *The Global Covenant: Human Conduct in a World of States* (Oxford: Oxford University Press).
> One of the most significant contemporary accounts of English School positions, written by a leading scholar in the field.

Jackson, R. (2005a, b) 'Solidarism' and 'Pluralism', in M. Griffiths (ed.), *The Encyclopedia of International Relations and Global Politics* (London: Routledge): 765–8 and 651–3, respectively.
> Both entries are very concise accounts of the two major currents of thought within the English School.

Knudsen, T. B. (2005) 'The English School: Sovereignty and International Law', in J. Sterling-Folker (ed.), *Making Sense of International Relations Theory* (Boulder CO: Lynne Rienner): 311–26.
> In this chapter, Knudsen traces linkages between law and sovereignty, as conceived of within the English School.

Linklater, A. and Suganami, H. (2006) *The English School of International Relations: A Contemporary Reassessment* (Cambridge: Cambridge University Press).
> An authoritative interpretation of the main characteristics of the English School, written by two eminent representatives.

Wheeler, N. (2000) *Saving Strangers: Humanitarian Intervention in International Society* (Oxford: Oxford University Press).
> The primary and most systematic account of the solidarist current of thought and its implications for our understanding of humanitarian interventions.

Websites for further information

www.leeds.ac.uk/polis/englishschool/
> The main English School website.

www.un.org/Overview/rights.html
> The UN Declaration of Human Rights.

www.un.org/aboutun/charter/
The UN Charter.

oregonstate.edu/instruct/phl302/philosophers/grotius.html
Hugo Grotius bibliography, at Oregon State University.

eprints.lse.ac.uk/archive/00000166/01/Vincent_finalAGP_BB.pdf
An article in strong favour of solidarism.

www.pwe.org.pl/pdf/sa/sa00600.pdf#search=%22pluralism%20
english%20school%22
An introduction to the English School, and to the pluralist and solidarist
currents.

www.bu.edu/ir/faculty/jackson.html
The Robert Jackson website.

www.icrc.org/Web/eng/siteeng0.nsf/iwpList2/Humanitarian_law
A wide range of links on international humanitarian law collected by the
the International Committee of the Red Cross.

Chapter 6

The International Political Economy Tradition

The study of globalisation has to embrace the study of the behaviour of firms no less than other forms of political authority. International political economy has to be recombined with comparative political economy at the sub-state as well as the state level.

(Susan Strange 1999: 354)

In the previous chapters we have seen that international political theory, liberalism, realism and the English School are theoretical traditions which primarily focus on international politics. By contrast, the international political economy (IPE) tradition focuses on the linkages between international politics and economics. This simple shift in focus produces a number of distinct theoretical currents and a rich theoretical domain in which the issues addressed and questions asked differ significantly from politics-centred traditions. In negative terms, IPE is not economics, because the discipline of economics does not usually show much interest in either the economics–politics relationship or in politics. IPE is not the study of politics, because this field of study tends to neglect the role of international economics.

As just emphasized, IPE addresses the multifaceted relationship between international politics and economics, that is, the relationships between states and markets as well as between states and civil society actors, for example, firms, NGOs and a range of commercial interest groups. At the heart of the IPE tradition, we will therefore find important issue areas such as the production of commodities and services as well as the politics of trade, currencies, financial flows and export control regimes. IPE also includes topics such as globalization, foreign direct investment, development, competitiveness, economic sanctions, regional economic blocs and environmental regulation.

When characterizing the relationship between politics and economics, we have in principle three fundamentally different options. Some believe that politics basically controls economics. Others believe that economics determines politics. Still others believe that the two spheres of social action mutually influence each other. Among IPE theorists, all three options have very

Box 6.1   Some major classical political economists

Mercantilists regard the economy as the continuation of politics by other means. In other words, they make a plea for making use of the economy to achieve political ends.

Francois Quesnay (1694–1774) was one of the first modern economists, co-founder of the Physiocratic school of thought.

A. R. J. Turgot (1727–1783) made very few, yet cutting-edge, contributions to political economy. He is best known for the short but brilliant book, 'Reflections on the Formation and Distribution of Wealth' (1766). He is also considered a Physiocrat, though he did not always agree with Quesnay.

Adam Smith (1723–1790) was a fierce critic of mercantilism and one of the prime promoters of free trade.

David Ricardo (1772–1823) created the theory of comparative advantages, a prototype theory of free trade and globalization.

Karl Marx's (1818–1883) work on capitalism was significantly influenced by David Ricardo and other classical economists. In a certain sense, he extended their findings and produced a distinct mixture of economics and a politics of liberation.

vocal proponents, something contributing to the diverse and contested nature of IPE. In addition, the IPE tradition is cultivated differently in different parts of the world, and the present chapter reflects this diversity and pluralism concerning different focal points, approaches and dominant ways of employing different kinds of theory. To some degree, scholarly attention follows the volume of economic activity, implying that research interest in the politics of international economic activities within the wealthy North is significantly greater than the attention to the political economy of the less well-off South.

Genealogy

The intellectual roots of the study of international political economy can be traced back to 17th-century doctrines of mercantilism and 18th- and 19th-century classical political economists such as Francois Quesnay, A. R. J. Turgot, Adam Smith, David Ricardo and Karl Marx.

Concerning the 20th century, the genealogy of IPE can usefully be divided into three main phases. The first phase covers the period until the mid-1940s. In this period, Marxist approaches to IPE play a significant role, for

> ## Box 6.2 Karl Polanyi
>
> Karl Polanyi (1886–1964) was a Hungarian sociological-cultural economist. He was born in Vienna and became part of the extraordinarily rich scientific milieu that characterized the final years of the Austrian-Hungarian Empire. He fled Austria in 1933 and settled in London for some time before moving to the US and ending up in Canada. His best known publication, *The Great Transformation* (1944), was prepared in London but completed and published in the US. Polanyi has been very influential for subsequent IPE developments, known not least for his three arguments: (i) the modern state and market economies are two sides of the same coin; (ii) economies are embedded in society and culture; and (iii) if left to themselves market economies are unsustainable or, put differently, *laissez faire* economies are thoroughly planned.

example, setting the research agenda on key issues such as the nature of international capitalism, relations between capitalist and pre-capitalist modes of production and, finally, the dynamics of imperialism. Both Marxist and others emphasize that international political economy is influenced by technological change, in particular because such changes have an impact on economic developments. The invention of tractors, for example, has obviously had a profound impact on rural economies and the rapid development of the Internet has enabled the dot.com industry to thrive. Outside the Marxist tradition, specialized institutes for area studies were established during this period, often devoted to the study of the political economy of colonial possessions. Economics and political science were not yet as specialized as these disciplines are at present, implying that the disciplinary split between political science and economics did not characterize research to the extent it does today.

During the second phase, after World War II and until the early 1970s, Marxism was a source of inspiration for scholars developing dependency theory and theories of regulation. Marxism also became the dominant ideology of the communist world, characterized by state-led economies. Outside the Marxist tradition, modernization and development studies have focused to some degree on international political economy. During this phase, professional economists continued to pay serious attention to political factors, thereby making possible the launch of IPE as we know it today (Cooper 1968; Kindleberger 1973; de Cecco 1974; Schonfield 1976; Cohen 1977). Studies like these simply made it easier to bridge the two disciplines. However, the dominant trend within economics is to produce ever more specialized and formalized studies. In general, this phase was shaped by developments in the world economy itself, for example, changing patterns of open and closed (communist) economies as well as highly uneven degrees of economic development.

The third phase begins in the early 1970s and represents an important milestone in IPE development. Two initiatives proved to fundamentally reshape our conception of IPE and the third phase is therefore essentially characterized by a deep split between two contemporary versions of IPE. The first contemporary version of IPE was initiated by Susan Strange, who in 1970 published an influential article provocatively entitled, 'International Economics and International Relations: A Case of Mutual Neglect?'. Basically, she argues that given the developments within the global economy, it is both unnecessary and undesirable to keep the two disciplines apart; there is much to gain from bringing them together. In other words, she makes a strong plea to bridge the two disciplines. Furthermore, by founding a network of scholars – the IPE Group – she contributed to institutionalizing the bridge. She deliberately avoided prioritizing any particular discipline, theory or method – inviting political scientists, economists, international lawyers (and many others) to focus on IPE, each from their respective perspective. Her vision *anno* 1970 of a future IPE is remarkably similar to contemporary IPE, at least as it is cultivated outside the US.

This leads us to the second contemporary version of IPE, which is particularly cultivated within American scholarship (Katzenstein, Keohane and Krasner 1998; Cohen 2007; Lake 2006). According to this conception, IPE is a relatively young field of study that was launched during the 1970s (in the US) and matured during the 1990s. In order to make this conception plausible, Jeffrey Frieden and Lisa L. Martin (2002) point out that the first IPE textbook was published as late as 1977 and that it has become increasingly common to offer courses on the topic since then. Furthermore, they claim that a consensus on theories, methods, analytical frameworks and research agendas has developed over the course of the last two decades of the 20th century. However, this claim should be seen in the context of the fact that American positivist scholarship alone is reviewed. David Lake (2006) shares both the narrow focus and the perception of the characteristics of the field. Notably, he regards American scholarship as providing the dominant approach – labelled 'Open Economy Politics' – and finds that the emerging inter-discipline, though relatively young, is rapidly maturing. IPE 'made in the US' is typically conceived of either as a subset of International Relations or as a combination of International Relations and Comparative Politics. Hence, the debates within IR and/or Comparative Politics define the analytical framework of IPE enquiry, whereas the dominant understanding of social science standards provides the epistemological and methodological baselines.

This genealogy demonstrates that IPE is a highly contested field of research that can be seen as on the one hand an old tradition of thought, reaching back to the classical political economy tradition of the 17th and 19th centuries and on the other hand a relatively new tradition characterized by a narrow conception of both the subject matter and a small family of approaches. IPE is thus characterized by contending images of the identity of IPE, implying that there is fundamental disagreement about whether it is a sub-discipline of IR, an inter-discipline or a discipline in its own right. In order to understand the trajectories of IPE during the 20th century, it is important to keep the disciplinary distinction between economics and political science in mind. IPE is simply an attempt to bridge the ever-wider gap between these two social sciences that seems to exist in worlds apart. In a certain sense, IPE simply owes its existence to this split and is characterized by highly contrasting ideas about the nature of the subject matter and the form and standards of enquiry.

Currents of IPE thought

There is a clear pattern in how IR theoretical traditions handle the linkages between international politics and economics. Thus, the English School, the international political theory tradition and the post-positivist tradition (see Chapter 7) hardly comprise any such linkages and will therefore not be examined in this section. By contrast, both the liberal and realist traditions include currents of thought in which politics–economics linkages are at the centre of attention. In addition, Marxists have made a significant contribution to international political economy, and they can be said to constitute a current of their own. Finally, there is a current of thought which can be referred to as the eclectic current. It is characterized by the key idea that several disciplines in the social science and humanities have something important to say about international political economy. It is therefore not quite a homogeneous current, yet a considerable number of scholars subscribe to the idea. Each of these four strands of IPE – realist, liberal, Marxist and eclectic – is characterized by specific features, conceptual understandings and genealogies. Combined, they provide intriguing yet contending perspectives concerning the role of economics, the relationship between international politics and economics and contemporary trends in the world economy. Theorists from all four currents are engaged in important debates both inside the tradition and with theorists from other traditions.

Realist IPE

Realist IPE is often seen as a version of mercantilism. Hence, we will begin this section by examining the different meanings of mercantilism; subsequently we will move on to realist IPE as such.

Figure 6.1   *Timeline: some key works in international political economy*

1902	John A. Hobson, *Imperialism: A Study*
1926	Fritz Sternberg, *Imperialism*
1944	Karl Polanyi, *The Great Transformation*
1952	R. G. Hawtrey, *Economic Aspects of Sovereignty*
1957	Paul A. Baran, *The Political Economy of Growth*
1967	Andre Gunder Frank, *Capitalism and Underdevelopment in Latin America*
1968	Richard Cooper, *The Economics of Interdependence: Economic Policy in the Atlantic Community*
1970	Susan Strange, 'International Economics and International Relations: A Case of Mutual Neglect?', *International Affairs*, vol. 46
1973	Charles Kindleberger, *The World in Depression, 1929–1939*
1974	Immanuel Wallerstein, *The Modern World System: Capitalist Agriculture and the Origins of the European World Economy in the Sixteenth Century*
1976	Andrew Schonfield (ed.), *International Economic Relations of the Western World*
1977	Benjamin Cohen, *Organizing the World's Money: The Political Economy of International Monetary Relations*
1987	Robert Gilpin, *The Political Economy of International Relations*
1991	Craig Murphy and Roger Tooze (eds), *The New International Political Economy*
2000	Jan Aart Scholte, *Globalization: A Critical Introduction*
2005	Nicola Philips (ed.), *Globalizing International Political Economy*
2006	B. R. Weingast and D. A. Wittmann (eds), *The Oxford Handbook of Political Economy*
2007	Benjamin Cohen, 'The Transatlantic Divide: Why are American and British IPE So Different?', *Review of International Political Economy*, vol. 14

Anyone who combines Reagan, Bush, Clinton, Korea, China and the EU, respectively, with mercantilism and 'Googles' the six pairs of concepts (Reagan and mercantilism, Bush and mercantilism etc.) will find that mercantilism is a popular but not quite positive term in the public discourse on international economic affairs. However, 'Googling' everyday language is not our business. The task is to become familiar with discourses of theory, and, in the present context, figure out how academic currents of thought explore international political economy. In this context, it is significant that mercantilism is basically a political doctrine dating back to 16th-century Europe. Mercantilism was a popular economic philosophy and state practice in Europe for two centuries, the 16th and 17th. The newly established Westphalian order and mercantilism go hand-in-hand, and the era of European absolutism was also the era of mercantilism. During the 18th century, Adam Smith and other free trade theorists attacked mercantilism and it slowly began to wither away. During the 19th century, however, mercantilist theories and political practice resurfaced in Germany and the US. This new wave is sometimes referred to as neomercantilism. Finally, the policy prescriptions of Marxist *dependencia* theorists were taken directly from the mercantilism manual. Brazil, India and many other Third World countries all bought the argument and adopted mercantilist policies; a tempting policy for most late developers, that is, countries that try to catch up with the global economic avant-garde. Due to a failure to deliver, these policies were gradually abandoned and substituted by free trade policies. At this point and given these developments, one important question remains to be answered. If the mercantilist doctrine is more than 200 years old and if the late 19th-century neomercantilist experiments in Germany and the US have given way to free trade and new deal economics and, if *dependencia*-informed policy-making in the Third World has undergone a U-turn, then why devote several pages to a seemingly dated doctrine?

There are two eminently good reasons for doing so. First, while some of the historical forms of mercantilism are long gone, mercantilism-informed policies remain in place around the world. They influence contemporary Europe, Asia, Africa and North America. Even Japanese overseas development aid (ODA) is claimed to fit Japanese mercantilist aims. The EU is marked by a fundamental divide between 'free traders' and protectionists. Similarly, there is an equally significant divide concerning the attitudes to state control of key industries. Some are deeply reluctant to reduce such state control, whereas others are prone to practice liberalization, also concerning these industries. The United States, probably the strongest proponent of international free trade strategies, has in practice proved less than willing to drop high tariffs on agricultural commodities, open up for foreign direct investment in strategic industries, drop subsidies to home market industries and abandon attempts at extra-territorial legislation. Outside public policy-making, policy recommendations of important segments within the anti-globalization movement are also deeply informed by protectionism.

Second, mercantilism has been refined and given the form of a theoretical current. How does this work? Realist IPE is often referred to as mercantilism. Like political realism, economic realism emphasizes the conflict-ridden nature of the politics of international economics. As we saw in Chapter 4 (on realism), states are supposed to prefer relative rather than absolute gains. Mercantilism also implies a strong dose of state intervention in domestic economics, for example, in the form of state-owned companies. Power is at the centre of attention, because the aim of mercantilist policy is to increase state power; not only by military means (as offensive realists suggest), but also by means of economics. As explained by Robert Gilpin, possibly the best-known of the contemporary mercantilists:

> I knew there was a connection between politics and economics, and I knew I was not a Marxist ... I was, for example, greatly influenced by Hawtrey's book *Economic Aspects of Sovereignty*. He was a monetarist theorist in the 1920s, and wrote a wonderful book on the interplay of economics and politics, and I then discovered a book on mercantilism and said to myself: 'Ah! That's what I am!' I began to realize that you could have a realist view of world economics without being a Marxist. (Gilpin 2005: 368)

He adds that '[t]he postwar age of multilateral liberalization is over and the world's best hope for economic stability is some form of benign mercantilism' (Gilpin 2005: 368). Gilpin reaches this conclusion by means of an impressive examination of political and economic developments affecting money, trade, development, finance and multinational corporations. Thus, he draws a distinction between benign and malign (or aggressive) mercantilism. The former version is typically represented by countries such as the US, whereas aggressive mercantilism has been adopted by countries such as China and South Korea.

Liberal IPE

Many scholars consider the field of IPE to be the heartland of liberal theorizing. Which arguments justify such a view? In the first place, the origins of economic liberalism were traced to 18th-century criticism of mercantilist doctrines, characterized by their emphasis on protectionism and the notion that the national economy should serve the objectives of power politics. As an alternative to mercantilism, liberal theorists promoted free trade, and free trade is to the bone about intersections between international politics and economics. Furthermore, as we saw in the chapter on liberalism (Chapter 3), the main dimensions of liberal international thought were identified: interdependence liberalism, republican liberalism and neoliberal institutionalism. These currents of liberal theorizing are perfectly compatible with a focus on the intersections between international economics and politics. Though conditions of interdependence can have several sources – for example, economic, security and ecological – liberal theorists usually have the economic dimension in mind, arguing that economic interdependence has a positive impact on international politics, especially because the costs of political conflict will increase while the benefits decrease. Studies emphasizing the effects of the internationalization or globalization of production often represent extensions of interdependence liberalism.

The line of argument concerning republican liberals is possibly less direct but nonetheless very present and influential. Liberal theorists are prone to argue that free trade causes economic growth which, in turn, stimulates processes of democratization. At this point, republican liberal theorists can join the causal chain, not least because their key argument is that democracies are more peaceful than non-democratic states, for which reason processes of democratization should be supported. From this perspective, it makes sense to integrate China in the world economy and encourage Chinese membership of international economic institutions such as the WTO. Chinese economic growth is supposed to create a new middle class, aiming at democratizing China.

Concerning neoliberal institutionalism, it is worthwhile noting that it applies to general processes of institutionalization, including international economic institutions. In other words, the (failed) ITO, the GATT and the WTO were all meant to promote free trade and provide common norms and rules concerning international trade. Similarly, the IMF and the World Bank were created with political ends in mind, which were to be achieved by means of economic instruments. In the case of the IMF, the original political objective was to secure stable currency relations, particularly because unstable currencies harm international trade and economic growth. Subsequently, the purpose of the IMF has been redefined and broadened. Even seemingly non-economic international institutions, such as the World Health Organization (WHO), play a key role in the international political economy. The immediate purpose of WHO is obviously to secure a high level of health globally, including fighting pandemics such as SARS and bird flu. International health has a considerable economic dimension (just ask the pharmaceutical industry or investment consultants), however, and regulating this health economics is an important task for politicians and officials.

In summary, then, all three layers of the liberal theoretical 'cake' – interdependence liberalism, republican liberalism and neoliberal institutionalism – are designed to analytically handle intersections between international politics and economics. Such intersections do not merely represent an optional 'add on' analytical gadget; they constitute an intrinsic aspect of the theoretical currents. In addition, purely economic theories – such as international trade theory – can be seen as sub-contracted constructs that are essentially part of the liberal package, though without including the political-ideological wrappings that characterize the liberal theories of inter-national political economy. Combined, this prompts some to argue that liberal IPE is probably the strongest theoretical platform for understanding contemporary international political economy.

Marxist IPE

Marxism is a general theory of political economy and a general theory of capitalism specifically. This might not be surprising, as it simply means that Marxists focus on what they regard to be the main determining factor for societal development and leave epiphenomenal factors to idealists of various sorts. In other words, Marxists see strong causal arrows leading from modes of production to the superstructure of capitalist society; superstructure understood as political, religious and ideological spheres. Tellingly, Marx's main work is entitled *Das Kapital (The Capital)*. In his understanding, comprehensive knowledge of the general laws of capitalist accumulation provides a necessary key to understanding all of the other derived societal and state phenomena. As a leading analyst of political economy, Marx plays an important role for these analytical interventions. In addition, he provided a theory of political action and, thus, combined analysis of things as they are and how they can possibly be changed by the employment of strategies of emancipation.

The outcome of World War II meant that Western European socialist and communist parties returned to some of their past prominence. These parties played a significant part in the resistance movements across Europe and managed to become part of the leading political forces in Western Europe after the war. However, Marxism was no longer in the same position as was previously the case. Western European communist parties balanced between Soviet Marxist dogmatism and more independent stances. Impressed by the process of de-colonization, some analysts transferred their hopes concerning social change or revolution from the industrialized West to the Third World. They supported various national liberalization movements and failed to see that most of these movements were nationalist forces first and Marxist or socialist second. It took the student protests and general social commotion of the 1960s to reinstall Marxism as a major grand theory. Throughout the late 1960s and 1970s, Marxism was reintroduced in Western European universities. A thorough reconsideration of the Western Marxist tradition was part of the agenda, in part because the tradition had largely been forgot-ten (Anderson 1973). Moreover, the current state of capitalist affairs was analyzed, including imperialism, *dependencia*, Americanization and the creeping internationalization of the means of production.

Among the main schools within the Marxist IPE tradition we find the Amsterdam School, the Toronto School and the World Systems Theory

---

Box 6.3   The Amsterdam School

The Amsterdam IPE School is a remarkably long-standing school of thought. For some time, Andre Gunder Frank was part of the school. Other leading figures include Otto Holman, Henk Overbeek and Kees van der Pijl, whereas the younger generation includes Bastiaan Apeldorn, Andreas Bieler and Angela Wigger.

School, the latter based in North America. The Amsterdam School is named after the relatively strong group of Marxist scholars in Amsterdam, whereas the Toronto School refers to a research community at the University of York in Toronto, Canada. The two schools share several characteristics. Both of them represent a so-called neo-Gramscian approach to international political economy. Ironically, Antonio Gramsci did very little work on economics, emphasizing instead the relatively autonomous role of politics vis-à-vis economics. Members of the Amsterdam and Toronto schools do exactly the opposite. Furthermore, the two schools focus on the dimension of hegemony, yet are far from the emphasis on cultural and ideological dimensions that characterized Gramsci. Despite these critical issues, the two schools are recognized for their belonging to the Marxist tradition and Gramsci's role has been conceptualizing, for instance, hegemony, which the neo-Gramscians subsequently have applied to international affairs. The Amsterdam School in particular can point to a long tradition of IPE studies spanning three generations or more. World system theory will be introduced below in the 'Main variants' section

The eclectic IPE current

The eclectic conception of IPE implies that scholars from almost any discipline – for example, political science, sociology, geography, economics, MBA schools, law – with an interest in the relationship between international politics and economics are accepted – indeed welcome – to join the joint venture. The common point of departure is exclusively the subject matter in all its complexity. Scholars within the current therefore employ a plethora of conceptions, approaches and perspectives. The major advantage is that, in principle, all analytical opportunities can be pursued, that is, no analytical opportunity should by necessity be left unexplored at the roadside. This feature seems well suited to a truly complex subject matter such as international political economy. Some of the perspectives cultivated within this heterogeneous eclectic conception of IPE produce insights that are hardly achievable by any other means. Among the analytical disadvantages, two are particularly important to consider. Given the different languages that scholars from different disciplines are trained to use, it is often difficult to read across disciplines. Many insights are lost in translation or remain known to limited segments of the research community. Similarly, given the absence of common criteria for best practice scholarship, it is difficult to determine what exactly the state of the eclectic IPE art is, in other words, what exactly has been achieved in terms of understanding international political economy.

Kinds of theory

Contrasting perspectives on the identity of IPE produce logically different bundles of studies, each representing different kinds of theory. Three main perspectives have come to shape the field of study.

First, when IPE is seen as a subset of IR and political science, it is only to be expected that IR theories and theoretical debates characterize how IPE studies are conducted. Hence, much of what has been described in the previous chapters on the liberal and realist traditions, for example, also applies to the IPE tradition, exactly because IPE is seen as no more and no less than these other traditions *plus* a consistent focus on relations between international politics and economics.

Second, especially in the US, IPE studies are predominantly couched in a particular form of positivist- and empiricist-conceived social science. Given that American political science often draws heavily on methods developed within economics, the exact same feature characterizes IPE. Tellingly, Barry Weingast and Donald A. Wittman (2006) believe that political economy simply *is* a set of rationalist approaches and nothing more. 'In our view, political economy is the methodology of economics applied to the analysis of political behaviour and institutions. As such, it is not a single, unified approach, but a family of approaches' (Weingast and Wittman 2006: 3). Similarly, David Lake is keen to point out that normative principles need not be analyzed by means of normative theory. They can be converted 'into externalities simply by adding into an individual's utility function a desire, say, not to see children exploited' (Lake 2006: 767). Rationalist standard operating procedures can thus be employed by means of simply circumventing the ontology of norms. Though Lake does not consider the opposite convention process, that is, from utility functions and externality to norms, it should be a feasible analytical move, thus enabling studies of economic phenomena by means of applying normative theory and methods. Finally, choice-oriented approaches (Frey 1984; Lake and Powell 1999) count as a similar vintage IPE. Combined, these sources of inspiration produce a highly homogenized – though narrow – form of IPE. The advantage is that cumulative progress is both feasible and at least to some degree also achieved. Furthermore, due to the highly stylized form of research, it is relative easy for newcomers to figure out the state of the art and subsequently 'board the train', so to speak. The disadvantages are that a range of analytical opportunities have been lost in the process of homogenization, that is, certain questions cannot possibly be asked, potentially fruitful conceptions cannot be used and entire research agendas cannot be addressed. If, for example, preferences are assumed, then we cannot and need not explore their formation; if focus is exclusively on social reality, then material reality is beyond our research programme; if a given theory is couched in a timeless fashion, then any sense of historical direction becomes meaningless.

Third, the Marxist tradition, including to a certain extent approaches derived from Marxism, is so broad and multifaceted that it is difficult to summarize the key theoretical features. Concerning the kinds of theory, however, there are basically no limits. Explanatory, interpretive and normative theories have all been used. Although key concepts might be different from rationalist studies of international relations, Marxists often share both materialist and positivist underpinnings with their rationalist peers. Such underpinnings lead some Marxists – though rarely Marxists with an interest in IPE – to draw on rational choice. Likewise, Marxists share with political realists an interest in the relationship between power and wealth. Hence, it is hardly surprising that economic realists, Robert Gilpin (1987) in particular, include Marxist scholarship in their theoretical synthesis conception of IPE. The mixed presence of explanatory, interpretive and normative theory often makes it difficult for readers to determine which dimension is at play. Furthermore, the burden of belonging to a tradition also shows within the Marxist tradition. Paradigmatic conceptions are left under-questioned and therefore run the risk of becoming dogma. Normative concerns are present, yet the particular analytical language is broad-brushed and conceptual innovation is lacking. Theoretical over-determination often rules over a deep knowledge of the subject matter. Finally, the Marxist tradition is characterized by a stubborn adherence to 'mutually agreed, respectable' theories and methods. In this respect, however, the Marxist tradition is hardly different from any other theoretical tradition, the English School, realism and rationalist approaches included.

Main variants of theory

Within the IPE tradition and its various currents, theorists have developed a range of more specific theories. In the following sections, we will consider five such specific theories, selected because they illustrate the rich variation of theorizing within IPE. We will soon see that some of the theories are universal theories applied to the international politics of economic matters (e.g. regime theory), whereas other theories have been developed with specific economic issues in mind. We will also see that some of the theories are actually a cluster of theories, such as theories of imperialism.

Theory of hegemonic stability

The origins of hegemonic stability theory date back to Charles Kindleberger who, in *The World in Depression, 1929–1939* (1973), analyzed the economic instability of the 1930s. Basically, Kindleberger argued that the world economy is inherently unstable and therefore needs a hegemonic manager. In the words of Robert Gilpin, 'Charles Kindleberger was the originator of what Keohane subsequently called the theory of hegemonic stability. The argument was that there would be economic instability if there were no leading power managing the world economy' (Gilpin 2005: 368). Subsequently, the theory was further developed by Robert Gilpin, Robert Keohane and Susan Strange. According to the hegemonic stability theory, a hegemon is simply the dominant power in the international system, provided that the power in question is ready to pay the costs of the position. Furthermore, the theory asserts that systemic stability is not provided by means of a balance of power or international cooperation. On the contrary, the theory claims that a hegemon is a precondition for the functioning of a highly integrated world economy, not least because hegemons are willing to pay the price of leadership (side payments, endlessly being blackmailed by lesser powers, exchanging short-term costs for long-term benefits). In applications of the theory, Great Britain is typically viewed as the hegemon of the 19th century and the United States as the hegemon of the second half of the 20th century. In between these two (Western) eras of hegemony, there was an interregnum, no hegemon and, therefore, a world in depression. After the US defeat in the Vietnam War, there was debate during the 1980s addressing the decline of the US power. Some asked why the system seemingly continued to function, even after hegemony (Keohane 1984). Others claimed that the decline of hegemony was a myth (Strange 1987) or that the conception of a decline in US power was a fatal misperception (Nye 1990). The picture today is more blurred, as the current state of world affairs is highly contested. Are we in a situation of unipolarity, or does it make more sense to identify a range of issue-specific hegemons? Some argue that the EU provides most of the services that a hegemon is supposed to provide. While the Union does not supply security for global markets, it does provide a large market, an international currency and considerable loans to the world economy. Furthermore, within climate policy, the EU functions as a hegemon securing a collective good, whereas the US for some time preferred to free ride. Finally, the Union's unilateral 'Everything But Arms' initiative can be interpreted as a side payment to the least developed countries, expecting them to subscribe to EU positions in WTO negotiations.

> ## Box 6.4   The EU 'Everything But Arms' initiative
>
> In February 2001, the Council of the European Union adopted the so-called 'EBA (Everything But Arms) Regulation' (Regulation (EC) 416/2001), granting duty-free access to imports of all products from least developed countries without any quantitative restrictions, except to arms and munitions. At present, 49 developing countries belong to the category of LDCs. The provisions of the EBA Regulation (Council Regulation (EC) No 416/2001 of 28 February 2001) have been incorporated into the GSP Regulation (Council Regulation (EC) No 2501/2001). (Europa 2009)

Classic theories of imperialism

Karl Marx and Friedrich Engels devoted most of their time to thoroughly analyzing capitalism. To the degree that they analyzed colonialism, it was considered to be an aspect of the capitalist mode of production. However, Marx and Engels did not develop a Marxist theory of imperialism. This task was left to other leading Marxists, particularly Rudolf Hilferding (1909), Rosa Luxemburg (1912), Nikolai Bucharin (1917, 1924), Vladimir Lenin (1916) and Fritz Sternberg (1926). Rudolf Hilferding (1909) made an important distinction between production and finance capital. On this basis, he argued that the accumulation of capital would lead to fewer and fewer – but larger and larger – companies. In turn, these ever-larger companies would be dominated by finance capital. This development of capitalism would eventually comprise the entire globe and imply an unprecedented degree of imperialism. Furthermore, the new configuration of capitalism would have derived effects at the political and ideological levels, specifically in the form of an ideology of social Darwinism and warfare.

In *The Accumulation of Capital* (1912), Rosa Luxemburg argues that capitalism without territorial expansion is unsustainable. In order to survive and thrive, capitalism must conquer pre-capitalist territories and dominate the populations living there. Hence, imperialism is necessary for capitalism. Once again, we see a clear linkage between the analysis of capitalism and the explanation of imperialism. To intellectuals such as Hilferding and Luxemburg, World War I came as no surprise. It was also not a surprise that the West was bound to create colonies in most parts of what is today known as the Third World. Capitalism simply requires such expansion for its processes of accumulation. Vladimir Lenin (1916) also recognizes a connection between capitalism and imperialism. He addressed one of the classical issues in International Relations – the causes of war –

particularly the causes of World War I. Basically, he shares much of Luxemburg's analysis, famously claiming that imperialism is the highest stage of capitalism. He predicted that investments would gradually be transferred to the colonial areas, thereby depriving the working classes in the capitalist metropoles one of the preconditions for societal progress and human emancipation. Basically, capitalists would attempt to bribe part of the working class, thereby reducing the interest of the workers in revolutionary political action. Lenin concluded that if a world revolution happened, it would most likely happen in the semi-periphery, not in the capitalist metropoles. His conclusion was clear: let us try out revolution in Russia. And so he did. After the Russian revolution and several failed revolutions in Central Europe, the Marxist concern about imperialism changed somewhat. Fritz Sternberg's *Imperialism* (1926) is about the last study coming from the Marxist tradition of imperialist studies.

These classical Marxist studies of imperialism were produced by theorists who were also revolutionary politicians. They developed theories as part of their political vocation. This dual engagement also shows in their fate. Hilferding, Luxemburg and Bucharin were all killed by their political opponents, and Fritz Sternberg was forced into exile in the US during the era of Nazism and fascism in Europe.

Dependency theory

As European and American colonies were dismantled during the process of de-colonization after World War II, the gap between developed and developing countries received increased scholarly and political attention. Global inequality was difficult to ignore, and the gap even seemed to widen. People asked: why is this so? A diverse group of theorists consisting of European, Latin American and African scholars created dependency theory in order to provide answers to this intriguing question. The theory was promoted within the political climate of the 1970s, which also advanced the political vision of a new international economic order (NIEO). The UN Economic Commission on Latin America was instrumental in building a caucus of scholars, and the prominent role of Latin American scholars explains why the theory is sometimes referred to as *dependencia* theory. Karl Deutsch has summarized dependency theory in the following way:

> [T]he theory says that the poverty of the underdeveloped countries is the result of the present international economic system which by its automatic operation has underdeveloped the poorer nations of the world, keeping them as poor as if they were still colonies. This system, says these theorists, is by its very structure the equivalent of the old system of colonial empires. (Deutsch 1978: 270)

Some of Hilferding and Luxemburg's ideas were thus brought into a new setting, in particular the notion that the capitalist North needs the poor, pre-capitalist South for its development.

As mentioned above, dependency theorists make a heterogeneous group. Among Latin American scholars, we find Raul Prebisch, Enzo Faletto and Fernando Henrique Cardoso. The latter worked on dependency theory – while in exile – in the 1960s and 1970s, before becoming President of Brazil (1995–2003). Prebisch argues that there is a direct correspondence between poor and rich countries: it is simply a zero-sum game, implying that richness simply produces poorness. Among the other prominent dependency theorists are Samir Amin, Andre Gunder Frank and Johan Galtung. Andre Gunder Frank and Cardoso in particular played an important role in the development of the theory and are the ones who popularized the theory. Like Fritz Sternberg and others, Frank and his family fled Europe and went into exile in the United States. Hence, Frank was educated at American universities. Given his left radical mindset, it is somewhat a paradox that his teachers include Milton Friedman at the University of Chicago. Among Frank's main works within the field of dependency studies, we find *Capitalism and Underdevelopment in Latin America* (1967). Samir Amin, whose work primarily focuses on Africa, was brought into the circle of dependency theorists in order to provide insights on the case of Africa. In general, in the words of Robert Jackson and Georg Sørensen, dependency theory is 'an attack on late capitalism. It is an effort to provide the theoretical tools by which third world states can defend themselves against globalized capitalism' (Jackson and Sørensen 2003: 205).

World systems theory

World systems theory addresses some of the same issues characterizing the classical theories of imperialism and dependency theory. Immanuel Wallerstein (1974) and Giovanni Arrighi (see Arrighi and Silver 1999) are among the prominent representatives of world systems theory. In contrast to classical Marxists, world systems theorists do not believe that capitalism implies a transfer of investments from core countries to peripheral countries. On the contrary, it is the *absence* of such transfers and *unequal* transactions that keep developing countries in their unfavourable situation. Furthermore, the notion of 'developing countries' is a euphemism designed to conceal the fact that these countries are forced to remain underdeveloped. The policy prescriptions of both dependency and world system theorists highlighted the potentials of South–South trade and are often close to the doctrines of mercantilism (see above). In this context, it is interesting to note the paradox described by Karl Deutsch (1978), that mercantilist theorists (e.g. Friedrich List and Henry Carey) lost the argument to free trade economists, whereas

European states at the time increasingly practiced mercantilist or protection-ist strategies. Free trade strategies remain the dominant doctrine in contem-porary international economic diplomacy, cf. policy prescriptions flowing from international financial institutions such as the IMF and the World Bank, whereas major economic powers, such as the US and the EU, preserve some aspects of mercantilism, for example, tariff barriers vis-à-vis outsiders.

Economic theories

For a theoretical tradition focusing on the intersections between politics and economics, advances in economic theory are obviously far from irrelevant. On the contrary, economic theories contribute new options for theorizing linkages between economics and politics. Whereas the original economic theory of comparative advantages is among the origins of the entire IPE field, subsequent IPE theoretical constructs have been able to draw on advances in economic trade theory, including the Heckscher–Ohlin and Stolper–Samuelson theorems (see Box 6.5). Contemporary emphases on the distinc-tion between inter-industry and intra-industry trade patterns offer novel options of theorizing the linkages between economics and politics. In general, a primer in modern economic theory accompanied by a conception of politics that is based in economic assumptions makes a very strong analyt-ical package. It is a coherent combination that has the advantage of being in tune with the models used by major international financial institutions such as the IMF, the World Bank and the European Central Bank.

Embedded liberalism

John Ruggie (1982) coined the concept 'embedded liberalism' in the early 1980s, thereby generating a vigorous debate regarding the nature and dynamics of international economic orders. Since then, the concept has remained one of the most influential conceptions in IPE, IR, law and else-where. The concept has been called many things. For some, it is thus 'one of the most powerful metaphors in international relations' (Wolfe and Mendelsohn 2004: 261), whereas others regard it as a 'story' (Lang 2006: 81). No matter the labelling, in order to understand its significance, it is useful to specify its nature, the context in which it emerged, its theoretical underpinnings and its status in contemporary IPE theorizing.

The notion of embedded liberalism plays a key role in Ruggie's reflections on the processes of change and continuity in international political economy. The concept refers to a grand social compromise, primarily in the OECD world, according to which free trade abroad (internationally) is promoted and accepted, yet conditioned on welfare programmes at home (domesti-cally). In other words, we are talking about a liberal conception of interna-

Box 6.5   Three economic theorems

According to David Ricardo, comparative advantages emerge when two or more countries specialize in the production of different goods and subsequently trade these goods. Ricardo's classic example is Portugal producing wine and England producing cloth. If Portugal and England produced both these goods and did not trade, they would be worse off. Ricardo's theory of comparative advantages can be seen as a prototype of free trade theory and a theory explaining the benefits of globalization.

The Heckscher–Ohlin theorem extends Ricardo's theory of comparative advantages by claiming that a country's export and import patterns are determined by the distribution of factors of production. China has many inhabitants, for which reason China tends to export labour-intensive products while importing capital-intensive goods.

The Stolper–Samuelson theorem claims that a causal link exists between output prices and the price of the factors going into production. Hence, if the price of labour-intensive products increases, wages are likely to increase. If the price of capital-intensive products goes up, the price of capital is likely to increase.

tional political economy, but it is a specific kind of liberalism. This specific kind of liberalism is embedded, more precisely embedded in social purpose, legitimacy and authority. We are therefore also considering a triangular relationship between markets, states and civil society actors. Following Karl Polanyi's key argument, markets are, if on their own, self-destructive and unsustainable. Concerning the states, they should secure social welfare and societal consent as well as promoting free international trade.

Combined, the concept of embedded liberalism and Ruggie's general argument comprise a critical response to the theory of hegemonic stability. As we have seen above, the latter theory produces expectations about economic (in-)stability based on the international distribution of power. By contrast, Ruggie argues that though power is important, it should be understood in the context of legitimate social purpose and political authority in the international system. While both Great Britain and the United States have enjoyed hegemonic status, the open trading systems they sponsored differ significantly. The British system was based on (planned) *laissez faire* liberalism, whereas the American system is based on embedded liberalism. It follows that the great economic depression of the 1930s was not caused by the absence of a hegemonic state, but instead by the decline of legitimate social purpose, for which reason Britain increasingly experienced a lack of political authority in the international system. The objective of being a response to the hegemonic stability theory is important, because it implies that we can compare the two theories, highlight their differences (and similarities), and make a list of the research questions each theory is capable of generating.

The concept of embedded liberalism is perhaps not a theory in the narrow meaning of the term, but it has strong theoretical underpinnings. We have seen that the key notions include social purpose, legitimacy and authority. Furthermore, the fact that Ruggie draws on Karl Polanyi's synthesis of economic and sociological insights concerning the world economy suggests that the underpinnings include interpretive and sociological strategies of enquiry. Finally, the concept is underpinned by constructivist analytical commitments (see Chapter 7).

Processes of globalization constitute a serious challenge to an international economic order based on embedded liberalism. Ruggie (2003) explains why:

> For the industrialized countries, it is a fact that embedded liberalism presupposed an *international* world. It presupposed the existence of *national* economies, engaged in *external* transactions, conducted at *arms length*, which governments could mediate at the *border* by tariffs and exchange rates, among other tools. The globalization of financial markets and production chains, however, challenges each of these premises and threatens to leave behind merely national social bargains. (Ruggie 2003, emphases in the original)

Against this background, the intellectual and political task is therefore to redefine social purpose, legitimacy and political authority in a world characterized by an unevenly globalized world economy.

Main intra-tradition debates

Concerning the theoretical debates on the intersections between international economics and politics, IPE is a diverse and rich tradition that is characterized by several important debates. However, given the multiple identities of the tradition, it is difficult to draw a clear distinction between intra- and inter-tradition debates. It is thus important to keep the split identity of IPE in mind. For those who consider IPE to be IR traditions with a special view to economics, many of the intra-theoretical debates that were introduced in Chapters 2–5 are highly relevant even replayed in the context of IPE. Thus, the theorists within the IPT tradition have been deeply involved in analyzing the intersections between international economics and politics, for example, focusing on international distributive justice (Beitz 1979; Pogge 2002). Thomas Pogge has been consistently engaged in debates on these issues. Notably, just like many anti-globalization campaigners, Pogge is highly critical of liberal international policies and prescribes mercantilist/protectionist strategies as a suitable alternative. Turning to the liberal tradition, we realize it has a strong built-in advantage to handle the intersections between international politics and economics. Why? Because the tradition includes currents of thought such as interdependence liberalism and neoliberal institutionalism, and these currents have a strong focus, if they are not directly defined by means of the intersections between politics and economics. If we continue to the realist tradition, we can observe that neorealist criticism of traditional, classical realism also is represented in IPE. Essentially, the criticism is the same as the criticism introduced in Chapter 4, this time simply applied to international political economy. The debates among the theorists from these theoretical traditions are just as much on international political economy issues as they are about international politics. With these particularities of the IPE tradition in mind, we can proceed to the following three debates which have been particularly influential in shaping the tradition.

In the first place, we have debates on the nature and desirability of theoretical enquiry. Contending perspectives strongly characterize this issue. On the one hand theorists from the eclectic current of thought tend to emphasize the limits and negative aspects of theorizing. They believe that theorizing might turn out to be an obstacle in the processes of accumulating knowledge about international political economy or that theorizing takes attention away from the substance matter. They clearly fear the formalization and stylization that often go hand-in-hand with processes of theorizing and with theory metamorphosing into dogma or orthodoxy. They implicitly seem to cherish 'happy empiricism' that is untainted by theoretical reflection. In contrast, theorists cultivating IPE in the fashion that is predominant in the US make pleas for the exact opposite perspective. They argue that the 'happy empiricists' approach IPE in a way that is guided by implicit theoretical frameworks. They resist discussing these frameworks, partly because they are not theoretically minded, partly because of resistance to homogenizing endeavours.

Second, liberal theorists and economic realists emphasize the role of different actors and highlight different causal processes. Being a premier liberal theorist, it is hardly surprising that Francis Fukuyama has been an ardent critic of mercantilist strategies. First, he points out that 20th-century Latin America has 'inherited many of the feudal institutions of seventeenth- and eighteenth-century Spain and Portugal. Among these were the Spanish and Portuguese crowns' strong disposition to control economic activity for their own greater glory, a practice known as mercantilism' (1992: 104). Furthermore, he emphasizes that the upper classes were 'protected by their own governments from international competition through import-substitution policies adopted by many Latin American governments from the 1930s through the 1960s' (Fukuyama 1992: 104). Finally, he is aware of the irony that progressive forces in Latin America – labour unions and *dependencia* theorists – also recommended mercantilism as a means to secure social justice. Fukuyama's criticism concerning Latin America is to the point, but this is possibly due to Latin America being a soft case. Would the cases of Korea, China, the EU or the US bring about similar conclusions?

Third, the issue of development has triggered several critical encounters. Andre Gunder Frank was caustic in his criticism of modernization theory (as represented by the Research Center on *Economic Development and Cultural Change*, as well as by the journal *Economic Development and Cultural Change*). According to Björn Hettne, Frank 'went out to show that the modernization perspective ... was (a) empirically untenable, (b) theoretically insufficient and (c) practically incapable of stimulating a process of development in the Third World' (Hettne 1995: 71). Basically, Frank deconstructed modernization theory and provided an alternative explanation of underdevelopment. Frank argued that underdevelopment was not 'an original stage but a created condition' (Hettne 1995: 71). In contrast, dependency theory has never been without its critics. Tony Smith (1979) talks provocatively about the underdevelopment of development literature and uses dependency theory as an illustrative case. His main point of criticism is that dependency theory fatally overestimates the ability of international factors to determine developments in the South and, consequently, that the theory underestimates 'the real influence of the South over its own affairs' (1979: 249). Other critics have pointed out the fact that a major group of countries have actually managed to leave their former peripheral status behind, for example, the Scandinavian countries and the so-called tiger economies of South East Asia. Currently, East Central Europe might be successful in catching up with Western Europe, and both China and India are more often than not considered future economic superpowers. Other emergent economies can also be spotted on future horizons. In any case, the heyday of *dependencia* theory is a thing of the past. Arlene B. Tickner (2003) has examined the impact of the Latin American *dependencia* theorists and argues that, despite important insights, they 'failed to produce a viable solution to situations of dependence, short of revolution, the adoption of socialist forms of production, or the acceptance of skewed, dependent development' (2003: 330). In this context, it is relevant to ask whether this failure is caused by *dependencia* theory as such or by the policy prescriptions *dependencia* theorists forwarded. Finally, Björn Hettne (1995) emphasizes that in most countries the quasi-mercantilist policy prescriptions, forwarded by several dependency theorists, have not worked out. On the contrary, they have produced economic disasters and underdevelopment. In this perspective, dependency theory has been part of the problem rather than the solution. In the same fashion, the liberal *Zeitgeist* of globalization prescribes free trade and open economies, not autarky and protectionism. Debates regarding the merits of dependency theory are therefore as vigorous as ever, even if the classical theorists are not as prominent as they were in the 1960s and 1970s.

Research agenda

In this brief overview, the account will be structured by a distinction between three different levels of enquiry: macro, meso and micro. Fields of application include at the macro level the politics of international economic relations among the rich OECD countries, the politics of north–south relations and the politics of south–south economic relations. Each of these relations is really a cluster of research agendas. At the meso level, we find important issues such as the political economy of war and conflict providing important insights to the dynamics and rationality of conflict. Furthermore, we find the politics of representation in international financial institutions such as the IMF and the World Bank. Finally, we find the political economy of climate change, energy supply and food (safety). Decisions concerning the trade of CO_2 quotas are inherently political, whereas the derived consequences of such decisions are economic in nature. At the micro level of political economy, there is an IPE problematique concerning every single commodity and service that is traded internationally. Such single commodity/service studies often tell fascinating stories about how the world of politics and economics hang together. The production, trade and consumption of, say, bananas, oil, automobiles, wine, cocoa, missiles and, finally, to quote Iggy Pop, 'sex and drugs and rock'n' roll' make up a huge and really interesting part of the contemporary research agenda.

The task of further theory building constitutes a crucially important issue on the research agenda. Thus far, the tradition has proven incapable of producing more than a limited number of applicable theories. Somehow theorists have either formalized the tradition too much, thus approaching the dominant research techniques within economics, or they have formalized the tradition too little, sticking to rather lethargic, general and vague theoretical or conceptual constructs. Concerning the former case, analysts appear to believe that the methods of a discipline that has no sense of politics can be used to analyze the intersections between politics and economics. Concerning the latter, analysts seem to be satisfied with cultivating the ontological dimension of theorizing. The unfortunate outcome of this too much/too little theorizing has been that the tradition has been unable so far to develop its full theoretical potential.

Conclusion

Historically, intersections between international economics and politics have been of paramount importance, and it seems safe to predict that these intersections are here to stay. The IPE tradition is therefore nothing less than one of the indispensable theoretical traditions. No matter whether IPE is seen as a tradition in its own right, an inter-discipline or as an important added dimension to other traditions, IPE has much to offer. Theoretical debates and the wide research agenda make IPE a huge field of study. Accordingly, it is somewhat misleading to conceive of IPE as merely a minor 'add-on' dimension. Rather, IPE is a tradition that at least squares the domain of IR. The shifting boundaries of purely national, interdependent and globalized modes of production and consumption constitute an increasingly dynamic dimension of IPE. In turn, this novel feature has an indirect impact on the boundaries of politics and economics. As economists and political scientists continue to specialize, producing more and more knowledge about less and less, the continuous *raison d'être* of IPE becomes increasingly clear. It is also clear that the balance between the two disciplines is bound to remain on the agenda of the split tradition.

Questions

- How would you characterize the relationship between IPE and other theoretical traditions?
- Through which phases has the IPE tradition evolved?
- Which theoretical debates do you think are most promising concerning the future development of IPE?
- How does IPE relate to other theoretical traditions?
- Do you think that the hegemonic stability theory (HST) has been developed for a specific purpose or group?
- On which main actors, structures and processes do the main strands of IPE focus?
- What are the characteristics that enable us to recognize mercantilist foreign economic strategies? Make a top-five list of contemporary examples of mercantilism strategies.
- How are offensive realism (see Chapter 4) and mercantilism similar?

Further reading

Cohen, B. J. (2007) 'The Transatlantic Divide: Why are American and British IPE So Different?', *Review of International Political Economy*, 14: 197–219.
    An intriguing review of American and British approaches to IPE.

Lake, D. A. (2006) 'International Political Economy: A Maturing Inter-discipline', in B. R. Weingast and D. A. Wittman (eds), *The Oxford Handbook of
Political Economy* (Oxford: Oxford University Press).
>   A contribution representing one specific conception of IPE, somewhat
>   opposite to Murphy and Nelson, see next.

Murphy, C. N. and Nelson, D. R. (2001) 'International Political Economy: A
Tale of Two Heterodoxies', *British Journal of Politics and International
Relations*, 3: 393–412.
>   In this article Murphy and Nelson outline what it means to cherish diver-
>   sity and pluralism.

Philips, N. (2005) '"Globalizing" the Study of International Political Economy',
in N. Philips (ed.), *Globalizing International Political Economy* (Basingstoke:
Palgrave Macmillan).
>   A book discussing the ramifications of globalizing not only political and
>   economic affairs but also our theoretical perspectives.

Strange, S. (1970) 'International Economics and International Relations: A Case
of Mutual Neglect?', *International Affairs*, 46, 304–15.
>   The article by means of which Susan Strange made a plea to (re-)establish
>   the international political economy tradition.

Underhill, G. R. D. (2003) 'State, Market, and Global Political Economy:
Genealogy of an (Inter?) Discipline', *International Affairs*, 76: 805–24.

Websites for further information

www.oecd.org
>   The website of the OECD.

www.worldbank.org
>   The website of the World Bank.

www.imf.org
>   The website of the IMF.

www.ecb.int
>   The website of the European Central Bank.

www.wto.org
>   The website of the World Trade Organization.

www.oxfam.org
>   The website of a British interest group working on development issues.

www.eadi.org
>   The website of the European association of scholars working on develop-
>   ment issues.

www.uni-kiel.de/ifw
>   The website of the Institute of World Economy at Kiel University.

www.ft.com
The *Financial Times* website.

www.economist.com
The website of the *Economist*.

www.bruegel.org
The website of a Brussels-based think-tank.
europa.eu.int

Chapter 7

The Post-Positivist Tradition

During the last two decades of the 20th century and onwards, a wealth of post-positivist approaches went beyond conventional perspectives. When characterizing the tradition in general terms, it is important to remember that positivism is a philosophy of science. Hence, the name of the post-positivist tradition refers to contending views within philosophy of science and, significantly, to the ramifications these different views might have for our understanding of international relations. Proponents of post-positivist approaches share a basic dissatisfaction with what are typically referred to as 'orthodox' or 'mainstream' theories; in addition they share at least some sources of inspiration; and they obviously do not subscribe to positivist criteria for knowledge production.

However, the prime characteristic of the tradition is *difference*; indeed, some post-positivists would hate the idea of belonging to a tradition. In a sense, such reluctance is justified, because the sources of inspiration are exceptionally diverse. Thus, some draw on the so-called linguistic turn within philosophy (whether represented by philosophers Ludwig Wittgenstein, John L. Austin or John R. Searle) and study the role of language, speech acts and institutional (or social) facts in world politics; others draw on French philosophers – whether Michel Foucault, Jacques Derrida or Jean-Francois Lyotard – and produce genealogical, discourse analytical or deconstructive studies; still others draw on the tradition of critical theory, such as the Frankfurt School, and investigate the international political community or explore dimensions of world society, while seeking to identify emancipatory strategies. Finally, some draw on sociological theoretical insights, exploring patterns of interaction and the constitution of international and global society.

In this way, hitherto neglected dimensions of international relations have received the full analytical spotlight, sometimes motivated by normative concerns and sometimes not. A significant aspect of post-positivist scholarship has been the critique of mainstream perspectives on international relations, but the output in the form of substantive studies of world politics – in a very broad understanding of this term, that is – has been even more significant.

Genealogy

The post-positivist tradition emerged during the 1980s in the context of the so-called 'fourth great debate' (see Box 7.1).

The oft-nominated yet hotly contested 'winners' of the debates are highlighted. The fourth debate has no clear winner, as positivism has metamorphosed into rationalism, and post-positivism has proliferated into several currents of thinking, some broadly recognized and others less so.

The origins of perspectives that have gradually become known as the post-positivist tradition are thus to be found in a critical reconsideration of the trajectories and ends of the discipline. A wide variety of starting points were employed, and the departure from positivism was about the only feature that was shared. The post-positivist tradition has roughly developed through four main phases. The first phase was primarily characterized by meta-theoretical critique of other theories. Kicking the tradition off, Richard Ashley (1984) presented a devastating criticism of neorealism. Essentially, Ashley criticized the pronounced state-centrism of neorealism, its unclear conception of structure and the underlying utilitarianist assumptions. Ashley's criticism was essentially an application of post-structural methods of deconstruction. At the level of argument, the newly arrived and self-conscious theory – neorealism – was, if not totally destroyed, at least seriously damaged. At the level of scholarly practice, many decided to neglect Ashley's criticism, and neorealism survived the 1980s, only to be challenged in the 1990s by the collapse of the Soviet Union and the end of the Cold War.

Subsequently, Friedrich Kratochwil and John G. Ruggie (1986) presented a well-argued critique of the dominant way of theorizing international regimes. Essentially, they pointed at massive inconsistency between a field of study focusing on social ontological attributes such as norms, principles and rules and the employment of an epistemology that is claimed to be unsuitable for the purpose of producing knowledge about the social ontological dimensions of regimes. The role of norms, principles and rules cannot be understood by means of the rationalist registers that characterized research on regimes at the time, in particular because their existence is dependent upon the shared understanding among actors creating, reproducing and giving meaning to them.

Soon after, the first collection of post-structuralism-informed IR analysis emerged, entitled *International/Intertextual Relations* (Der Derian and Shapiro 1989). The contributors imported discourse analysis from the Humanities and applied it in studies of international relations. The distinction between classical data sources (e.g. foreign policy speeches or official documents) and new sources (e.g. spy novels or cartoons) no longer played a significant role. At about the same time, Alexander Wendt's first publication (1987) emerged, signalling a distinct take on constructivism. Many more examples could – but need not – be included. The argument is simply

---

Box 7.1   Four debates co-constituting the discipline

1	Idealism vs <u>realism</u>	1940s–1950s
2	Traditionalism vs <u>behaviouralism</u>	1960s–1970s
3	Inter-paradigm debate (<u>realism</u>–<u>liberalism</u>–globalism)	1980s
4	Positivism vs post-positivism	1980s-

---

that the origins of the post-positivist tradition date back to the 1980s and that they had little to do with the third debate, that is, the so-called inter-paradigm debate (Banks 1985). Rather than being empirical research on international relations, meta-theoretical criticism of mainstream IR theory predominantly characterized the first wave of the new tradition. The criticism in question concerned the very foundations of the existing theories and was thus anything but superficial scratches in the surface.

During the second phase, some post-positivists began to engage in developing an empirical research agenda. Though not a post-positivist himself, Robert Keohane has been instrumental in triggering this interest in empirical research. In 1988, Joseph Nye and Robert Keohane inadvertently raised two milestones of significant consequence for subsequent developments. Joseph Nye (1988) carried out a meta-theoretical comparison of neorealism and neoliberalism. He concluded that the two theoretical perspectives share a remarkable range of foundational assumptions and, furthermore, that the two theories had undergone a truly novel rapprochement. In other words, they agreed on almost everything. Nye concluded that a neo-neo synthesis had been accomplished. Robert Keohane (1988) claimed that there are two main approaches to the study of international institutions. Nye identified one of these approaches: the neo-neo synthesis. Keohane coined the term 'rationalism' for this position, and he called the other approach 'reflectivism'. Because theories as such had hardly been developed, the empirical studies were often guided by either conceptual frameworks or meta-theoretical categories and characterized as being based on barefoot empiricism (Ruggie 1998b). It is therefore natural that the first examples of methodological concerns were raised (Milliken 2001).

During the third phase, post-positivists increasingly aimed at theorizing and theory application. An increasingly broad range of theories were created or imported from other disciplines and an extensive research agenda was formulated (for a review, see Finnemore and Sikkink 2001). In addition, there was an increasing awareness of the crucial differences among post-

Box 7.2   Declarations of intellectual danger

'The declarations of intellectual danger directed at so-called postmodernists (a term with which I still have many, many problems) by the self-declared guardians of international relations ... have not abated ... If anything, their intensity and frequency have increased and appear to be directly correlated with a stubborn avoidance of intellectual engagement. It appears that the consequences of ceasing attempts to delegitimize perspectives they find abhorrent are feared.' (Campbell 1998: 210)

positivists, and intra-tradition debates unfolded in addition to the ever-present inter-tradition debates. Especially the boundary zone between constructivism and post-structuralism has been explored (cf. Campbell 1998; Ruggie 1998b; Fierke 2001).

In the fourth phase, social constructivism is increasingly recognized by mainstream scholars as a significant part of the theoretical landscape (Katzenstein, Keohane and Krasner 1998). Other post-positivist currents remain in the margin of the discipline, although post-structuralism has gained prominence, particularly in Great Britain. The field of critical security studies, partly inspired by post-structuralism, also plays an important role (Krause and Williams 1997; Wæver 1995; Hansen 1997).

When outlining the development of the post-positivist tradition, it is significant that the label 'neo' is beginning to lose credibility. Thus, neorealism dates back to the 1970s, neoliberal institutionalism is more than two decades old and the term neo-Marxism does not connote the same degree of modernity that it did in various corners during the 1970s. Ironically, the label 'neo' is beginning to signal 'retro' rather than anything modern and contemporary. This also applies to the new post-positivist tradition, which is not as new as it once was. As mentioned above, the entry of post-positivist approaches to the discipline dates back to the 1980s. This also applies to critical theory, which was introduced to the discipline in the 1980s, even though critical theory as an intellectual current can be traced back to the 1920s (Jay 1973). Since the 1980s, some of the currents and theories have moved from the periphery of the discipline to centre stage, almost constituting part of a new mainstream.

Currents of thought

As mentioned above, the post-positivist tradition is very diverse and characterized by a rather limited number of common features. Furthermore, the

Figure 7.1   *Timeline: some key works in the post-positivist tradition*

1981	Richard Ashley, 'Political Realism and Human Interest', *International Studies Quarterly*, vol. 25
1981	Robert Cox, 'Social Forces, States and World Orders: Beyond International Relations Theory', *Millennium*, vol. 10
1982	Andrew Linklater, *Men and Citizens in the Theory of international Relations Theory*
1987	James Der Derian, *On Diplomacy*
1989	Nicholas Onuf, *World of Our Making: Rules and Rule in Social Theory and International Relations*
1989	Friedrich Kratochwil, *Rules, Norms, Decisions: On the Conditions of Practical and Legal Reasoning in International and Domestic Affairs*
1989	James Der Derian and Michael J. Shapiro eds., *International/Intertextual Relations: Postmodern Readings of World Politics*
1990	Andrew Linklater, *Beyond Realism and Marxism: Critical Theory and International Relations*
1992	Alexander Wendt, 'Anarchy is What States Make of it: The Social Construction of Power Politics', *International Organization*, vol. 46
1993	Rob Walker, *Inside/Outside: International Relations as Political Theory*
1995	Cindy Weber, *Simulating Sovereignty: Intervention, the State and Symbolic Interchange*
1996	Steve Smith, Ken Booth and Marysia Zalewski, *International Theory, Positivism and Beyond*
1996	Peter Katzenstein, *The Culture of National Security: Norms and Identity in World Politics*
1999	Alexander Wendt, *Social Theory of International Politics*
1999	Jenny Edkins, *Post-structuralism and International Relations*
2001	Christine Sylvester, *Feminist International Relations*
2001	R. Wyn Jones, *Critical Theory and World Politics*

tradition is recently established, meaning that longer-lasting features have yet to be settled or consolidated. Finally, it draws on a wealth of very different sources of inspiration. Given all these features, its currents of thought can be categorized in several different ways. The following sections are based on a common distinction between constructivist, post-structural and critical theory currents of thought. These currents have simply been the most significant, although in markedly different ways.

Social constructivism

Let us begin this introduction to constructivism in a negative fashion by claiming that constructivism is frequently introduced in a superficial and misleading manner. It is superficial in the sense of being presented as a substantive theory and misleading in the sense of being presented as a coherent position. Constructivism is neither a substantive IR theory nor does it have its origins in International Relations. Constructivism ought to be understood as a broad approach to social theory, capable of generating a range of specific substantive theories about a range of social relations. Furthermore, despite the frequent use of the phrases such as 'Constructivists argue ...' and 'Constructivists claim ...', the fact of the matter is that constructivists rarely agree on substantive or non-substantive issues. Maja Zehfuss (2002) has brilliantly demonstrated the foundational differences between three constructivist schools of thought as represented by Nicholas Onuf, Friedrich Kratochwil and Alexander Wendt, respectively. Constructivism thus represents a rich current of thought that embodies an entire range of very different perspectives.

During the last two decades, constructivist work has flourished, and chapters on social constructivism have been added to most major textbooks introducing IR theory. Such additions demonstrate that constructivism has become a recognized part of the discipline, although, like in diplomacy, recognition does not necessarily imply amity.

Constructivism plays significant analytical roles at four different levels of theoretical reflection: philosophical, meta-theoretical, theoretical and empirical-analytical. As an example of the philosophical level, philosopher John Searle (1995) has formulated a general theory of social ontology and social institutions. He manages to sort out complex differences between social and material reality in a most concise fashion and emphasizes the crucial importance of keeping ontological and epistemological issues separated. Focusing on social reality (in contrast to material reality), he eminently outlines specific features of social reality, including the master proposition that social reality depends on human agreement for its existence. Thus, if we do not agree that money is money, then the social reality of money ceases to exist. The same goes for such international social realities as sovereignty, statehood and diplomacy.

As an example of constructivism at the meta-theoretical level, Alexander

Wendt (1987) has used structuration theory to characterize and evaluate major IR theories of international relations. Structuration theory tries to escape the dilemma between choosing agent- and structure-oriented approaches, proposing that agents and structures are mutually constituted. Both philosophical and meta-theoretical conceptions of constructivism offer important general tools, but they are not substantive theories of international relations. We will therefore leave the philosophical and meta-theoretical levels behind, and, by changing focus, we arrive at the level of theory. At this level, constructivism acquires a role that is significantly different from the role it has at the philosophical and meta-theoretical levels. Paradoxically, perhaps, it retreats somewhat into the background. In other words, it functions behind the scenes and, like an *eminence gris*, may well stop over-using the term 'constructivism'. Why not? After all, Kenneth Waltz (1979) did not present his theory as a 'positivist' theory of international politics, and Robert Keohane (1989) did not market his theoretical perspective as a 'rationalist', utilitarian theory of neoliberal institutionalism. The categories 'positivism', 'rationalism' and 'utilitarianism' are nevertheless features that provide theoretical perspectives with their philosophical or meta-theoretical underpinnings. Notably, it was by means of Joseph Nye's (1988) meta-theoretical analysis that the neo-neo synthesis was discovered.

As mentioned above, constructivism is capable of generating a range of specific substantive theories about a broad range of international relations issues. One way of generating new specific substantive theories is to arrange encounters between constructivism and existing substantive theoretical positions. Three examples illuminate this point. First, in contrast to Robert Jervis (1998), who clearly regards constructivism as a competitor to realism, Henry Nau (2002) has demonstrated that realist and constructivist theories of power and identity can be considered complementary theoretical positions capable of working together fruitfully within a single analytical framework. In other words, the two perspectives may well be established on different assumptions and contribute different insights, but their relationship is not necessarily competitive or conflicting. Actually, the relationship can be complementary and contribute to enhancing our understanding of, for example, American foreign policy. Indeed, we can go one step further, arguing that a fusion of constructivism and realism is possible. Hence, it is possible to develop, for example, a constructivist realist balance of power theory (Barkin 2003). Second, Alexander Wendt's (1999) theory of international cooperation can be considered to represent a constructivist liberal theory of international cooperation (see Chapter 3). Third, Charles Manning's (1962) theory of international society can be considered a constructivist theory of international society (cf. Suganami 2001a).

As we have previously rejected the view that constructivism is a theory, why continue investigating the status of constructivism at the theoretical level? The answer, quite simply, is that while constructivism is not a substantive theory, theories informed by constructivism are, as we have just seen, absolutely feasible. Such a solution, however, opens a veritable Pandora's Box of new problems and challenges. How should theory building be conducted? If not all types of theory are feasible, which kinds of theory *are* feasible? Do we proceed in a deductive or inductive mode? Or do the philosophical and meta-theoretical underpinnings of constructivism enable us to transcend this distinction? In principle, first-order theorizing can follow two major avenues. The first option is to examine constructivism and existing IR theory, which in some cases leads to a reformulation of existing theories. Kratochwil and Ruggie (1986) chose this approach in their path-breaking reformulation of regime theory. Wendt adopts a similar approach when transforming an existing (material) systemic theory into a social systemic theory (1994, 1995, 1999). Jutta Weldes (1996) also adopts a reformulation strategy in her attempt to rethink the bureaucratic politics model.

The second option is to employ various constructivist 'generic' theories, that is, theories such as J. L. Austin's (1976) and John Searle's (1969) theory of speech acts, Habermas's (1984) theory of communicative action, Luhmann's (1997) version of modern systems theory, sociological interactionist theory and many more theories of a similar stature in the development of analytical frameworks. For instance, studies on diplomacy can incorporate notions of 'communication', 'signalling', 'communicative action' and 'identity and interest formation'. Such notions have surely long been present in studies of diplomacy, but employing constructivist perspectives can provide them with a novel and elaborated theoretical grounding.

Constructivism is alive and kicking. Work in progress constitutes a new generation of IR constructivism, a generation that will be less preoccupied with strategic moves vis-à-vis seemingly competing perspectives. IR constructivist scholarship has become more diverse and cultivates different currents of constructivism. The employment of constructivist perspectives has brought about a significant improvement of our knowledge of international relations, and the discipline has become more pluralist. Constructivist research is based on philosophical and meta-theoretical platforms radically different from a considerable part of traditional IR research. The approach generates research programmes which would be unthinkable within traditional IR research. One illustrative example is the team directed by Peter Katzenstein and their research on national security cultures, a field that is supposed to be a *domaine reservée* for material power-oriented research (Katzenstein 1996). Furthermore, the constructivist research programmes under construction, so to speak, have moved closer to the substance of international relations. Hence, it is hardly surprising that constructivism has gained recognition as a part of the standard repertoire in sciences which do not hesitate to use 'social' as an adjective in front of the noun 'science'.

The constructivist current has been split between so-called ontological and epistemological constructivists. Ontological constructivists aim at complementing material ontology with ideational or social factors, such as norms, identity or culture. 'Complement' indicates that they do not support a massive rejection of materialism; instead, they work in favour of an extension of the research agenda and hope for a possible division of labour between material- and ideational-focused research agendas or possibly a grand synthesis. In order to illustrate how ontological constructivists argue, Peter Katzenstein's seminal *The Culture of National Security* (1996) will be used as an example. When outlining the theoretical framework and design of the book, Jepperson, Wendt and Katzenstein make sure to point out their distance to postmodernism and French philosophers. Furthermore, they deliberately avoid confrontation concerning material factors, arguing that the relationship between social and material factors is a question of both-and, not either-or.

Similarly, they have no interest in becoming entangled in epistemological issues and therefore do their best to avoid confrontation concerning epistemological and methodological issues. Hence, they reject the argument that research addressing social ontology requires special epistemologies and instead accept what they call standard criteria for sound normal science. They also argue that methodology is a non-issue for them, implying that they do not see any need for special interpretive methods flowing from their preoccupation with social ontology. They choose a hard case, security policy, which is intuitively seen as the heartland for material or realist theories. The main argument is that cultural or social factors can contribute significant insights in this issue area and often contribute insight that other theories are unable to produce.

Epistemological constructivists argue differently than ontological constructivists. They claim to complement a material ontology with a social ontology, but they also substitute part of the material factors with a social ontology. In other words, epistemological constructivists are more confrontational and less accommodating than ontological constructivists. Second, they claim that social ontology requires a (partial) change in epistemology. Their readiness towards compromise, synthesis and compromise is less than ontological constructivists, and they draw what they regard as logical, consistent epistemological consequences of choosing a social ontology.

This account of two major schools within constructivism demonstrates that constructivism is far more than just a methodological position. Though features known from the so-called 'second great debate' are present – indeed invite a sense of *déjà vu* – constructivism is far from exclusively addressing methodological issues. Constructivism is first and foremost an invitation to include social ontologies in our research on global politics and economics.

Such issues include the role of identity, ideas and values in the development of foreign policy, the importance of norms in international regimes and normative enquiries of fundamental principles. In general, the constructivist position has been enriched by this internal constructivist debate between so-called ontological and epistemological constructivists. Both versions of constructivism have been applied in research of dynamics at global, regional and national levels.

Post-structuralism

Post-structuralism in international relations is an important current of thought. It is born critical and in opposition to so-called mainstream approaches. The primary source of inspiration is post-structuralist philosophy, a significant source of inspiration because it is directly related to and part of important 20th-century developments within Western philosophy. Before exploring post-structuralist approaches in IR further, it is necessary to take a closer look at post-structuralism as such. Post-structuralism is 'post' because it aims at going beyond and being in opposition to structuralism, a philosophy that developed during the first half of the 20th century (indeed, well into the 1960s and 1970s), and whose impact it is difficult to underestimate. Structuralist approaches were introduced to both the humanities and the social sciences, for example, linguistics (Ferdinand de Saussure, Louis Hjelmslev), cultural studies (Roland Barthes), anthropology (Clause Lévi-Strauss), neo-Marxism (Louis Althusser, Immanuel Wallerstein) and sociology (Talcott Parssons and Niklas Luhman). This version of structuralism is characterized by being strongly deterministic and a-historical. It prioritizes (determining) structures over agency and change. In a sense, it is the antithesis to rational choice approaches.

Philosophers such as Michel Foucault, Jean-Francois Lyotard, Jacques Derrida and Jean Baudrillard responded to structuralism by creating a post-structuralism characterized by historical sensitivity, an understanding of politics as a form of social action and a focus on the dynamics of identity politics. Post-structuralist philosophy became prominent during the 1980s. None of the philosophers mentioned above have paid much attention to international relations; instead, they mainly analyzed topics such as knowledge, sexuality and prisons. Jean Baudrillard has written about America (1986) and the first Gulf War (1995, first published in French in 1991), but it is slightly difficult to determine whether the outcome is literary fantasy or scientific study (cf. Hughes 1990).

A diverse grouping of scholars took on the task of applying post-structuralist philosophy in International Relations. First, they targeted dominant theories of international relations for profound criticism, then increasingly began to reflect on important aspects of international relations. They insist that professional IR scholars are far from alone in possessing abstract knowledge about international relations; politicians, civil servants, military leaders, activists and journalists also have such knowledge. In this context, we should consider our own cases. We probably know more about the world as conceptualized by journalists than by professional IR scholars. Remember that we read this book as part of an introductory course to IR. Hence, we should ask ourselves: what do we know and where does this knowledge come from? Returning to IR scholars, theorists in particular create such worlds of abstract knowledge. Hence, the previous chapters (2 through 6) all describe different conceptions, assumptions and theories, which have been coined, made and developed by theorists. The worlds *of their making* vary considerably, and these worlds often differ significantly from the worlds created by others.

Post-structuralist IR scholars insist that post-structuralism is not a theory, a grand theory or a paradigm about international relations. Rather, it is a commitment to certain analytical principles and should foremost be regarded as a critical approach. Nothing, if not critical. According to Stefano Guzzini, 'poststructuralism is a theoretical framework which combines a meta-theory of intersubjective interpretivism with a moral theory of radical scepticism' (1998: 228). Guzzini continues by emphasizing that moral critique is intertwined with conceptual critique to such a degree that the one cannot be imagined without the other. Hence, when post-structuralists forward criticism of IR theories, they are deeply engaged in a normative pursuit.

Post-structuralists devote particular interest to three broad themes: identity, knowledge/power and representations/interpretation. As described above, post-structuralism should be seen as an attempt to move beyond structuralism. Hence, it is only natural to pay close attention to issues related to identity and identity politics, which is precisely what IR post-structuralists have done. Some have analyzed the linkages between identity and foreign policy (Campbell 1998), whereas others have studied the relations between 'manly' states and international relations (Hooper 2001). Linkages between knowledge and power were part of the agenda of post-structuralist philosophers such as Foucault and Lyotard. Post-structuralist IR scholars follow the paths of their intellectual fathers and explore how the linkages between power and knowledge are important for international relations. Concerning representation, we are used to talking about representative democracy, that is, the system in which elected representatives represent voters. Within post-structuralism, representation is understood in a broader fashion and also includes symbolic and metaphorical representations. Given the nature of representation (see Box 7.3), it seems uncontroversial to claim that interpretation strategies are indispensable.

One example is Jenny Edkins (1999), who dislikes most things taken-for-granted and, by consequence, likes to repoliticize the IR discipline. She considers post-structuralist approaches ideal tools for this endeavour of

Box 7.3   Symbolic representation

Discussing the symbolic representation of boundaries, Anthony B. Cohen explains that '[t]o say that community boundaries are largely symbolic in character is, though, not merely to suggest that they imply different meanings for different people. It also suggests that boundaries perceived by some may be utterly imperceptible to others' (Cohen 1985: 13).

repoliticizing our field of study. She also claims that we tend to employ an excessively narrow conception of politics (elections, parliaments, states, international institutions etc.), thereby disregarding the power to determine what is considered politics and what not, thus identifying the shifting boundaries of the political (cf. Maier 1987). Finally, Edkins has a strong interest in the two historical instances that produce social orders. In this context, she reflects on the grand genesis of social orders as well as the numerous micro practices contributing to the reproduction of social orders.

In a certain sense – and somewhat paradoxically – the post-structuralist current is among the most state-centric approaches one can imagine. This ironic observation is due to the aim of post-structuralists at understanding inside–outside dynamics, that is, politics and culture on both sides of state boundaries. Furthermore, they reject regarding the state in an a-historical fashion. Instead, they focus on the genesis and historical development of states, including the contemporary variety among states, including post-colonial states. Finally, by employing a broader notion of politics, they seek to achieve a more nuanced understanding of the processes through which the state is regarded by many IR perspectives as the most important actor in international relations.

The discipline's post-structuralist critics have had a significant influence on the development of the discipline. Richard Ashley, Rob Walker, Ole Wæver, David Campbell and James Der Derian have all had a significant impact on the direction of the discipline. The reason for this key role is that they have functioned as ice-breakers for other post-positivist currents and theories. The fundamental critique of mainstream theories produced an intellectual vacuum that other theorists knew how to fill. This means that the discipline is now more pluralistic and less homogeneous than ever before. A wider repertoire of theories and approaches is at our disposal. Lively debates take place, including diverse points of departure and perspectives. However, there is little evidence indicating that the post-structuralist critics will play an equally prominent role in future debates or in major research programmes. They have succeeded in breaking the ice, and their greatest service to the discipline has been to make a redirection of the discipline possible. It is most likely that they will continue to publish and, being eminent scholars, we should expect major works from them. But their role as 'discipline revolutionaries' would appear to be a thing of the past.

Critical theory

This current of thought – perhaps an intellectual tradition in its own right – can be traced back to the intellectual and academic environment of the Weimar Republic of the 1920s. Given that it was institutionally situated in Frankfurt, it simply came to be known as the Frankfurt School and its theory was called critical theory, thereby signalling a detachment to both the classical and Soviet orthodox versions of the Marxist tradition. However, the official name of the school was the more neutral Institute for Social Research. It was affiliated with the University of Frankfurt and thus became one of the first Marxist institutes within a proper academic institution. The first director of the institute, Carl Grünberg, brought with him one of the key Marxist journals, *Archiv für die Geschichte des Socializmus und der Arbeiterbewegung* (Archive for the History of Socialism and the Working-class Movement), a relationship that suggests linkages back to the classical Marxist tradition (Jay 1973; Anderson 1973).

However, the Marxists who worked at the institute or were part of the research community affiliated to it had a fundamental impact on the Marxist research agenda. They also introduced modern research methods and accomplished a strategic – yet heretical shift – from material to ideational explanatory factors. Though this shift is significant, it should not be overstated. Thus, studies of the dynamics of capitalist accumulation were continued, at least for some time. In addition to empirical social research, the institute also further developed the philosophical dimensions of Marxism and consequently downplayed the close relationship between analysts and intellectuals/politicians, a unique relationship that characterized the early phases of the Marxist tradition (Anderson 1973).

Given the context in which the institute found itself, concern about the rise of fascism (in Italy, Spain and Portugal), Nazism (in Germany) and authoritarian regime forms (in major parts of East, Central and Southern Europe) soon prompted the institute to engage in identifying the causes of such ideologies and politics. By the mid-1930s, the institute and its affiliates were forced into exile in the United States where, under the wings of Columbia University in New York, a new school of social research was established. After the end of World War II, the 'new school' continued its programmes in New York, but most affiliates of the Institute of Social Research returned to Frankfurt while becoming increasingly philosophically oriented, as Marxism as a social theory with a strong accent on economics and as a theory of action was deliberately downplayed.

The critical theorists of the Frankfurt School have produced a rich conceptual, theoretical and philosophical platform of social theory. With a few notable exceptions, however, they did not spend much time on research on international relations. The idea of using critical theory in order to understand and change the nature of international relations was not introduced in a systematic manner before the 1980s. When the idea was finally introduced, critical theory basically came in two main versions. One version draws directly on the Frankfurt School, particularly on contemporary representatives such as social theorist Jürgen Habermas and with a special view to his theory of communicative action (Hoffman 1987; Müller 2001; Humrich 2006). Andrew Linklater (1990) also draws on critical theory in his reflections on (international) political community. Nicholas Rengger has summarized the importance of this strand of thought:

> it is the Frankfurt School influenced critical IR theorists who have provided the most general orientation for critical theory in international studies as far as emancipation is concerned, and it is this orientation that essentially drives the critical project in international relations. (Rengger 2001)

The other main version of critical theory was introduced by Robert W. Cox in the early 1980s (1981, 1983, 1987). Cox draws on the writings of the Frankfurt School – especially Max Horkheimer's distinction between traditional and critical theory – and Italian Communist Party leader Antonio Gramsci. Cox's theory is basically an updated version of historical materialism with special emphasis on the role of critical theory, social forces, hegemony and world order. According to the theory, social (class) forces constitute states, create hegemonies of ideas based on consent, and aim at projecting the outcome beyond state borders, in turn shaping world orders.

German scholars have paid close attention to the merits of post-positivist approaches and particularly to the potentials of critical theory. Thomas Risse (2000) has usefully synthesized the German debate and introduced it to the English-speaking world. Christoph Humrich (2006) points out, critically, that these interpretations have lost much of their critical edge in translation. In other words, what remains is a highly diluted version of critical theory, including vague notions of emancipation.

Narrowly conceived critical theory remains the least widespread of the three major currents of post-positivist tradition. It is a kind of niche production. However, analysts favouring critical studies of security, critical geopolitics, critical political economy – even critical realism – are somehow part of this strand of thought. If their studies are included, it is an increasingly important intellectual current of thought. In this wider sense, critical theory is vibrant and has a significant role to play within the discipline.

Kinds of theory cultivated?

Similar to other traditions, theorists within the post-positivist tradition employ a range of different kinds of theory. For better or worse, it is probably the richest and most diverse tradition of all in terms of the number and markedly different nature of theories in play. The following four kinds of theory are among the most prominent: meta-theory, interpretive theory, normative theory and explanatory theory. In the following paragraphs, each kind will be briefly outlined.

In many cases, post-positivists prefer to make use of meta-theory, both in their critical studies of other theories but also in their empirical studies. Meta-theory is quite simply (second-order) theory about (first-order) theory. It includes a number of categories that can be used in state-of-the-art or stocktaking studies. Meta-study has usefully been defined in the following fashion: 'If primary study is a long journey to an unfamiliar place, then meta-study involved frequent pauses for rest, identifying directions, revising travel plans, or even having second thoughts on the final destination' (Zhao 1991: 381). One example is Walter Carlsnaes (2002) who has usefully reviewed a comprehensive sample of research on foreign policy by means of meta-theoretical categories. Second, meta-theory can also be employed directly in empirical studies. Compared to first-order theory applied in concrete studies, the outcome of meta-theory-informed research is perhaps less precise but potentially more path-breaking and innovative. This is because meta-theory invites reflection on fundamental issues rather than simply shuffling and reshuffling a limited number of rather well-known variables. It concerns strategic analytical issues, not the tactical analytical issues that theory as such addresses so well. One example of meta-theory applied in empirical research is structuration theory, that is, the acknowledgement of social structures need actors to be created and reproduced, for which reason strictly actor- or structure-oriented theories are characterized by severe limits. Structuration theory is an attempt to solve the so-called agent–structure problem (Christiansen and Jørgensen 1999). A second important example is Michel Foucault's genealogical method employed in research on world politics, for example, in studies analyzing the chemical weapons taboo and in studies of sovereignty (Price 1995; Bartelson 1995).

Interpretive theory has been widely used within the post-positivist tradition. Within the constructivist current, there have been important examples of interpretive theory right from the beginning. Kratochwil and Ruggie (1986; see also Ruggie 1991, 1998b) made a plea for using interpretive theory in research on international regimes, arguing that norms and principles require strategies of interpretation. Given their focus on the role of symbolic and metaphorical representations in international relations, post-structuralists are bound to employ interpretive approaches. Critical theorists, especially the Frankfurt School orientation, also widely apply interpretive theory in their studies, for example, in Habermas's (1999) interpretation of Kant's *Perpetual Peace* and the prospects for global governance (see also Haacke 2005; Diez and Steans 2005). All three strands of thought are bound to engage in interpretation once they begin to reflect on the role various philosophers or social theorists might play in international studies. In other words, the insights of Habermas, Foucault or Searle require interpretation and application, as they do not engage themselves.

Normative issues and concerns are strongly present in post-positivist scholarship. Both critical theorists and post-structuralists reject the view that analysts can be neutral bystanders. Instead, they claim that theories are marked by their creators and the environment in which they have been formulated. Constructivists are split on the issue as some follow the above argument whereas others believe that some detachment is possible. They emphasize that a preoccupation with social constructions necessitates neither a critical perspective nor a normative position of desirability.

The move beyond positivism does not necessarily imply any abandonment of explanatory or causal theory. Ron Jepperson, Alexander Wendt and Peter Katzenstein's (1996) exploration of cultures of national security offers a prominent example. Their starting point is based on a massive, complex model of causal relationships, beginning at the level of the global cultural environment and subsequently proceeding to state identity, interests and policy-making, respectively. In an ambitious attempt to synthesize key constructivist insights while displaying a complete lack of interest in non-normal social science, they fully embrace standard explanatory theory. Tellingly, Paul Kowert and Jeffrey Legro's (1996) primary criticism of the project is not the choice of explanatory theory, but rather the direction of causality, specifically the structural version of explanatory theory embraced by Jepperson, Wendt and Katzenstein. Post-structuralists and critical theorists largely reject the option of using explanatory theory, yet causal reasoning is difficult to avoid and can often be found to play an implicit role.

Main variants of theories

In general we should not apply constructivism, post-structuralism or critical theory as such in our empirical studies. Being currents of thought, they are inapplicable. When we want to apply theory in theory-informed studies, then we should choose specific constructivist, post-structuralist or critical theory theories or conceptualizations. However, this presents certain problems.

When it comes to variants of theory, the post-positivist tradition reveals its truly diverse nature, in the first place, because the feasibility or desirability of theory building is deeply contested. Some post-positivists reject the possibility or desirability of theory as such. Post-structuralists in particular are often criticized for prioritizing critique of existing IR theory rather than formulating one or more theories of their own. But theory building is not their project, and criticism for not being interested in providing a theory is really misplaced.

Second, for some, the post-positivist rejection of positivism includes the theory–hypothesis–data package and also theory building. Sometimes it is emphasized that rejection only concerns the narrow social scientific conception of theory, but alternative options remain largely unspecified. Some leave the door open for generalization. Thus, having conducted a critical analysis of American foreign policy, David Campbell does not entirely rule out the possibility that:

> Similar specific readings could be offered from a range of cultural, national, and political sites, and while *Writing Security* does not offer a universal theory of Foreign Policy (at least not in the narrow social-scientific sense), these reflections suggest that the argument does offer a means for interpreting cultural contestations and political issues implicated in foreign policy/Foreign Policy in domains other than the United States. (1998: 208)

Third, some have imported concrete theories from other disciplines and proposed that they make sense in the context of international relations. Others have not stopped at the phase of proposing but actually applied such theories, demonstrating their value for scholarship in international relations. In the following sections we will briefly examine three universal theories, which are applicable in research in international studies. Combined, they demonstrate the wide horizons of the post-positivist tradition.

Theory of securitization

Within the field of security studies, the theory of securitization is among the most widely applied. It has been developed by Barry Buzan, Ole Wæver and Jaap de Wilde (1998; see also Wæver 1995). The theory draws on speech act theory in general and the notion of *performative* speech acts in particular. The latter notion is used for acts that are not purely descriptive but constitutive of the objects of which they speak. In addition, securitization theorists employ a broad notion of security, specified to five main sectors: military, political, economic, society and environment. Issues within these five sectors – and possibly beyond – can, in principle, be securitized. Instead of taking security threats at face value, analysts describe how actors try to securitize various phenomena, including missiles, religion, migration and climate. According to the theory, actors securitize ordinary issues by declaring that they consider issue x, y or z an issue of security. Not merely an ordinary issue of security but actually an existential security threat, for which reason the employment of extraordinary means is mandatory and therefore legitimate. Finally, it takes more than the performative speech act to securitize an issue; the reception of the act by one or more relevant audience(s) needs to be favourable. In summary, analysts applying securitization theory ask questions such as: who securitizes? Which issues do they securitize? Which existential threats do actors point to? Which extraordinary means do actors suggest? While Ole Wæver (1995) has built this theory, Jeff Huysman (1996) and Rens van Munster (2009) have made important contributions in terms of applying it.

Discourse theory

In the world of world politics, discourses are ubiquitous. While discourse theory is not directly a theory of world politics, it can nonetheless help us to better understand these discourses. Discourse theory is a generic term, an umbrella term comprising several different, competing discourse theories. Hence, it is too vague or insufficient to claim that in order to analyze a given research question, we will use discourse theory. It is necessary to specify which discourse theory we will be using.

Before we review what discourse theory can do for us, we need to look into the meaning(s) of the key term 'discourse'. This is best done by means of unpacking the term. We can begin by emphasizing that discourse analysis is a rather old form of enquiry. Throughout centuries, philosophers have analyzed discourse: Machiavelli did it; Kant did it; Jürgen Habermas does it, just to give a few examples. Edward Said (1979) famously analyzed the genesis of Western discourses on the Middle East and coined the term 'Orientalism' for the outcome.

Discourses simply concern the meaning of things and words. Put differently, discourse is made by means of 'social representations', that is, systems of values, ideas and practices. For example: what is the meaning of the European Union? In some British discourses, the EU represents a regulatory, Brussels-based bureaucracy, quasi-socialist. By contrast in some French discourses, the EU represents a neoliberal, capitalist agent of globalization and therefore a threat to French identity and interests. The point is not necessarily which discourse is right (if any) but the existence of contending social representations from which policies flow. Furthermore, what is a nation? Benedict Anderson (1991) has suggested a nation is an imagined community, underpinned by political and cultural symbols.

Different discourse theories make different claims regarding the genesis and function of discourses; their nature and significance. In the present context, we limit our account to just two widely used theories: critical discourse analysis (CDA) and structural discourse theory (SDT).

Critical discourse analysis is interdisciplinary and based on a considerable variety of inspirational sources (e.g. Louis Althusser, Michel Foucault, Mikhail Bakhtin and Frankfurt School philosophers). Furthermore, and as a consequence of the variation of underpinnings, CDA comprises a number of different approaches, each with its own characteristics, emphases and understandings of theoretical and methodological issues. One of these approaches, the 'discourse-historical approach', has also been called the Vienna School, yet the research centre was forced to close in 2003 (See *Times Higher Education Supplement* November 2003). In general, CDA assumes that discourse is a form of political action, sometimes called social practice. Furthermore, CDA theorists claim that discourse should be analyzed as a dialectic movement between context (shaping discourses) and intent (discourses shaping the context or environment). Finally, to be critical means in general not taking things for granted; some CDA analysts assume that discursive practices can be analyzed from a neutral, 'true' position – hence, 'critical' means pointing out discursive deviations from how things 'really are'.

According to SDT, the starting point is the existence of discursive structures and their constraining or enabling impact on agency, that is, the available options for political actors. Like most structural theories, structural discourse theory is leaning towards structural determinism. Hence, political actors are expected to stay within the constraining limits of what can be said (without political costs). It is clear that there is a considerable risk of *post hoc* deductive reasoning, that is, beginning with the known outcome of a political process and then using the social discursive structures to explain the outcome, arguing that actors could only do what they actually did.

In the present context, we will not go into methodological issues, just emphasize that different discourse theories require the employment of different methods and research techniques (Milliken 2001).

Identity theory

Identity theory is a generic term comprising several specific theories. Post-positivist scholars have employed identity theory in three major ways. In the first place, they have explored where interests come from. In other words, instead of assuming the existence of timeless national interests (the classical realist position), geographically determined interest (the old-time geopolitics position) or exogenously given interests (the rational choice and neorealist positions), post-positivists make the genesis of interests part of their research agenda, arguing that the politics of identity is where we should search for the origin of interests. Hence, when we aim at explaining a certain policy, the question is not whether an interest-based or an identity-based explanation is the better option. The question is how a certain identity causes a set of interests and subsequently, how these interests are translated into policy (Finnemore 1996; Jepperson, Wendt and Katzenstein 1996). Second, some scholars argue that identity-based explanations are complementary to power-based explanations, for which reason the two should be employed together; that an analysis of one without the other is bound to miss a few but very important features (Nau 2002). Finally, identity plays an important role in post-colonial studies, that is, the field of study focusing on the significant major part of the world that consists of formerly colonized countries. In their enquiries into the post-colonial condition, these scholars ask whether the previously colonized should aim at developing a so-called authentic, precolonial identity, explore the degree to which they are suffering from inferior complexes or, discuss the characteristics of a 'creolized' or 'hybridity' identity. In any case, the politics of identity is a key concern within post-colonial studies.

Main intra-tradition debates

Given that the post-positivist tradition is characterized by foundational diversity, it is hardly surprising that the tradition is also characterized by several important internal debates. Mark Neufeld (1993) has rightly predicted that debate within the post-positivist tradition may prove to be as vigorous as debates between this and other traditions. In the following we will review five major issues that have been addressed by contending perspectives.

The first controversial issue concerns positivism. While the post-positivist tradition is obviously defined by its critical relationship to positivism, this relationship remains nonetheless somewhat unclear or contested. Thus, the relationship between critical theory and positivism is inherently contested. Whereas some theorists believe that critical theory has left positivism behind (Linklater 1990; Brown 1992; Smith 1996: 24), others maintain that critical theory never really abandoned positivism (Hoffman 1987). The constructivist position is marred by a similar uncertainty about the relations to positivism. On the one hand most constructivists do not subscribe to a positivist philosophy of science; indeed, the rationale of their project is often to move beyond positivism, to explore post-positivist analytical options and potentials. On the other hand a leading constructivist such as Alexander Wendt claims that compromise is possible. In other words, it is possible to combine a post-positivist ontology with a positivist epistemology. Specifically, he declares that, 'in fact, when it comes to the epistemology of social enquiry I am a strong believer in science – a pluralistic science to be sure, in which there is a significant role for "understanding", but science just the same. I am a "positivist"' (Wendt 1999: 39, see also 47–91). In this context, it is note-worthy that John Searle (1995), one of the leading constructivist philoso-phers, vigorously defends the correspondence theory of truth. These contending understandings within critical theory and constructivism clearly have implications for debates with the post-structuralist theorists who seem entirely unaffected by such dividing views regarding one of the key features of the post-positivist tradition.

The second issue that has generated important debate is whether emanci-pation is part and parcel of the post-positivist tradition. On the one hand some post-positivist scholars claim that the endeavour of emancipation is a both necessary and desirable dimension of the post-positivist tradition. It is noteworthy that post-structuralists and critical theorists agree on the pres-ence of emancipation yet disagree regarding the kind of emancipation they aim at. Critical theorists have a tendency to think emancipation in universal terms, whereas post-structuralists are leaning towards more specific concep-tions of emancipation. On the other hand other post-positivist scholars respond that – at least concerning social constructivist approaches – there need be no emancipatory endeavours. Constructivist studies need not be politicizing. In the words of Kubálková, Onuf and Kowert, there is nothing in constructivism that 'mandates an "emancipatory" or "critical" politics' (1998: 4). As they explain,

> [c]ontructivism is normative in the sense that it takes normative phenomena – rules – as the foundation of society but Onuf's claim that rules always result in a condition of rule has earned him criticism from scholars who believe that a post-positivist position is necessarily 'criti-cal'. (1998: 19–20; see also Jørgensen 2001)

Martha Finnemore presents a similar view, arguing that, 'there is nothing inherently "good" about social norms. Social norms can prescribe ethically reprehensible behavior – slavery, violence, intolerance – as well as charity and kindness' (1996: 32). Thus, even if constructivism is more open – compared to various a-historical approaches – to aspects of 'change' or 'transformation' in world politics, it does not follow that the 'change' in question will necessarily be progressive, that is, constitute a change for the better. Nicholas Onuf concludes that 'under the broad mantle of construc-tivism, there is no justification in making emancipatory commitments a political test' (2001: 254).

The third issue that has been addressed concerns the nature and very possibility of theory. Responding to an oft-voiced criticism for not making their own theory, post-structuralists respond by explicitly rejecting the possi-bility of theory building, arguing that the post-positivist point of departure is incompatible with social science theory. By contrast, constructivist scholars usually aim at theory building, most clearly in the case of Alexander Wendt who first outlined a structural, state-centric theory of collective identity formation (1995) and subsequently engaged in building a theory of international cooperation (1999). Emmanuel Adler claims that '[u]nlike idealism and post-structuralism and post-modernism, which takes the world only as it can be imagined or talked about, constructivism accepts that not all statements have the same epistemic value and consequently that there is some foundation for knowledge' (2005: 11, see also 89–105). Likewise, theorists belonging to the critical theory current have no objection to the scientific task of theory building. However, they do draw a distinction between traditional (or problem-solving theory) and critical theory (Cox 1981). The two kinds of theory share the aim of understanding and explaining international relations, yet critical theory also aims at changing or transforming its subject matter. This brings us to a very important point. Audie Klotz and Cecily Lynch (1998) rightly suggest that 'there can be realist and liberal variants of constructivism, since it offers an ontological and epistemological approach, rather than an explanatory theory of international politics'.

Fourth, methodology has proven to be a contested issue, triggering in turn an important debate on methodology. Of course, as long as explorations of constructivist analytical options stay at the philosophical or meta-theoretical levels, there are no acute needs to consider methodological issues. It is telling that, on the one hand, Jepperson, Wendt and Katzenstein (1996) write about 'methodological nonissues', arguing that a constructivist stance does not disturb the standard operating procedures of a 'normal science'. Apart from a shift in the social ontology of research, scholars are invited to employ the 'same procedure as last year'. On the other hand, Kratochwil and Ruggie (1986; see also Ruggie 1998b), among others, argue that just as ontology rules over epistemology, theory rules over method, meaning that not just any method goes with any theory. Finnemore states this very succinctly: 'method should serve theory, not the reverse' (1996: 26). The question then remains which criteria, standards and conventions are available for post-positivist empirical research? Some criteria, which some take for granted as being positivist, seem, in reality, to be rather standard scientific standards, cf. Peter Berger's remark, 'I don't see why an insistence on the falsifiability of sociological propositions makes one a "Popperite". I rather think that, while the *term* is Popper's, the *methodological principle* is one accepted by the vast majority of social scientists' (1986: 233).

Finally, we have the more general issue about the relationship between the three main currents of thought. According to Steve Smith (2001), theoretical developments crystallize in three different positions: rationalism, constructivism and reflectivism. In his view, the position of constructivism is unsustainable. It is bound to either accept most of the basic premises of rationalism and subsequently be subsumed by rationalism, or radicalize in order to be accepted by reflectivists. There are four problems with this image of the theoretical landscape. First, the category 'reflectivism' seems to be a residual category including almost everything except rationalism and constructivism. The only thing these approaches have in common is that they are different from constructivism. They do not share a common programme, and variations concerning ontology, epistemology and normative preferences are significant. Second, several so-called reflectivist approaches have characteristics that indicate they are closer to constructivism than to anything else. This includes some of the normative theorists, modernist feminists, most historical sociologists and a fair share of critical theorists. What is left of reflectivism? Postmodern theorists of various sorts, plus a few more approaches! It is even possible to discuss where Michel Foucault, the founder of the genealogical method, belongs. Given all this, it is very difficult to maintain reflectivism as a dominant position in the contemporary theoretical landscape. Third, constructivism is far more than Alexander Wendt's otherwise eminent work. Surely, he originally coined the term and represents a prominent variety. However, he does not represent the linguistically inspired version of constructivism. Furthermore, Nicholas Onuf has developed a rules-based version of constructivism which differs significantly from Wendt's version of constructivism (Zehfuss 2002). Fourth, the expectation that constructivism ends up being rationalist is based on an either/or image. In contrast, Christiansen, Jørgensen and Wiener (2001) claim that constructivism is a mediating and very flexible position (cf. Figure 7.2). Hence, it makes more sense to think in terms of a spectrum than in terms of an either/or image. In general, the debate between post-structural and constructivist scholars is among the liveliest and most enriching for the discipline.

Research agenda

It would be wrong to describe the contemporary research agenda of the post-positivist tradition as anything but wide and very diverse. This has not always been the case. When constructivism was launched, for example, it was easy to dismiss it with reference to its limited number of empirical studies. In other words, even if the meta-theoretical critique of extant international theory forwarded by constructivists were considered legitimate or helpful, constructivism could not be expected to have a future unless it delivered an empirical research agenda (Keohane 1989). Constructivists have delivered ever since, making it a downright impossible task to summarize the studies published in recent decades. Instead, the following paragraphs will focus on the four most pronounced contributions to the contemporary post-positivist research agenda.

Figure 7.2   *Situating the constructivist middle ground*

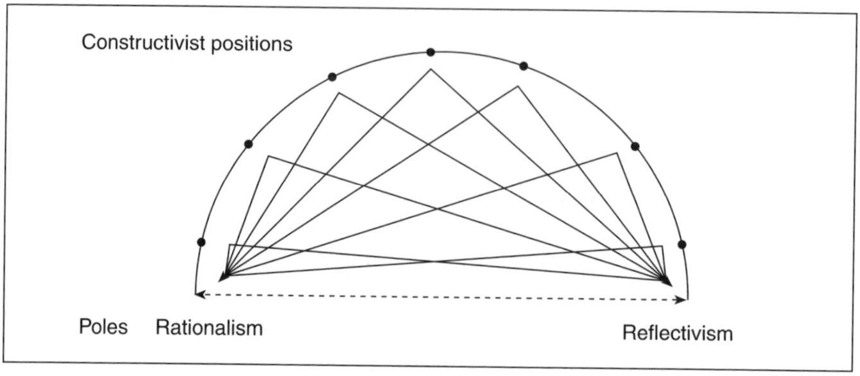

Source: Thomas Christiansen, Knud Erik Jørgensen and Antje Wiener (eds) (2001) *The Social Construction of Europe* (London: Sage): 10.

First, part of the research agenda can be summarized under the heading, 'enduring themes, changing conceptualizations'. Key concepts such as anarchy, power and security have always played a significant part in both theorizing and analyzing international relations. Post-positivists have taken their point of departure in these old concepts yet given them a new meaning. Whereas the causal power of anarchy is the starting point in most realist and some liberal theories, Alexander Wendt has diffused the causal explanatory power of anarchy, arguing forcefully that it is indeterminate; that 'anarchy is what states make of it' (Wendt 1992c). Michael Barnett and Raymond Duvall have thoroughly extended the meaning of power, and studies of securitization have emphasized that security threats are sometimes socially constructed rather than objective conditions of life. In short, reappraising traditional foundational concepts has been a major preoccupation among post-positivist theorists. In addition, new concepts or concepts just new to the discipline have been coined or examined: securitization, identity, hegemony, emancipation, security culture and social 'facts'.

Second, rather than regarding meta-theoretical reflection as the destination from whence no traveller returns, post-positivists tend to focus more on the deeds than the vices of meta-study. This is hardly surprising given their focus on foundational issues, including the philosophical or social theory underpinnings of IR theories and the future directions of the discipline. The very name of the tradition suggests that its representatives are entirely uninterested in issues associated with the shuffling and reshuffling of a limited number of rather inferior variables. It follows from the early constructivist theoretical deficit that procedures for empirical research often have been some sort of deduction from – or bridge-building between – philosophical or meta-theoretical positions and real-world empirical issues, potentially leading to the same sort of problems as when Giddens's structuration theory is applied without theoretical mediation, specification or methodological operationalization.

Third, meta-theoretical reflections are sometimes merged with critical concerns. Thus, post-structuralists insist that meta-theoretical criticism is a necessary part of the post-positivist research agenda; indeed, they reject the strict separation between theory and political and cultural practice. In general, engagement in reconceptualization, reconstruction of theories and extensions of research agendas etc. is usually motivated by a critical endeavour. It is the assessment of the state of the art that prompts scholars to try to improve what they consider to be in need of improvement.

Fourth, many scholars within the post-positivist tradition are no strangers to empirical studies, yet insist that there is a crucial difference between 'empirical' and 'empiricist'. Over the course of three decades, representatives of the post-positivist tradition have contributed to an empirical research agenda that is far more comprehensive than it is possible to account for in the present context (Finnemore and Sikkink 2001). David Campbell (1998) points out, that major conflicts, such as Bosnia and the Gulf War, have been analyzed by means of post-structuralist approaches. Within the field of foreign policy analysis, we have also seen the emergence of studies that have been informed by post-positivist perspectives (Wæver 1994; Weldes 1996; Campbell 1998). Some would still regard the notion of 'applied constructivism' as a contradiction in terms. In a certain sense it is. It is not possible to apply constructivism as such. It is possible, however, to apply given constructivist substantive theories. The problem, as we have just seen, is that during the early years of the post-positivist tradition only a relatively limited number of constructivist substantive theories were developed, cf. Martha Finnemore who argues that:

> [d]emonstrating the utility of a constructivist approach vis-à-vis dominant, interest-based paradigms is the first step in establishing a constructivist research program. The second step will be to elaborate that set of normative arguments in ways that provide more, and more easily testable, hypotheses and research questions for the future. Simply claiming that 'norms matter' is not enough for constructivists. They must provide substantive arguments about which norms matter as well as how, where and why they matter. (1996: 130)

The same argument goes for research on 'discourses' and 'identity'. It is insufficient to point out that discourses or identity matter – specification is required (cf. Milliken 2001).

Conclusion

The post-positivist tradition is very much alive and kicking. It has proven to be far more than a 1990s fad. Post-positivist theoretical approaches may appear slightly diffuse and lacking common main features. The new theories may also appear slightly difficult to grasp and characterized by a lack of clear hierarchy. Hence, it remains difficult to trace the contours of a clear profile and conclusion, that is, a conclusion to the questions addressing the accomplishments of the representatives of the somewhat new tradition. Which theories have proven to be sustainable and which ones have faded away or remained at the margins of the contemporary theoretical landscape? Despite these uncertainties, it is possible to conclude that the development of the tradition demonstrates that the representatives of the tradition cultivate a wider range of enquiries than do the theorists in most other traditions. Thus, movement between philosophical, meta-theoretical, theoretical and empirical levels of enquiry analysis is commonplace. This intellectual capacity implies potentials for more rigorous studies across levels of abstraction than analysts who only master one or two levels. The potential downside is that advances become difficult to pin down, because too many things are going on in too many different corners and in too many different directions; and not always in mutually compatible or supportive ways.

On the one hand the main currents of thought as well as the different kinds of theory employed contribute to a very rich tradition. On the other hand this pronounced diversity is not necessarily an advantage when post-positivists engage in debate with representatives from other traditions (cf. Chapter 8). The tradition is characterized by lively internal debates. Thus, there is a lively debate concerning the question whether a focus on non-material phenomena should have epistemological consequences; if yes, then which consequences? This issue has created a sharp split between so-called ontological and so-called epistemological constructivists. The post-positivist tradition focuses strongly on non-material factors. These factors can be seen as competing or complementing factors. There is an equally lively debate on the possible methodological consequences of studying social ontology.

The number of new arrivals has clearly diminished. The situation is no longer characterized by the maxim 'Let a hundred flowers blossom'. Rather, we see consolidation, extension and application in a wide variety of concrete studies. Concerning research agenda, the post-positivist tradition has rendered an impressive range of important research questions possible. These issues would not – and could not – have been addressed without the tradition, including its three currents of thought. Hence, the tradition implies a profound value added to the discipline and thereby to our understanding of world politics.

Questions

- What is the relationship between positivism and post-positivism? Why is this relationship significant for the post-positivist tradition?
- Which major sources of philosophical inspiration do the theorists of the tradition draw upon?
- How would you describe the trajectories and phases of the post-positivist tradition?
- Why is there no international post-structuralist theory?
- Why do post-structuralists consider it controversial to engage in theory building and empirical research?
- Which main intra-tradition debates have evolved? Is it possible to outline consensus positions, or are the positions incommensurable?
- Which issues on the contemporary research agenda can solely be attributed to scholars representing the post-positivist tradition?
- Why is methodology a contested issue?
- In which sense can the post-positivist tradition be said to be beyond positivism?
- What are the main pro and con arguments of treating the above theoretical perspectives as a tradition?
- Why do some theorists object to being categorized within a tradition?
- What is the relationship between philosophy and the post-positivist tradition?
- Is constructivism a perspective, a theory or a method?
- Is the relationship between tradition, currents of thought and concrete theories different from other traditions?
- Which main intra-tradition debates are the most important? Why?
- Why is the post-positivist tradition predominantly Western?

Further readings

Campbell, D. (1998) *Writing Security: United States Foreign Policy and the Politics of Identity* (Minneapolis: University of Minnesota Press): 207–27.
  A post-structuralist interpretation of the dynamics of American foreign policy.

Der Derian, J. and Shapiro, M. J. (eds) (1989) *International/Intertextual Relations: Postmodern Readings of World Politics* (Lexington, MA: Lexington).
  One of the first books cultivating a postmodern reading of international affairs.

Fierke, K. M. (2001) 'Critical Methodology and Constructivism', in K. M. Fierke and K. E. Jørgensen (eds), *Constructing International Relations: The Next Generation* (Armonk, NY: M. E. Sharpe).

In this chapter, Karin Fierke addresses methodological issues in the context of the constructivist turn.

Guzzini, S. (2000) 'A Reconstruction of Constructivism in International Relations', *European Journal of International Relations*, 6, 2: 147–82.
One of the most widely cited articles on the constructivist theoretical and meta-theoretical issues.

Ruggie, J. (1998b) *Constructing the World Polity: Essays on International Institutionalization* (London and New York: Routledge).
A collection of essays by one of the leading liberal and constructivist scholars in the field.

Searle, J. R. (1995) *The Construction of Social Reality* (New York: Free Press).
In this book the prime constructivist philosopher outlines a general theory of social ontology and social institutions.

Smith, S., Booth, K. and Zalewski, M. (eds) (1996) *International Theory: Positivism and Beyond* (Cambridge: Cambridge University Press).
One of the first books exploring the diverse post-positivist tradition.

Taylor, C. (1978) 'Interpretation and the Sciences of Man', in R. Beckler and A. R. Drengson (eds), *Philosophy of Society* (London: Methuen).
A treasure on epistemology, specifically on social ontology and the necessity of interpretive approaches.

Walker, R. B. J. (1993) *Inside/Outside: International Relations as Political Theory* (Cambridge: Cambridge University Press).
A famous book by Walker in which he, as one of the first, analyzes IR theory as political theory.

Weber, C. (1994) 'Good Girls, Little Girls, and Bad Girls: Male Paranoia in Robert Keohane's Critique of Feminist International Relations', *Millennium*, 23: 337–49.
Weber's part of a dialogue on feminist theory and international relations.

Zehfuss, M. (2002) *Constructivism in International Relations: The Politics of Reality* (Cambridge: Cambridge University Press).
In this book, Zehfuss analyzes three leading constructivist scholars and points to the significant differences that characterize their positions.

Websites for further information

socrates.berkeley.edu/~jsearle/articles.html
Click here for articles by the philosopher John Searle. The site includes a downloadable important article on social ontology.

polisciprof.blogspot.com/2006/03/some-thoughts-on-poststructuralism-in.html
A brief article on the merits of post-structuralism in IR theory.

plato.stanford.edu/entries/critical-theory/
An introduction to critical theory.

www.ifs.uni-frankfurt.de/english/history.htm
The Frankfurt School website.

Chapter 8

Contemporary Inter-Tradition Debates

Thinking is also research.

(Hedley Bull 1977: x)

One can learn more from a first-rate thinker with whom one disagrees than from a thinker who simply ratifies or reinforces what one already knows.

(Terence Ball 1995: 61)

Paradoxical perhaps, but exaggerated reliance on methodological rules and procedures for research tend to lax the mind. It is likely that Hedley Bull had this risk in mind when coining his famous reminder, emphasizing that even when applying a highly ritualized methodology, we should continue to think. Political theorist Terence Ball points out a similar risk: leaning on 'agreeable' positions alone can impede learning. In other words, we should not forget to learn from our opponents and from contending, perhaps counter-intuitive theoretical positions. In the context of the present chapter, these statements are highly relevant because the chapter focuses on debates among theorists from contending theoretical traditions.

Whereas the previous six chapters have introduced distinct traditions of IR theory, the present and following chapters will address issues that go across these traditions. With an emphasis on contemporary debates, the present chapter introduces the debates between traditions. It is widely agreed that the IR discipline has developed through a number of inter-tradition debates and is therefore thoroughly marked and characterized by such debates. It is exactly when challenged that theorists are forced to present or defend their positions in the most succinct and efficient fashion. Furthermore, it is when challenged in such debates that theorists reach for their strongest arguments. Finally, some theorists are actually compelled on occasion by arguments that lead them to change their minds, indicating that they are prepared to be proven wrong.

Apart from identifying the strongest arguments for and against a given tradition or parts of it, the chapter is intended to counter camp-thinking, that is, a tendency to exaggerate differences and downplay shared features or perspectives. In previous chapters, we have seen that traditions and currents of thought appear to be neatly bounded containers of ideas and reflections. They are relatively easy to understand and reproduce, and their contours and trajectories are easy to describe. Hence they are perfect for heuristic introductory purposes. The main disadvantage is that these images are slightly misleading in the sense of downplaying instances of overlapping or shared features as well as the potential of complementary perspectives or synthesis. The risk is that theoretical contention and theorists may appear more simple-minded and homogeneous over time than they actually are. The aim of this chapter is therefore twofold: to demonstrate the richness of theoretical debate and to draw attention to the nuances or multiple facets of theoretical reflection.

The premise of the chapter is that both intra- and inter-tradition debate can potentially contribute to progress in the discipline. In this context, three things are certain. First, such progress is not in any way guaranteed, especially because debates may degenerate into yelling among etched-in-stone positions, highly developed 'groupthink' and ritualized exchanges. Second, there are no obvious alternative paths leading to such progress. And finally, the very nature of progress is essentially contested, not least because what counts as progress in one tradition may appear most problematic from a different perspective. Should we, for instance, celebrate or deplore the existence of a plurality of theoretical traditions?

In principle, the encounters between six traditions make fifteen inter-tradition debates possible (cf. Figure 8.1); however, not all inter-tradition debates have thrived equally. Thus, liberal and realist theorists have been engaged in a century-long lively debate, whereas there has hardly been any encounter between, for example, the English School and IPE theorists. Hence, there are no good reasons to introduce the debates in an even or egalitarian manner, and the uneven account of the debates presented in the following reflects this state of affairs.

Liberalism–realism

Debates among realist and liberal theorists have been numerous and have contributed to fundamentally shaping the development of the discipline. In many ways, the 20th century began with a fierce liberal attack on 19th-century European power politics. Some liberal thinkers, such as John Hobson (1902), criticized colonialism and imperialism. Others criticized the prevailing mindset among those who make a deed of war or who cultivate a narrowly conceived national self-interest. Friedrich Kratochwil (1982) has demonstrated how German thinkers in the late 19th century defined the national interest in ever-more selfish terms. Zara Steiner (2003) has pointed out that contrary to the self-image of being a peace-loving empire, Great

Figure 8.1   *A hexagon of debates*

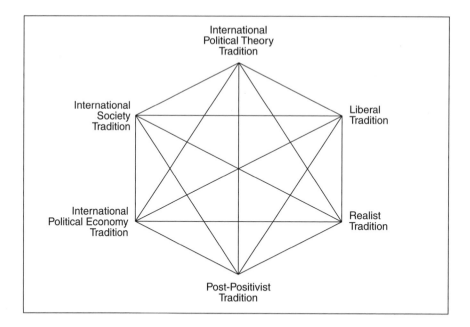

Britain had its considerable share of old-fashioned warmongers. Still others pointed out the diminishing economic returns of territorial conquest. Thus, Norman Angell (1909/2009) wrote critically against the so-called 'Machiavellians', a grouping of *Realpolitik* thinkers also portrayed by Friedrich Meinecke (1924).

After the creation of the Nobel Peace Prize in 1901, it is telling that it was consistently awarded to liberal thinkers during its first years. Liberal contributions to conceptualizing world politics include terms that now are taken for granted, including international anarchy, interdependence and international institutions.

During the early 20th century, one of the strongholds of liberal criticism of European-style *Realpolitik* was the United States, where criticism of Old World power politics was plentiful and an essential element in American identity politics. The version of liberalism represented by President Woodrow Wilson, who had a past as a professor of political science, was merely the tip of the iceberg of American liberalism. At the same time, to be sure, the US consolidated its military power and extended its strategic reach (Sloan 1988). World War I served as a grand vindication of the relevance of liberal criticism, although it should not be forgotten that national-liberal ideology has a certain share of the blame for the war.

The rise of fascism and Nazism in Europe, Japan and elsewhere understandably made a fundamental impact on the intellectuals of the time. The outbreak of World War II further contributed to considering or reconsidering the state of international affairs. It was a time of power politics in its crudest form, a time characterized by the failure of liberalism-informed international reform (League of Nations, collective security, etc.; see Chapter 3). E. H. Carr (1939) was among the first to present a comprehensive critique of what he dubbed 'utopian liberalism'. It should be noted, however, that Carr presented his realist position along with pleas for an appeasement-like foreign policy. Hans Morgenthau published similar criticism. Having fled Europe in the late 1930s due to the rise of Nazism, Morgenthau began his splendid career in the United States. In the summer of 1940, he gave a talk on liberalism and foreign policy at the New School for Social Research in New York. The recent fall of France fresh in mind, he presented a lengthy, devastating critique of the liberal tradition. His first book, *Scientific Man vs Power Politics* (1946), originates from that lecture. Right from a citation to arch-conservative Edmund Burke on the first page, Morgenthau focuses on the relationship between human reason, human nature and international politics. He demonstrates how the liberal tradition is based on key assumptions about human reason, a strong belief in the role of science in reforming both domestic and international society and a very specific notion of politics. In contrast, Morgenthau evokes the realist tradition from Thucydides to Disraeli, emphasizes the perpetual struggle for survival and power, and points to intellectual, moral and philosophical competences as the only means that can potentially solve global problems. Most of the points of classical realist criticism of the liberal tradition can actually be found in these two books by Carr and Morgenthau.

It took a while for liberal theorists to respond. Ernest Haas (1953) contributed a devastating critique of the key realist notion of balance of power and subsequently developed neofunctionalism, a theory of international cooperation and integration with a special view to European integration. Karl Deutsch coined the term 'security communities', thereby criticizing the realist billiard ball mechanical image of international relations. John Burton (1965) takes issue with political realism, especially in his criticism of its unitary actor model. Burton's alternative is the so-called transnational cobweb model in which state and societal actors relate in a highly complex fashion. According to Burton, state-centrism and billiard ball images – states behaving mechanically in balance of power politics like bouncing billiard balls – are misleading and should be replaced by a cobweb model depicting multiple networks among a broad range of different actors. A contemporary synonym might be international network society. Burton draws on systems theory and cybernetics, particularly in his early books, thus having similarities with the some of the underpinnings of Karl Deutsch's (1957) transnational version of liberalism. Among contemporary liberal theorists, Alexander Wendt (1992a) has thoroughly criticized neorealism for its narrow focus on material structures.

Jeffrey Legro and Andrew Moravcsik (1999) are contemporary liberal theorists who bluntly ask, 'Is Anybody Still a Realist?' They focus on major weaknesses of contemporary realism, in particular the trend of contemporary realists explaining an increasing number of anomalies by means of a less determinate, less coherent and less distinctive realism. Legro and Moravcsik conclude by asking why the realist tradition – given all of its weaknesses – has not simply been abandoned. Put differently, what does it take before a failed tradition should be abandoned? Predictably, their criticism has provoked a spate of responses, and the exchange is a useful source for any student seeking a brief contemporary version of a century-old debate.

The most recent round of liberal criticism of the realist tradition was launched at the end of the Cold War. Charles W. Kegley summarizes:

> Well before the Cold War began to thaw – in the period when realism appeared applicable and accurate – many scholars warned that realism was incomplete, misdirected, non-rigorous, inconsistent with scientific evidence, conceptually confused, and incapable of accounting for international behaviour in all issue areas including even controversies surrounding the high politics of conflict, war and peace. (1993: 134–5)

Realist responses to this avalanche of criticism were attempted, cf. John Mearsheimer's (1995) critique of the false promise of international institutions, Waltz's (1999) critique of the much-overstated consequences of globalization and Jack Snyder's (1991) attempt to incorporate domestic politics in realist theory. Despite these and other responses, Kegley notes that realism is 'losing its grip on the imagination of those writing in our field and on policy-makers' thinking' (1993: 134). During the 1990s, the European Union and the Clinton Administration pursued largely liberal internationalist foreign policies. The arrival of the Bush administration did not really provide any support for the realist tradition, given its peculiar blend of idealism and predominant power. Leading realists such as John Mearsheimer and Stephen Walt (2003) felt obliged to strongly criticize American foreign policy for being adventurous and well beyond the confines of balance-of-power rationales. At the same time, leading neoconservatives criticized EU foreign policy for pursuing the tactics of the weak – or multilateralism – and for lacking the instinct for punching when necessary (Kagan 2003). In summary, the traditional fault lines of theoretical debate are anything but traditional, and the foreign policies of leading powers continue to reflect such traditional contradictory currents of thought. Assuming that world politics has an impact on theorizing, we should expect that the US/UK war on terrorism and non-democratic states will leave a fingerprint on theorizing at the beginning of the 21st century. Ironically, the continuous significance of the realist tradition is demonstrated by the fact that liberal theorists continue to find it worthwhile to engage in harsh criticism of the tradition (Legro and Moravcsik 1999).

Realism – the English School

Theoretical debate between realists and English School theorists is somewhat asymmetrical in the sense that the former largely neglects the latter, whereas the latter displays considerable interest in the former. Given that the English School is a kind of secessionist break-away tradition leaving realism behind, this asymmetry is perhaps not particularly surprising.

For decades, Martin Wight was a fairly typical classical realist in England, yet he gradually changed his mind, thereby becoming a founder of the English School. His criticism of realism was at the same time a factor that contributed to making sense of the English School. Though he never gave specific reasons for leaving realism behind in any comprehensive fashion, he did present discontent with the archetype dichotomy of realism and idealism/liberalism. Indeed, his criticism of the simple-minded bifurcation of international theory is among Wight's greatest contributions. When lecturing on international theory, he had two main objectives in mind:

> One has been to show that the two-school analysis of international theory is not adequate. It was in fact the reflection of a diseased situation ... [the] second aim has been to try to bear out Tocqueville's point which I made at the outset that there is very little, if anything, new in political theory, that the great moral debates of the past are in essence our debates. (1991: 267 – 8)

Wight is even open to the suggestion that rather than just three traditions, there are possibly four or more. Finally, Wight confesses to being a rationalist at heart: 'I find that I have become more Rationalist and less Realist through rethinking this question during the course of giving these lectures' (1991: 268). Retrospectively, it is perfectly possible to investigate the degree of Wight's break with realism. Sean Molloy (2003) argues that it was only a partial break-away and that important realist elements remain present in Wight's work.

In this respect, it is crucially important to understand that the aim of the English School is to explain *global* political dynamics, particularly among *states*. In other words, the English School is a tradition designed for research on phenomena at the systems level. The intellectual lighthouse of the English School, Martin Wight, is so global in his outlook that he can write the following:

> Practical problems of international politics are often described in terms
> of building a bigger and better state – a European Union [for example]
> without seeing that such an achievement would leave the problems of
> inter-state politics precisely where they are. (Wight 1960: 39)

Actually, many realists would share this argument; indeed it has been a standard argument in realist critique of the apparent advances of European integration.

Hedley Bull acknowledges the important contributions made by the realists. He emphasizes that 'the writings of the "realists", a name that some of
them claimed for themselves, were a reaction against those of the "idealists",
or rather against wider tendencies in public thinking of which the latter
provided an illustration' (1972: 36). Bull realizes that this debate was
confined to the English-speaking world, and he welcomes the realist antidote
to docile idealist legalism and moralism. Nonetheless, he also states that 'the
laws of international politics to which some realists appealed in such a
knowing way appeared on closer examination to rest in tautologies or shifting definitions of the terms' (1972: 36). Subsequently, he concludes that 'in
terms of the academic study of international relations, the stream of thinking and writing that began with Niebuhr and Carr has long run its course'
(1972: 39). In essence, Bull reaches a conclusion here that critics of realism
would repeat during the following decades.

In general, contemporary English School representatives do not engage
much with their realist peers. Instances of engagement can be found, but they
are few and brief. Thus, Robert Jackson (2000) claims that realism is based
on the misleading notion that it is value-free. According to Jackson, realism
does not just describe the world as it is; it contributes to reifying certain
foreign policy practices. Apart from such exceptions, it is significant that
systematic engagement with realism does not characterize any of the major
English School studies (Bull 1977; Jackson 2000; Wheeler 2000; Linklater
and Suganami 2006).

In a mirror fashion, realists are generally not impressed by the English
School 'secessionists'. Hans Morgenthau never seriously engaged with
English School theorizing and, according to Kenneth Waltz, English School
theorists are disqualified by default, because they 'did theory in a sense not
recognized as theory by philosophers of science' (Waltz 1998: 385). This
claim is absolutely correct provided that by 'philosophers of science' we
understand a specific kind of philosopher of science. If not, the statement
loses its relevance and the English School theorists could return the compliment to Waltz, encouraging him to find some new philosophers. Finally,
Dale C. Copeland (2003) has outlined an interesting critique of the English
School. Copeland basically diagnoses a plethora of English School weakness and outlines a recipe for curing the English patient. Among the weak-

---

> ## Box 8.1   Compatible, if not overlapping, positions
>
> Kenneth Waltz and his wife visited London in 1959 and came across an essay in the LSE library.
>
> > 'I read her a few sentences and I said to her "Who do you think wrote this?" And she said "You did!" I said, "No: Hedley Bull." We really were thinking in very much the same way in those days. Hedley's later development was in a different direction; not wholly incompatible.' (Waltz 1998: 385)

nesses, Copeland cites a lack of theoretical clarity and the role of rules and norms:

> As it stands, the English School is less a theory that provides falsifiable hypotheses to be tested (or that have been tested) than a vague approach to thinking about and conceptualizing world politics . . . the idea that international societies of shared rules and norms play a significant role in pushing states towards greater cooperation than one would expect from examining realist theories alone. (Copeland 2003: 427)

Copeland concludes by explaining that remaining 'at the level of typologies and vague generalizations about the impact of international society will not do the trick' (2003: 441).

Finally, it is noteworthy that encounters include transfers from one tradition to the other. Just like in the 1950s and 1960s, it is realists that move to the international society tradition. One example is Barry Buzan (1993) who during the early 1990s was engaged in reconstructing neorealism. In this context, reconstruction means carefully reconsidering neorealism's explanatory factors and actually extending the range of such factors. Buzan's reconstructed neorealism essentially employs a more nuanced repertoire of factors. One decade later, Buzan (2001) initiates a relaunch of the English School. In this fashion, it is once again a realist who leaves realism behind, this time not to found but to reconvene the English School.

Liberalism – English School

We have previously seen that some of the founders of the English School came from the realist tradition and thus had a close relationship with that tradition. This section examines relations between the English School and the liberal tradition. A first hint about the characteristics of the relationship comes from the English School's consistent insistence on being a *via media*, that is, an in-between theoretical tradition. In Martin Wight's conception of three traditions (cf. Figure 5.1), we have the Grotian international society tradition in the middle. On the flanks we have on the one hand the Hobbesian realist tradition and on the other hand the Kantian revolutionary tradition. This is important, because it demonstrates that the founders of the School were keenly aware of the liberal tradition yet also wanted to distance themselves from it. This deliberate distance, then, is the point of departure for the troubled relationship between the liberal tradition and the English School. In the following, the five most important instances of 'trouble' will be introduced.

The English School and the liberal tradition share an interest in the role of international institutions, the extension of international society and the impact of international norms, including human rights and the principle of non-intervention. The English School cultivates a distinction between on the one hand international institutions as international organizations and on the other hand international sociological institutions termed 'fundamental institutions' (see Chapter 5). In Hedley Bull's investigation of the sources of international order, the latter institutions were clearly most important. However, members of the English School also paid some attention to the role of international organizations, not least the United Nations (Roberts and Kingsbury 1988; Jackson 2000). This suggests that the research interests of the two traditions are asymmetrical. The English School has made a priority of the type of institutions that evolve evolutionarily so to speak, whereas liberal theorists tend to focus on so-called architectural institutions, international organizations, that can be designed, created and changed by means of political decision-making.

Second, strong liberals and solidarists share a remarkably large common platform, and there is a considerable overlap between the solidarist and strong liberal currents of thought. They are considerably less state-centric than their counterparts and pay special attention to individuals and global institutions. To a considerable degree, they share motivations, concerns and normative agendas. Both currents would therefore likely benefit from an intensified dialogue, perhaps even a merger. Pushing the frontiers of each current in order to overcome some of their limits could be accomplished by further specifying the relationship between individuals and international society, issues of human security and the UN-introduced 'responsibility to protect' principle (cf. Evans and Sahnoun 2001). Finally, an extension of the solidarist research agenda to include global economic and environmental issues would potentially further strengthen the links between solidarism and strong liberalism.

Third, liberal theorists do not have a common position vis-à-vis the English School. On the one hand some liberal theorists take a positive view on the English School or its individual members. Thus, Yale Ferguson (1998) has written a long paen to the work of Hedley Bull. On the other hand most American liberals seem to have serious problems with the English School, probably because the English School does not fit into the dominant image in North America of a 'Russian doll' consisting of a narrowly conceived social science, political science and IR. Robert Keohane (1989) has voiced serious criticism of the English School, claiming that it is necessary to search for the keys where the street light is – not in the dark. Martha Finnemore (2001) has formulated a brief yet caustic criticism of the School. She points out that to many non-English School scholars, it is nothing but a challenge 'simply figuring out what its methods *are*. There is remarkably little discussion of research methods anywhere in the English School canon' (2001: 509). Furthermore, she points out a second source of puzzlement, this time concerning 'the theoretical ambitions of much English School work. What, exactly, are its advocates offering? What, exactly, are they claiming theoretically' (2001: 510). This citation indicates that realists (cf. Copeland in previous section) and liberal constructivists, such as Finnemore, share agendas; at least when criticizing the English School.

Fourth, we have previously seen that liberal theorists, when theorizing international relations, place considerable emphasis on three features: domestic factors, domestic regime form and the possibility of progress. Hence, they are bound to criticize the English School, because it can only deliver disappointing – if not alarming – ignorance concerning all three features. By focusing exclusively on the international system or the international society, the School ignores the role of domestic politics. Furthermore, the School clearly pays no attention whatsoever to the democratic peace argument. Finally, the School is rather agnostic about the possibility of progress in international affairs. If forced to choose, however, the School's theorists would probably align themselves with the realist position.

Fifth, the blatant state-centrism makes it difficult for the traditional English School to contribute to our understanding of the role of major international NGOs, for example, in the creation of treaties on small arms, bans on landmines etc. Similarly, the role of private companies in spreading Western values is completely neglected. Apart from some of the newer contributions, the English School is predominantly state-centric, implying that interest groups, political parties or regional institutions play an insignificant role. Whenever the English School 'moves up' (i.e. somehow goes beyond the level of states) it arrives at international, yet 'fundamental' sociological institutions such as great powers, war, balance of power, international law and diplomacy. Despite the strong dose of the aforementioned state-centrism, the English School does focus on the *impact* of fundamental international (sociological) institutions. As pointedly put by Buzan, 'states live in an international society which they shape and *are shaped by'* (Buzan 2001a, emphasis added), that is, we witness a process of mutual constitution.

In summary, a few notable exceptions do not hinder us from concluding that encounters between liberal and English School theorists are more potential than really existing.

Liberalism and post-positivism

Before exploring the encounters between the liberal and post-positivist traditions, it is important to point out that there is a significant shared identity between the theorists in the two traditions. More specifically, in substantive terms, many post-positivists are liberal scholars who have simply left positivism behind. Historically, positivism has been the philosophy of a science vehicle that many liberal theorists employed in order to claim scientific legitimacy vis-à-vis their (traditionalist) realist or English School critics. Hence, there has been a close alignment for decades between liberal theorists and a positivism serving liberal emancipatory endeavours. Some post-positivists basically argue that the costs of using positivism as a philosophical underpinning vastly exceed the analytical benefits.

In order to illustrate the evolvement of the most recent and important encounters, more specific interventions will be introduced in the following. In a certain way, it all started with a critique of liberal regime theory; more specifically, a critique of a flawed relationship between ontology and epistemology in regime theory. Friedrich Kratochwil and John Ruggie (1986) argue that the focus on intersubjective phenomena such as norms and principles in regime theory require a post-positivist epistemology, for example, interpretive approaches. Robert Keohane responded with a criticism of post-positivism (1989), and his article actually proved capable of, if not setting the discipline's research agenda, then at least contributing to significantly shape it. The specific objective was a discussion of two different approaches to the study of international institutions, but it became a more general discussion of two approaches – rationalist and reflectivist – to the study of international relations. Basically, Keohane argues that reflectivists need to develop an explicit research agenda; otherwise their perspective will prove unsustainable and perish:

> [T]he greatest weakness of the reflective school lies not in deficiencies in their critical arguments but in the lack of a clear reflective research program that could be employed by students of world politics ... until the reflective scholars or others sympathetic to their arguments have delineated such a program and shown in particular studies that it can illuminate important issues in world politics, they will remain on the

> ## Box 8.2   A debate made up?
>
> 'This notion of the rationalist–constructivist debate is problematic. For a start, whilst German scholars have indeed discussed the merits of rational choice versus constructivism approaches at length, there is little evidence of a debate in the Anglo-Saxon context. In surveys of the state of the discipline in general and of constructivism in particular we are told time and again that this debate is happening and that it is crucially important. And yet we do not find exchanges between rationalist and constructivist scholars in key journals.' (Zehfuss 2002: 4–5)

> margin of the field, largely invisible to the preponderance of empirical researchers, most of whom explicitly or implicitly accept one or another version of the rationalistic premises. Such invisibility would be a shame, since the reflective perspective has much to contribute. (1989: 173)

Subsequent responses to Keohane's challenge vary considerably. In the first place, some liberal theorists argue that the new approach, reflectivism, is not particularly new. There was a strong sense of *déjà vu* surrounding this seemingly new approach (Sørensen 1991). Where had it all been seen before? In Europe, where ideational factors had never been abandoned to the same degree as in the US. Other liberal yet post-positivist theorists responded differently. Richard Ashley and R. B. J. Walker's response to Keohane's criticism was sharp and goes as follows:

> This is a fine admonishment. It is as direct as it is succinct. It is delivered without the slightest concealment of the privilege being arbitrarily accorded to a certain interpretation of 'empirical research', of the policing function being performed, or of the punishment that will come to those who fail to heed the admonishment delivered. But it could not be offered or plausibly entertained by anyone who has actually read and taken seriously the work of the 'reflectivists' admonished. (Ashley and Walker 1990b: 266)

By contrast, Alexander Wendt has systematically aimed at downplaying contrasts; essentially he attempts to de-escalate the contradiction between Keohane's position and, if not post-positivism, then at least constructivism. He claims that 'constructivism's potential contribution to a strong liberalism has been obscured . . . by recent epistemological debates between modernists and postmodernists, in which Science disciplines Dissent for not defining a conventional research program, and Dissent celebrates its liberation from Science' (Wendt 1992a: 393). In general, the empirically minded constructivists did not pursue the meta-theoretical issues, but simply launched, without much fanfare, a major empirical research programme (for a review, see Finnemore and Sikkink 2001). Some selected supposedly hard cases, such as national security, using them to demonstrate the usefulness of constructivist approaches (Katzenstein 1996).

In addition to triggering immediate responses, Keohane's intervention became a moment of truth, especially because post-positivists realized that – though they all share an interest in post-positivist approaches – they essentially want to pursue different research strategies. The intervention also signalled what has been acknowledged to be the discipline's main axis of theoretical contention since the 1990s, namely rationalism and constructivism (Katzenstein, Keohane and Krasner 1998). Jepperson, Wendt and Katzenstein (1996) do their best to reduce affinities with post-positivism, and they are keen to point out that their employment of the term identity does not 'signal a commitment to some exotic (presumably Parisian) social theory' (1996: 34). Furthermore, they emphasize that contributors do 'comparison across time and space, in ways now standard in social science. When they attempt explanation, they engage in "normal science", with its usual desiderata in mind' (1996: 65). Finally, they do their best to reduce methodological matters to non-issues and criticize epistemological constructivists for not explicating what an interpretive methodology would entail in practice or 'provided an empirical exemplar representing concretely the kind of work he has in mind' (1996: 67). They also explain that they part company with constructivists, who insist on 'the need for a special interpretive methodology' (1996: 67).

Despite the heated encounters between the two traditions, one should not lose sight of the fact that there is a considerable overlap in the sense of several post-positivists belonging to the liberal tradition but thoroughly refurbishing it by means of giving liberalism a post-positivist platform. Similarly, Keohane's self-image is that of a liberal theorist, and his criticism of reflectivism was more concerned with what he regards as proper research design than with substantive liberal concerns. The behavioural revolution mainly gave liberalism its positivist identity, which especially applies to the development of liberalism in North America. The behavioural revolution was less significant outside North America, implying in turn why the post-positivist response was strongest in North America. Outside the US, there was simply less to react to.

Post-positivism – realism

The relationship between post-positivism and realism is highly complex, and the sources of this complexity are many and varied. During the 1990s, neorealism enjoyed the privilege of being among the main targets of post-positivist criticism, especially because Kenneth Waltz's neorealism is couched in a scientist form, but also because a fair share of post-positivist theorists are basically liberal theorists employing arguments informed by post-positivism (see above section). Thus, we have another example of substance and form being intimately linked if not mixed. Post-positivist criticism of realism constitutes the origin of the tradition. Richard Ashley (1981, 1984) diagnoses 'the poverty of neorealism', emphasizing main problems such as reifying state-centrism, making use of a problematic agent–structure relationship and positivist underpinnings.

The response from leading realists has been swift and forceful. Robert Gilpin (1986) returns Ashley's compliments by pointing out the predominantly incomprehensible post-positivist language, which he finds intolerably convoluted and idiomatic. Thus, the substantive content of Gilpin's criticism is not particularly impressive. In a response to constructivist advances, Robert Jervis (1998) outlines the virtues of realism and the vices of constructivism. Like many realists, Jervis believes that constructivism is a competing substantive tradition in IR theory. Furthermore, that constructivists insist on ideational or social factors suggests to some realists that constructivism is a kind of political idealism couched in a fancy vocabulary. Hence, they believe they can reach for traditional responses to archetypical idealist positions. This might be particularly evident in John Mearsheimer's (1995) criticism of what is called 'critical theory' and proves to be a garbage can-like compilation of various new approaches. In other words, Mearsheimer lumps together a range of different theoretical currents, including critical theory, constructivism and ideas about collective security. Constructing a liberally naive and theoretically incoherent position makes it possible to employ traditional realist criticism of utopian liberal critical theory. To political realists, the notion of 'interpellation' may sound sexy, but most realists seem not to have a clue what the term actually means. The example represents the relationship between the two traditions. The overlap in terms of vocabularies is minimal, and these theorists have great difficulty discerning whether they agree or disagree in substantive terms.

How have post-neorealists responded to post-positivism? This is a most relevant and interesting question because, after all, both post-neorealism and post-positivism have been developed parallel to one another since the 1980s. The short answer is that responses have been very different. In the case of Stephen Walt (1987), there were no comments on post-positivism; perhaps unsurprising given the fact that the post-positivist tradition had hardly taken off at the time. However, the situation looks entirely different a decade later. Walt subsequently praises the increasing theoretical pluralism (realism, liberalism and constructivism) characterizing the discipline. He concludes that 'each of these competing perspectives captures important aspects of world politics. Our understanding would be impoverished were our thinking confined to only one of them' (1998: 44). However, the example is atypical as most post-neorealists do not encounter post-positivism.

As we saw in the chapter on realism, some analysts identify certain over-lapping or complementary features. One example is Richard Ashley (1984) who clearly is critical of neorealism, but he acknowledges that there is some value in classical realism. A second example is Henry Nau (2002) who demonstrates that realism and constructivism can be employed in a fruitful, complementary fashion in which power (realism) and identity (construc-tivism) factors each contribute to explaining American foreign policy. Robert Barkin (2003) goes a step further, suggesting that realism and constructivism are so compatible that it is possible to not only combine but actually merge the two, that is, a constructivist realist theory is in his view fully conceivable.

Post-positivism – the English School

Outlining the relationship between the English School and post-positivism is relatively simple, particularly because of the relatively limited nature of the relationship. This is possibly because relatively few theorists adhere to the two traditions; or perhaps the two traditions are too far from one another to really invite encounters. Much post-positivist criticism has been directed against neorealism, neoliberal institutionalism and rationalist or positivist approaches in general. By contrast, the English School has attracted rela-tively little attention or criticism. In the following, three encounters will be presented. First, Ole Wæver (1999) has traced lines of argument and streams of thought within the English School that are strikingly similar to the philosophers who informed parts of the post-positivist tradition. Wæver essentially argues that the reconvening of the English School deserves some attention if not support from post-positivist theorists. Second, Robert Jackson (2000: 51–5) criticizes post-positivism, focusing on critical theory, postmodernism and constructivism. Concerning critical theory, he notes the obsession with linkages between knowledge and power and the aspiration of emancipation. With no signs of approval, he acknowledges that Robert Cox's remark 'theory is always for someone and for some purpose' is 'frequently quoted' (2000: 52). In relation to postmodernism, Jackson singles out Robert Ashley and is mainly critical of relativism, that is, 'the anything goes' thesis and potential dangers of nihilism. Regarding construc-tivism, he believes there is an inherent contradiction between rejecting an objective outside world and the aspiration of constructivists to do 'proper' social science. If Jackson is critical of post-positivism, he attributes signifi-cant value to the pre-positivist English School's classical approach which he therefore engages in reconstructing. The third encounter is between James

Der Derian (1987) and Hedley Bull. Der Derian carried out his doctoral studies at Oxford University with Hedley Bull serving as supervisor. Notably, Der Derian's doctoral thesis is on diplomacy, one of the fundamental institutions in Bull's edifice of international order. Furthermore, Der Derian employs a post-classical approach. In short, substantive thematic continuities (diplomacy) and methodological discontinuities characterize the relationship between the English School and Der Derian's version of post-positivism.

The fourth example is the idea that the English School actually is based on constructivist underpinnings. The image of a layered cake comes to mind as the English School provides substantive propositions about the nature of international society and constructivism provides the ontological and epistemological analytical 'software'. The idea was first forwarded by Timothy Dunne (1995) and subsequently supported by Hidemi Suganami (2001b). If, for a moment, we accept the proposition, it is clear that the genealogy of constructivism within International Relations reaches back to the 1950s, or, put differently, that the English School can be seen as a kind of prototype constructivism. Apart from meta-theoretical underpinning, the English School pluralists and post-structuralists share a scepticism regarding issues such as humanitarian intervention, both currents cultivating a fairly conservative assessment of the desirability of humanitarian interventions.

All four examples can be seen as invitations to further explore the relationship, especially because there are strong indications that shared features are more widespread than one might intuitively think.

IPE encounters other traditions

In the chapter on the IPE tradition (Chapter 6), we saw how IPE has a deeply split personality. This feature has important consequences for the encounters IPE has with other traditions. In the first place, IPE can be seen as an interdisciplinary field of study, with each of the engaged disciplines contributing a range of intellectual traditions. In a heterodox and diverse fashion, IPE is the outcome of all sorts of encounters across disciplines and traditions; as long as the focus is exclusively on international economics and politics.

Second, IPE can be seen as a microcosmos of inter-tradition debates in IR, focusing on the linkages between international politics and economics. In other words, IPE is one long inter-tradition debate unto itself, and the inter-tradition debates are embedded in the tradition.

Third, we can explore debates between IPE and the five other IR theoretical traditions (IPT, liberalism, realism, the English School and PPT). As it is often the case, the volume and intensity of debate varies significantly. Concerning IPE and IPT, markedly different intellectual cultures and languages have kept these two traditions worlds apart, and inter-tradition debate has therefore been relatively limited. However, scholars with an interest in international distributive justice share a number of concerns with IPE scholars, leaving some room for future debate. Furthermore, debates between theorists of globalization and theorists of supra-national democratic governance could also be fruitful. The same can be said about debates between English School theorists of humanitarian intervention (Wheeler 2000) and theorists of the political economy of war and conflict. It is rather difficult to imagine IPE formulated in PPT terms, and leading PPT theorists have displayed limited interest in IPE (Walker 1993; Campbell 1998; Der Derian 1987; Kratochwil 1989).

There has always been a close encounter between liberalism and IPE, often actually characterized by a fusion of concern and approach. One of the first examples is John Hobson's analysis of the causal links between imperialism and the causes of war. In the second half of the 20th century, studies of transnationalism contribute to strengthen links between the two traditions. Further examples are provided by studies focusing on domestic interests as the primary sources of foreign economic policy (Katzenstein 1978). Finally, research on embedded liberalism (Ruggie 1991) and studies of multilateralism (Ruggie 1993) demonstrate the close encounter.

There is a largely unresolved relationship between scholars at home in the post-positivist and IPE traditions, respectively. On the one hand they share a vocation to 'critical' scholarship. On the other hand they tend to disagree about the merits of positivism. As Craig Murphy and Douglas Nelson point out:

> despite their character as a broad, oppositional churches, British IPE's major institutions – IPEG, RIPE, New Political economy, texts such as Stubbs and Underhill, and major summaries of theory such as Gill and Mittelman or Germain – rarely invite in the strong (and equally oppositional) post-structuralists and post-modernists who deny the possibility of the scientific project. (2001: 405)

Murphy and Nelson continue by pointing out the possibility that positivism, rather than playing a role as a perpetual other, can serve as an underpinning of critical approaches; a widespread role in the early phases of the Marxist tradition. By contrast, post-positivist scholars obviously do not regard positivism as a philosophy of science meriting further subscription.

Grand theories can be criticized both for what they are and what they are not. In the case of the English School, realists and liberals are inclined to criticize the School for what it is: a *via media* orientation that does not satisfy either of the competing traditions. The English School has also been criticized for what it does not include. As the presentation above makes clear, the English School focuses on the dynamics of international politics, and hardly a single reflection or sentence can be found regarding economics. Theorists working within the tradition of International Political Economy in particular find this focus almost perverse. They argue that, at the end of the day, the linkages between international economics and politics provide the key to properly understanding international dynamics.

Unsurprisingly, given the almost complete lack of English School interest in economics, there have been few examples of debate between IPE and the English School. IPE theorists tend to believe that the English School is merely a very conservative or traditional perspective on international politics. Susan Strange, who was a colleague of several English School theorists, has been very much aware of the School and vocal in criticizing its traditionalism, its negligence concerning the dimension of economics and its pronounced state-centrism. The two main currents within the English School, pluralists and solidarists, demonstrate no particular difference in their common negligence of economics. In principle, solidarism could be extended to economic solidarism, but that remains to be seen. Similarly, Hedley Bull's interest in the factors explaining international order could be extended to economic factors and the international economic order, but this has not been carried out.

Finally, there is a strange and partly unresolved relationship between IPE and realism. On the one hand there is considerable overlap between the two traditions. Thus, international political economy can be analyzed by means of realist theories, emphasizing state power and interests. Furthermore, mercantilism *is* realist thinking, although with a focus on both economic means and political ends. Robert Gilpin and Stephen Krasner are among the realists who have most convincingly demonstrated how IPE and realism need not be contrasting but rather complementary theoretical traditions characterized by complementarity as not only a possibility but also an option that has been successfully achieved. On the other hand we have the theorists according to whom the two traditions are mutually exclusive and contradictory. Among IPE scholars, criticism of the exclusive focus on politics in realism, state-centrism and the circular view on historical development is widespread. Some argue that realist scholars live in a bygone world and that it is time to wake up because the world has changed (Strange 1994). Among realists, many stick to purely state-centric perspectives and an exclusive focus on international politics. Pet topics among IPE scholars, such as interdependence and globalization, have been systematically neglected or rejected. Kenneth Waltz thus argues that interdependence does not have the causal role many interdependence theorists attribute to it and that the level of interdependence varies across time in ways that do not support the hypotheses generated by interdependence theory. Concerning globalization, it is typically a phenomenon that is explained away or the arguments concerning interdependence are repeated (Waltz 1999).

International political theory debates with other traditions

The revival of IPT has been accompanied by a general encounter between IPT and other theoretical traditions. Several IPT theorists – for example, Frost and Hutchings – have been engaged in securing IPT by means of criticizing the existing research practices. In this case, debates with theorists from other traditions constitute the vehicle of the IPT revival. In other words, IPT emerges partly by means of critical encounters. However, there has not been widespread response to this kind of criticism. It seems as though theorists from other traditions believe that they can continue to simply neglect IPT theorists and choose silence or benign neglect as their preferred response strategy. Given that IPT is ascending, this strategy does not appear to be sustainable in the long run.

Debates between IPT and the liberal traditions have been marked by the complex nature of their relationship. When political theory was pushed out of political science generally – and the IR discipline specifically – liberal theorists did not merely play a minor role; several were actually leading figures in the behavioural revolution. One of the first tasks during the revival of IPT has therefore implied a reconsideration of the warranted or unwarranted links between liberal IR theory and positivism. This obstacle should not hide the fact that the theorists from the two traditions share an unusually large common pool of interests. It is well known that liberal republican theorists have a strong interest in the domestic governance features of states and that several IPT theorists have a long-standing interest in democratic governance. Furthermore, the neoliberal institutional perspective on world politics and IPT scholars share an interest in processes of domesticating world politics; in particular the role of constitutions, rules and norms. Finally, the liberal tradition is the tradition of thought that probably pays most attention to processes such as interdependence and globalization. Both processes have a direct impact on the meaning of key terms in political theory, including democracy, legitimacy and justice.

The realist tradition has a close, yet often unacknowledged, relationship with political theory. Chris Brown insists that:

> a very great deal of what is traded in international relations as non-normative theory is steeped in normative assumptions. Such recent mainstream concoctions as the 'theory of hegemonic stability', or the neo-realist account of the balance of power, or Wallerstein's world systems approach are clearly grounded in normative positions, whether acknowledged or not. (Brown 1992: 3)

One of the main currents of the English School is defined by its understanding of justice, yet Terry Nardin (2006) is one of the international political theorists who has examined issues of international justice most comprehensively. The two traditions also share an interest in conceptual analysis and constitutive explanation.

The relationship between the post-positivist tradition (PPT) and IPT has been characterized by three different forms. First, the two traditions can be considered identical in some cases. At the general level, contemporary (I)PT has been developed in a form beyond positivism; indeed, contemporary political theorists are well aware of the role positivism served when political theory was pushed to the margins of political science, if not exterminated. The revival of IPT is therefore bound to be shaped by negative attitudes towards positivism. At the specific level, R. B. J. Walker, for example, simply considers IR theory to be political theory. In order to make this argument, he employs methods of post-structural deconstruction, thereby providing an excellent example of the two traditions being identical. Second, even in cases in which the two traditions are not identical, they are characterized by extensive overlapping concerns and conceptualizations. Thus, they both cultivate conceptual analysis, constitutive theorizing and engage freely in interpretations of important thinkers. Finally, there are cases in which the two traditions represent contending perspectives, and there are important examples of leading theorists engaged in fierce debates. Identical and overlapping characteristics cannot hide the fact that the two traditions also represent important contending perspectives on world politics. Many leading IPT theorists do not subscribe to the postmodern or post-structural underpinnings that unsurprisingly characterize a substantial part of PPT scholarship.

In summary, given that IPT is currently consolidating its newly gained ground in the discipline, it is most likely that the contentious zone of debate will become even livelier in the years to come. IPT seems highly suitable to challenge other traditions and currents of thought. By doing so, the tradition might be able to upgrade the theoretical reflection in the discipline significantly.

Conclusion

The kaleidoscopic presentation above focuses on the major axes of inter-tradition theoretical debate. If successfully conducted, such debates become dynamic and bring theoretical progress to the discipline. We have seen that most theoretical debates concern a relatively limited number of issues. Given that we are talking about theoretical debates, it is hardly surprising that the very nature of theory has been thoroughly discussed. As seen in Chapter 1, the range in the conceptions of theory is considerable, and mutually recognized kinds of theory are rare – if not entirely non-existent. An equally popular topic for debate concerns the ontology of 'the international', that is, the existence and appropriate blend of actors, structures and processes in the so-called international realm. However, not only the existence of things is important. In the context of analytical endeavours, it is equally important to discuss the precision of our knowledge about those phenomena that exist – with or without our agreement on their existence. The question of how we can know about actors, structures or processes is the essence of epistemology (cf. Chapter 1). Contending views on epistemology are as widespread as are views regarding ontology. The level of analysis issue concerns the level at which we can locate the phenomena we choose to include when explaining selected aspects of world politics. The number of levels and their relative merits has also triggered contending views. Methodology is the lowest rung on the ladder from theoretical abstraction to concrete analysis. Some consider methodology the master of the analytical game, implying that you cannot analyze topics that cannot be analyzed by means of what is considered the correct methodology. Others consider methodology to be the servant of theory and address issues of potential encounters between theory and empirical data. Within international political theory, methodology concerns somewhat different issues, such as the structure of coherent reasoning, the role of context.

The shifts in the fault lines of theoretical reflection across time may originate from changing fads and concerns within the discipline. In the 1980s, the introduction of regime theory first caused quite a splash but subsequently assumed a more adequate role in the study of international relations. A second cause can be found in the developments in other disciplines, such as political science, law, philosophy or sociology. Illustrative examples include the rise of rational choice within first economics and then political science and its spill-over into International Relations. Positivism is a branch of philosophy that has also spilled over to International Relations. Constructivism in International Relations has drawn on insights from sociology. A third cause can be located in developments in world politics or economics, that is, in the external environment of scholarly reflection.

Not all debates are successful in terms of generating new knowledge. Some can be characterized as dialogues of the deaf. Other debates are essentially endless debates marked by changing times but enduring positions. Some theorists consider their theoretical orientation to be a precious aspect of personal identity. Clearly, such theorists do not take criticism easy. Debates such as those presented in the above are anything but innocent. They are very much about the power of the mind, personal pride and scholarly prestige.

Questions

- Through which phases has the debate between liberal and realist theorists evolved? How would you characterize the current phase of this debate?
- In which different ways does PPT challenge other traditions? What responses to this challenge can you point out?
- Which debates have been more optional than actually existing? Which factors explain why these debates have been non-starters?
- How would you characterize the relationship between theoretical debates and theoretical progress?
- In which debates have English School theorists primarily engaged?
- What are the major ways in which the IPE tradition relates to other traditions?
- Why is the revival of IPT promising for conceptual and theoretical reflection on the discipline?
- Why are theoretical debates necessary?
- Why are the debates so uneven in terms of encounters between different positions?
- What is the good and bad news about theoretical debates?
- Are the debates of equal importance to the students of international relations situated in different parts of the world?
- What are the relations between the theoretical debates and progress in our understanding of international relations?
- What factors explain the rise and fall of theoretical orientations?
- Which debate(s) do you find most promising for the future development of the discipline? Why?

Further reading

Acharya, A. and Buzan, B. (2007) 'Preface: Why is There No Non-Western IR Theory: Reflections On and From Asia', *International Relations of the Asia-Pacific*, 7, 3.

> In this article, Acharya and Buzan discuss the uneven development of IR theory, especially the state of affairs in non-Western parts of the world.

Buzan, B., Held, D. and McGrew, A. (1998) 'Realism versus Cosmopolitanism', *Review of International Studies*, 24: 387–98.

> An interesting dialogue on the merits of realism and cosmopolitanism, respectively.

Keohane, R. O. (1986) *Neorealism and Its Critics* (New York: Columbia University Press).

> A collection of essays in which authors discuss the strengths and weaknesses of neorealism.

Keohane, R. O. (1988) 'International Institutions: Two Approaches', *International Studies Quarterly*, 32: 379–96.

>   An article in which Keohane outlines rationalist and constructivist approaches to the study of international institutions, including issues of research and design.

Walt, S. M. (1998) 'International Relations: One World, Many Theories', *Foreign Policy*, 110: 29–46.

>   In this article Walt discusses why we continue to have many theories about the same 'one world'.

Wendt, A. (1995) 'Constructing International Politics', *International Security*, 20: 71–81.

>   Essentially an article demonstrating that criticism might trigger concise elaborations of given theoretical positions.

Websites for further information

www.isanet.org

>   The website of the International Studies Association, including a gateway to useful resources for theorists.

www.leeds.ac.uk/polis/englishschool/default.htm

>   A website created to promote the further development of the English School.

Chapter 9

A Guide to Creative Theorizing

In the previous chapters, six theoretical traditions, 17 currents of thought and numerous examples of applicable theory have been introduced (cf. Table 1.1). The chapters contribute considerable evidence to frequent claims that there is 'One World, Many Theories' (Walt 1998) and 'One Field, Many Perspectives' (Hermann 1998). Furthermore, the chapters demonstrate and confirm that the discipline is truly diverse and characterized by numerous contending perspectives. Such diversity has been praised and celebrated (Lapid 1989) though also observed with various degrees of scepticism (Lijphart 1974; Holsti 2001). Finally, the previous chapters, especially Chapter 1, have addressed the issue: why theory? In the present chapter, a related issue will be addressed: how theory? How do we theorize? How do we learn to think theoretically?

In this context, it is important to point out the obvious, that 'theory' is a noun. It refers to something that can be approached and, in principle, can be comprehended. In our context, it is something we will find in introductions to IR theory, such as the one you are reading right now. In the introduction to this book, we were also introduced to the pros and cons of thinking theoretically. Indeed, it is possible to learn about and account for theories without developing the competence to think theoretically. However, the aim of this chapter is to further develop our skills in theoretical thinking. Hence, we proceed from *learning about* theories to an engagement in *active* theorizing. It is therefore useful to keep in mind that 'theorizing' is a verb. It is something you *do* and requires intellectual curiosity and engagement to be carried out successfully.

The chapter is based on the hardly controversial idea that theories should not be regarded as non-dynamic, a-historical intellectual constructs. On the contrary, all theories have been created by someone, somewhere and presumably for some purpose. Authorized theorists are not the only ones able to theorize. So can students. Actually, the prime aim of this chapter is to encourage students to engage in active theorizing.

The chapter is intended to serve as a kind of DIY manual and will therefore first introduce key aspects of the craft or art of theorizing, including illustrative descriptions of the process provided by prominent theorists. Second, it will outline the building blocks of theory. Subsequently, we will review a number of issues, each briefly introduced and followed by an exercise, specifically issues of complementary approaches, theoretical eclecticism, synthesis, reappraisals and theoretical 'shaping'. Finally, these aspects will be summarized in a DIY manual for active theorizing. In other words, readers will be introduced to a range of guidelines for active theorizing and a number of illustrative examples describing what theorists do when they theorize.

What do theorists do when they theorize?

The following mosaic of four reflections illustrates conceptions of the process of theorizing and is intended to trigger images of the creative art of theorizing. The first part of the mosaic employs a perhaps surprising metaphor of painting. Addressing the issue of what we do when we theorize, Donald Puchala emphasizes that:

> [t]he theorists are first and foremost conceptualizers, symbolizers, synthesizers, and abstract organizers ... what they have been doing as theorists is painting for us in their writings bold-stroked, broad-brushed pictures of social reality and telling us that the real world is their pictures. (Puchala 2003: 24)

This is a very apt description of what theorizers do. The painting metaphor is highly suggestive and Puchala is not the only one to use it. Kenneth Waltz also makes use of painting as a metaphor yet in a somewhat similar fashion: 'the neorealist's world looks different from the one that earlier realists had portrayed' (Waltz 1990: 32).

The second mosaic points to different characteristics. Terry Nardin, an international political theorist (see Chapter 2), is very specific in his view of what theory is and is not, as well as the role of theorists:

> Making relevance to current affairs a criterion of success in theorizing misunderstands the activity of theorizing and what it can contribute to our understanding of international affairs. The knowledge we call theoretical is by definition detached from factual contingencies and therefore from current affairs. The theorist finds relationships among ideas that are abstracted from the ever-changing spectacle of events ... The aim of the theorist of international justice, as a theorist, is not to prescribe policy; it is to clarify and make coherent the meaning of justice in an international context. (Nardin 2006: 449)

This view does not mean that a given theory cannot be used for policy predictions, only that linkages between theory construction and current affairs are weaker than, for instance, in journalism or week-to-week policy analysis.

Third, in his discussion about how economic theory became possible, Waltz points out that:

> [t]he first step forward was, as it had to be, to invent the concept of an economy as distinct from the society and the polity in which it is embedded. Some will always complain that it is artificial to think of an economy separate from its society and polity. Such critics are right. Yet the critics miss the point. Theory is artifice. A theory is an intellectual construction by which we select facts and interpret them. The challenge is to bring theory to bear on facts in ways that permit explanation and prediction. That can only be accomplished by distinguishing between theory and fact. Only if this distinction is made can theory be used to examine and interpret facts. (Waltz 1990: 22)

Waltz finds the means used to make economic theory important and interesting, especially because he uses very similar means to build his own theory of international politics.

Fourth, in their book on thinking theory thoroughly, James Rosenau and Mary Durfee reflect on the skills required to theorize. They claim that:

> [l]earning the skills underlying the design of theories is not, however, the equivalent of learning how to think theoretically. To move beyond the dos and don'ts of theoretical design, one has to acquire not a set of skills but rather a set of predispositions, a cluster of habits, a way of thinking, a mental lifestyle – or whatever may be the appropriate label for that level of intellectual existence that govern the use of skills and the application of values. (Rosenau and Durfee 1995: 178)

The key to this citation is the distinction between 'a set of skills' and the hard to pin down intellectual competence that governs the use of such skills. Is the act of theorizing an art or a craft? While the distinction can easily be overstated, the assumption behind this chapter is that theorizing is first and foremost a learnable craft. True, some fortunate people enjoy the ability to turn the craft into an art, but this quality does not necessarily depend on the age or status of the person in question. Not only professors master the art of theorizing,

If the four parts of the mosaic describe key aspects of the intellectual process, what, then, is the task we face? Think traditions. The theoretical traditions represent rich and wide-ranging ontologies, meaning that most of the building blocs are available for further theorizing. The traditions wait for a new generation of theorists who are ready to take up the challenge of theorizing. As emphasized by Jack Donnelly:

[t]he realist research program will continue to generate valuable theories. But the same is true for other research programs. The discipline needs non-realist theories no less than realist ones. Rather than adversaries, let alone enemies, we need to see each other as concerned scholars with different interest, insights and contributions. Rather than *Theory of International Politics*, we need *theories* of international politics, realist and non-realist alike, that together give us a chance to begin to come to terms with the multiple human purposes and complex practices and processes that make up world politics. (Donnelly 2000: 197–8, emphasis in original)

It is against this background that teaching how to theorize becomes relevant and feasible. Rosemary Shinko is a scholar who has introduced experimental teaching in her classes and claims that 'IR theory is fun and the underlying aim of this class is to allow students to sample the intriguing and engaging craft of the IR theorist' (Shinko 2006: 45).

Exercise: Find more illustrative examples – pieces of mosaics – and discuss the implications of each conception of theorizing.

Building blocks

Which building blocks do theorists use when building theory? Table 9.1 shows 14 components that are used repeatedly. It is difficult to imagine any theory that does not include three or more of these building blocks.

Table 9.1   *Some building blocks for theory building*

- assumptions
- claims or propositions
- concepts or sets of concepts
- levels of analysis
- definitions
- kinds of theory
- scope
- philosophical underpinnings
- hypotheses
- criteria for good theory
- specification of actors, structures and processes
- variables
- inductive and deductive reasoning
- eclecticism

In order to understand the nature and function of various building blocks, it is helpful to gain some experience in 'butchering' existing theories, for example, the liberal democratic peace theory (Chapter 3), the realist power transition theory (Chapter 4) or the IPE theory of hegemonic stability (Chapter 6). Once the components are on the table, we can begin viewing them as building blocks.

Keeping the purpose of our prospective theory in mind, we select from Table 9.1 the relevant components and make a choice in terms of theoretical ambition. All theories are built by means of a rather limited number of building blocks. If we think in terms of a spectrum, some theories can accomplish much with a very limited number of blocks, whereas other theories are very complex yet can do very little for us. Still other theories are simple and explain very little. Finally, some theories can accomplish much by means of a large number of building blocks. The prudent builder of theory will know how to navigate between or around these extremes.

Exercise: Deconstruct a given theory by identifying its building blocks.

Theoretical synthesis

Surely this form of theorizing does not invent everything *de novo*, but the process of combining existing theories or theoretical parts in new ways can be truly innovative and bring about some truly novel analytical options. Theory synthesis is not as straightforward as one might expect. On the contrary, it is an ambiguous and hotly contested way of theorizing that is less technical than first impressions might suggest (cf. Hellmann 2003). The first issue that triggers contention concerns the very meaning of theory synthesis. Some regard synthesis as the outcome of mergers or fusions, that is, as an integration process through which previously independent theories become part of a new composite theory. Others are less demanding and consider discrete theories situated on a common platform as synthesis, in other words, they think that a synthesis is a coherent theoretical framework. The second issue really concerns a clash of different analytical virtues. On the one hand it is common to consider theoretical parsimony a virtue. On the other hand comprehensive explanation is also considered a virtue. By necessity, theoretical synthesis implies a trade-off between these two virtues. Third, the appropriate level of synthesis is contested. Some syntheses comprise theoretical perspectives rather than discrete theories. One prominent example is the so-called neo-neo synthesis, which brings together neorealism and neoliberalism (Nye 1988; see also Wæver 1996a). Another example is Robert Gilpin's (1987) synthesis of realism and aspects of Marxist political economy. Other syntheses are strictly at the level of discrete theory, that is, involving theories such as those listed above in previous chapters (Chapters 2 through 7) in the variants of theory sections (see e.g. liberal intergovernmentalism in Chapter 3). Fourth, the issue of coherence is contested, because some believe that theories can be synthesized, provided that they are brought together on a common ontological or epistemological footing. Others do not believe that such a common footing is necessary.

The issue of commensurability triggers contending visions of theory synthesis. Some basically hate the idea of incommensurability and do their best to bridge or accommodate any contradictory perspectives. Others believe that incommensurability is a fact of life and that it is a futile endeavour to bring together theories that are bound to have separate functions and qualities.

As an illustrative example, we can see how Andrew Moravcsik accounts for his own attempt at theory synthesis:

> an example of structured synthesis, taken from recent empirical research on European integration, places major theories in sequence. In my analysis of major negotiations to create, develop, and amend the treaty structure of the European Union, liberal theory is employed to account for national preferences, rationalist bargaining theory (which could be seen as a non-coercive variant of realism) to account for the efficiency and distributional outcomes of negotiations, and institutionalist theory to account for subsequent delegation. (2003b: 43)

In this example no mergers or fusions take place. The outcome, labelled liberal intergovernmentalism, is rather a synthesis on a common (rationalist) footing (Moravcsik 1998). Frank Schimmelfennig (2003) provides a second example. In order to analyze the European Union enlargement process, Schimmelfennig brings together a rationalist theory of instrumental action and a constructivist theory of communicative rationality. Barry Buzan (1993), who reconstructs neorealism by means of adding further explanatory variables, provides a third and final example.

The choice for theory synthesis is often characterized as bridge building or dialogue, notions suggesting friendly accommodation, innocence, innovation and neutrality. In this context, however, it is worth keeping in mind that some mergers in the business world are frequently referred to as hostile takeovers. Similarly, some dialogues are conducted based on a range of different conditions, including conditions exclusively formulated by one of the dialogue partners. Theory synthesis can also be seen as a subsuming process, that is, a process implying extinction for one or more of the synthesized elements. If you decide to enter a dialogue and do not want to be extinguished, then the game is to make sure that you are the one who subsumes and avoid becoming subsumed.

Finally, one variant of the synthesis game is called 'add on'. Basically, the proposition is that a favourite theoretical perspective is claimed or assumed to explain most cases or the most important processes, yet an 'add on' perspective is required in order to handle residual cases and processes of a secondary order of importance. Gunnar Sjöstedt (1977) represents an illustrative example. Sjöstedt favours a rationalist approach in studies of the EU's 'international actorness' yet reluctantly acknowledges that ideational approaches must be added to the primary theoretical framework. The 'add on' option invites conclusions such as the following. Stephen Walt appears to represent a pluralist position, acknowledging a role for realist, liberal and constructivist perspectives alike. Nonetheless, he concludes the following: 'The "complete diplomat" of the future should remain cognizant of realism's emphasis on the inescapable role of power, keep liberalism's awareness of domestic forces in mind, and occasionally reflect on constructivism's vision of change' (Walt 1998: 44). Such a conclusion seems to be based on the idea that social reality only occasionally plays a role in world politics, for which reason it should be added on to the perspectives that enjoy the status of 'master' perspectives.

Exercise: Discuss the option of synthesizing, including advantages and disadvantages.

Reappraisals

Theoretical orientations come and go. Once upon a time, old-time geopolitics was an attractive perspective; and still is in some places. Later on, during the 1960s, the behavioural revolution swept parts of the Western world, eventually to be followed by the post-behavioural era. Currently, the English School is being 'reconvened', a notion suggesting that the School went through a 'dark ages' period, a period of relative decline between its foundation and the present. During the 1970s, particularly in Europe, Western Marxism was a respectable orientation. With a few exceptions, for instance the Amsterdam School and world systems theory, this is no longer the case. Since the 1990s, we have witnessed the constructivist turn and the decline of realism.

More examples could be provided yet the important point is that reappraisals of IR theory are unavoidable. The personal reappraisal is the most straightforward. For example, we can see how Robert Keohane became attracted to formal theories in the early 1980s, yet subsequently lost interest:

> as a result of my involvement in a collective attempt to understand 'cooperation under anarchy' through the use of simple precepts derived

from game theory, I concluded that it was unlikely that greater formalization of game theory would provide a clear structure for precise and
insightful investigation of world politics – and, in any case, that I was
intellectually unequipped and temperamentally unsuited to making a
contribution toward that enterprise. (1989: 29)

Personal 'aha' experiences are seldom synchronically accomplished across the
discipline. Keohane describes how, 'I can still remember the "aha" feeling, in
my fourth floor office at Stanford, when I glimpsed the relevance of theories
of industrial organization for understanding international regimes' (1989:
28). Karl Deutsch (1989) has described his coincidental yet crucially important meeting with Norbert Wiener, the famous inventor of cybernetics. Hans
Morgenthau has described his meeting with lawyer Carl Schmitt, as well as
the conclusions he reached when sitting in at the early Frankfurt School meetings. In this fashion, the rhythm of ebb and tide as well as the nature of the
waves vary across geographies – making it very difficult to synthesize 'main-
streams' of thinking and general patterns of intellectual development.

The notion of 'tradition' connotes continuity and long-term perspective,
whereas the notion of 'current' suggests a more dynamic, medium-term
perspective. When realists claim that the realist tradition reaches back to
Thucydides or Machiavelli, they are claiming to have access to some perpetual insights. Philosophy of science approaches draw on other criteria. This is
where philosophers such as Thomas Kuhn and Imre Lakatos enter the scene,
for instance in reviews of major international relations theories (Elman and
Elman 2003).

Each of these approaches produces a different narrative of the history of
the discipline. Obviously, however, none of them is ideal. Theoretical debates
are in part about dogma and progress. Hence, you should be introduced to
arguments and behind-the-scene manoeuvres. Without understanding the
arguments put forward, you are unlikely to understand theoretical debates
and, in turn, the current state of the art. Furthermore, without an introduction to the role of argumentative structures, you will never accept the idea
that the state of the art is a bundle of contending perspectives.

Shaping theories

Previous chapters have described how theories can be shaped, that is, given
different forms by means of a range of different epistemological commitments. In the words of Martha Finnemore:

Neither constructivism nor rational choice provides substantive explanations of international political behaviour until coupled with some

theoretical understanding of who or what are relevant agents and structures as well as some empirical understanding of what those agents might want and what the content of that social structure might be. (Finnemore 1996: 28)

The option of theory shaping, that is, the claim that, for example, constructivism can be merged with a substantive theoretical orientation, can be generalized. In other words, it is possible to fuse constructivist perspectives together with most theoretical traditions, currents and theories. Alexander Wendt's (1999) theory of international cooperation can thus be considered a constructivist liberal theory of international cooperation (see Chapter 3). Realists have not necessarily argued against the theory because it is constructivist; rather, they might have targeted its liberal elements. In general, to the degree that they have criticized constructivism and liberal theory, they first and foremost criticize the liberal features. Thus, John Mearsheimer (1995) regards 'critical theory' (including constructivism) as a set of propositions – garbage can-like – that he happens not to share. In turn, he turns the richness of perspectives within critical theory into a 'mashed potato' version of theory that probably does not satisfy anybody. Furthermore, he sees an old-time idealist version of liberalism lurking and therefore activates E. H. Carr's prototype realist criticism of utopian liberalism or idealism. By contrast, Jeffrey Barkin (2003) argues that it is possible to fuse realism and constructivism, that is, he basically argues it is possible to develop, for example, a constructivist realist balance of power theory.

The option of shaping can be generalized in a second fashion. Constructivism is not the only approach that can be combined with major substantive traditions. There is a similar option for other second-order theories, including rational choice, behaviouralism, positivism and scientific realism. Let us consider a few examples. Peace research was originally introduced in parallel to – or rather as part of – the behavioural revolution, implying that peace research drew on behavioural armaments when criticizing 'traditional' perspectives, in particular realist traditionalism. David Singer's contribution is but one example and the *Journal of Conflict Resolution* another. Hans Morgenthau's version of realism is informed by continental European political thought, ranging from Friedrich Nietzsche to the German 19th-century *Machtschule* (Guzzini 1998; Williams 2005). However, Morgenthau is sometimes categorized as a prototype positivist, particularly because his famous six principles were cast in that fashion. Robert Gilpin explains their origin and function:

When Morgenthau wrote *Scientific Man* he was not at Chicago. When he went to Chicago, however, he found it dominated by the social science fashion of the time; he apparently realized that if he were to make an impact, he had to learn and write social science. He decided that international politics had to become an objective science; I think he was influenced by those in comparative government and other subfields pushing the idea of an objective science of politics. Paradoxically, when you get to the end of *Politics Among Nations* it is a moral tract on how states should behave. (Gilpin 2005: 365)

Like other rich traditions, realism has been cast in all sorts of meta-forms, ranging from the classical approach, behaviouralism (cf. Vasquez 1983) to rational choice (Waltz 1979) and constructivism (Barkin 2003).

The theorizing mode of shaping is not without its problems. Popular images of various substantive theories will inevitably be challenged. John Mearsheimer (2006) believes that there are no European realists. He has reached this conclusion due to his peculiar conception of realism; as the conception's criteria are not fulfilled, he is bound to conclude that whatever European scholars represent, it is not realism. Furthermore, if not realism, then it has to be the default 'other' orientation, that is, idealism (liberalism). Thus reassured about the enduring nature of IR theory, he activates realism's standard operating procedures for encountering liberal thinking. In fact, he effectively joins Robert Kagan (2003) in criticism of liberal thought, European vintage (America is from Hobbesian Mars, Europe is from Kantian Venus).

The shaping option is likely to short-circuit such well-established certainties, which can be considered good news because it promises theoretical reflection and innovation.

Complementary or competitive approaches?

In contrast to Robert Jervis (1998), who clearly regards constructivism as a competitor to realism, Henry Nau (2002) has demonstrated that realist theories of power and constructivist theories of identity can be considered complementary theoretical positions capable of working together within a single framework of analysis. In other words, the two perspectives are established on different assumptions and contribute different insights, but their relationship is not necessarily competitive or conflicting. The relationship can actually be complementary and contribute to our understanding of, for example, American foreign policy (cf. Nau 2002). Martha Finnemore reaches a similar conclusion:

The cases may give the impression that constructivism as a theoretical approach stands in opposition to realism and liberalism. This is not so: the relationship is complementary not competing. My argument is not that norms matter but interests do not, nor is it that norms are more important than interests. My argument is that norms shape interests. Consequently the two cannot logically be opposed. (Finnemore 1996: 27)

Whenever students face a research question, they also face the problem of identifying a suitable theoretical framework. In case more than one theory has been chosen, it is compulsory to specify their relationship. Are the two or more theories competitive or complementary?

The issue of complementarity takes us to the potentials of eclecticism. On the one hand theoretical eclecticism is often dismissed because: (i) it is said to be an example of mixing apples and oranges; (ii) eclectic analytical frameworks aim at approximating the real world thereby missing the benefits of simplified theoretical propositions; (iii) causal or constitutive logics soon intensify in terms of complexity, making subsequent operationalization difficult. Hedley Bull quite simply warned that 'in the present controversy, eclecticism, masquerading as tolerance, is the greatest danger of all' (1966a: 377). On the other hand there have been several pleas for eclecticism. One of the most elaborate cases for analytical eclecticism emphasizes that the gladiatorial approach to theoretical competition has proved to be less than useful. Research traditions should instead be seen as at least partly complementary. If so, a given research question can usefully be answered by means of drawing on two or more research traditions. Hence, the art of theorizing becomes the art of choosing and mixing selected parts of research traditions or parts of specific theories; of describing how the adequate balance of selected parts should be and how they hang together (Katzenstein and Sil 2004). Having made the case for eclecticism, Katzenstein and his team demonstrate how it can be used in the context of rethinking Asian security. Similarly, an eclectic approach has been used to analyze foreign policies in the Middle East (Hinnebusch and Ehteshami 2002).

Best Western?

Despite the discipline, the diversity and the progress, Amitav Acharya and Barry Buzan have raised the following key question: 'Why is There No Non-Western International Relations Theory?' (2005). Across the six continents, it is increasingly recognized that IR theory is a form or field of study predominantly cultivated in the United States and Europe (Hoffmann 1977; Kahler 1993; Crawford and Jarvis 2001; Jørgensen and Knudsen 2006; Tickner and Wæver 2009). In most other parts of the world – Australia and Canada constitute a couple of important exceptions – the art of theorizing is hardly on the agenda. This is the case in, for example, Latin America

(Tickner 2003), China and Japan (Song 2001; Callahan 2001; Chan 1999; Inoguchi and Bacon 2001), South Asia (Behera 2007), the Middle East and Africa. Is this a problematic state of affairs? Let us begin our examination of the issue by pointing out that part of Acharya and Buzan's argument is not without its problems. According to Hedley Bull (1991), the term 'international theory' is misleading, because it is not the theory but rather the subject matter that is international. A somewhat similar criticism can be directed at Acharya and Buzan's conception because the IR theories in question are not necessarily 'Western', even if created and institutionalized in the West. Furthermore, Acharya and Buzan might be wrong in asserting the absence of theory in the non-Western world. Could it be that, for instance, scholars from the Third World employ different concepts or understands traditional IR concepts differently? That the worlds of their making are so markedly different from the ones cultivated by Western minds that the easy exit route is simply to ignore such a-typical conceptions. Arlene Tickner (2003), writing from a conflict-ridden Columbian perspective, emphasizes that Third World scholars look fundamentally different on IR and also the meaning of key terms, such as war, the state and sovereignty, is markedly different.

In the following exercise, you are invited to imagine that you are an analyst of international affairs based in Beijing, Brussels or Bogota – Taipei, Teheran or Tokyo – Cotonou, Cairo or Catania – Mexico City, Moscow or Male. Make your choice! Perhaps you will conclude that the geography of theory building is utterly unimportant for the form and substance of your theory. After all, you will find realist, liberal and English School theorists around the globe, and you will find rational choicers, constructivists, positivists and post-positivists in most corners of the world. If this is the case, there simply is no Western, Eastern, Northern or Southern theory. The search for a theory with Chinese characteristics is futile (cf. Song 2001), just as African students – despite claims to the opposite (see Gordon 2002) – do not need radical political economy approaches rather than – or at the expense of – realist or liberal theories (see also Dunn and Shaw 2001).

By contrast, you may conclude that the economic, political, institutional or cultural contexts do have an impact on the theorizing process. The artifice characterizing theories may be shaped differently depending on both your experience and the collective experiences characterizing the area you are based in. If this is your conclusion, there is a long way to go in terms of reconsidering the existing theoretical traditions as well as exploring the options of complementing the existing body of theory with theories drawing on non-Western experiences. The reconsideration requirement also comprises theory application. While American policy advice is based on a well-known offensive realist position (cf. Mearsheimer 2003), which advice would an offensive realist give to the EU, China, India or Russia?

A DIY manual in theorizing

Having passed the above waypoints, it is now possible to proceed and put everything together in an 11-step manual. While each step is important in itself, it is perfectly possible to skip one or more steps. In order to optimize the process for your purpose, it might be an idea to browse the steps and reorder the sequence of steps.

1. Problem-driven theorizing

Perhaps theorizing is fun. In this context, it is useful to keep in mind that Rosenau and Durfee (1995) emphasize the importance of being professionally 'playful' in the course of the theorizing process. Their point is well taken. Theorizing does require a dimension of playfulness, for example, trying on for size counter-intuitive reasoning. However, this section focuses on problem-driven theorizing; it emphasizes that you engage in theorizing because you have a given problem in mind. You engage in theorizing in order to better understand or analyze a given problem. Hence, you reflect on the key features of a specific analytical tool that you subsequently intend to use in an instrumental fashion. Instrumental theory building might pursue the following four-step procedure. First, begin by briefly describing how the international political agenda has changed in each decade throughout the 20th century. Subsequently, make your own personal top-three list of world politics issues that you believe are the most important. Explain briefly why you think these issues belong at the top of the contemporary international agenda. Subsequently, discuss proposals in class in order to reach a consensus conception. Second, consider existing theories. Identify their building blocks and the cement binding the bits and pieces together. The following elements are likely to pop up: actors, structures, processes, levels of analysis, propositions, claims, assumptions, concepts or sets of concepts (cf. Table 9.1). Even more building blocks can possibly be identified (if so, which ones?). In any case, it appears as though a relatively limited number of key elements can be found in all theories. Once these elements have been identified, it all becomes a question of arranging or rearranging the deck chairs, that is, the building blocks. Third, you want to better understand the top-three issues on the political agenda. Explain how you think your theoretical tool-box should look in order to help you analyze and better understand the issues of your concern. In other words, build a theory that you believe can help. Fourth, consider whether the top-three issues contain any normative dimension. Do you have a preferred solution or outcome in mind? If so, which likely role will this normative dimension play in your theory? Finally, does your theory include any constitutive elements?

2. Scope

At some point you need to take a strategically important decision: specifying the scope of your theory. In the present context, scope refers to the ambition of the theory you have in mind, specifically whether you aim at creating a general theory, a mid-range theory characterized by a narrow or specific area of concentration. Obviously, your choice should be consistent with the purpose of your theory. Before deciding, please keep in mind that most attempts at building *general* IR theories have failed and that the interest in the relatively few that have been created is rapidly declining.

3. Kinds of theory

Once you have decided on the scope of theory and explained your choice, you can continue by deciding what kind of theory you want to build. In the previous chapters, you have been introduced to a number of different theories, and you know that each kind of theory has its strengths and weaknesses. Furthermore, you know that explanatory, interpretive and normative theories are designed fundamentally differently. Given what you now know about these options and features, what is your choice?

4. Procedures of theory building

You can now consider which procedure of theory building you want to follow. The options include the following four procedures:

- The case study approach invites an inductive approach to theorizing (George and Bennett 2005). Given that your primary interest is in theory construction, you probably do not have time to conduct a sufficiently high number of case studies yourself. This is not necessarily a problem, because you can use the case studies conducted by other analysts and simply summarize or synthesize findings. In other words, you can use other researchers as a kind of sub-contractor and skim their findings for theoretically relevant insights. For you, this is a rewarding form of theorizing, because you get to know the substance of multiple case studies yet are able to maintain your focus on innovative synthesizing and summarize findings, an analytical task that most case study analysts tend to avoid; in part because case studies are very time consuming, in part because many analysts do not aim at theorizing.
- The pros and cons of theory synthesis have been presented above and there is no need to go further into detail about this procedure. Hence, consider if you find synthesis an attractive option.
- The option of reconstructing existing theories is a procedure of theorizing implying both criticism and construction, and the former is usually instrumentally used for the latter. In other words, the point of departure is a given body of theory that, in one way or another, is deemed internally

incoherent or insufficient or unsatisfactory for application purposes. An attempt to reconstruct neorealism was presented in Chapter 4 (Buzan 1993). Barry Buzan aimed at reconstructing neorealism by adding a couple more explanatory variables.

- In many cases, conceptualizing is the first step in theorizing; in some cases the only step. In other words, it is difficult to underestimate the crucially important role of concise conceptualization. Kenneth Waltz once acknowledged that in *Theory of International Politics* (1979), he 'slipped into using "sovereignty" for "autonomy"' (Waltz 1990: 37). In this manner, he acknowledges the importance of conceptual precision. When theorizing, keep in mind that you leave everyday language behind and engage in more or less professional discourses of theory. Words have meanings, some even have multiple meanings and some have contested meanings. When conceptualizing, you should therefore remember to explicate and specify the meaning of the concepts you have decided to employ.

5. Building blocks

In a previous section (cf. Table 9.1) you were introduced to a range of different theoretical building blocks. It is now time to identify the relevant building blocks, that is, the bits and pieces of theory that you deem relevant. At least for a start, it is recommendable to limit the number of building blocks. You can always add further bits and pieces if you deem doing so necessary or fruitful.

6. Important features

Sooner or later you are bound to identify important actors, structures and processes, explaining connections between them as well as specifying their relative importance. The first part, focusing on actors, is probably the easier part. In most international relations theory, (major) states count as important actors. The question is how many different kinds of actors you want to include when building your theory. Among other kinds of actors, we find actors such as companies, NGOs and other interest groups, as well as entire civil societies. The challenge is to find an appropriate balance between inclusion and exclusion. In this context, you may find Kenneth Waltz's comment thought provoking:

> Should one broaden the perspective of international political theory to include economics? An international political-economic theory would presumably be twice as good as a theory of international politics alone ... A political-economic theory would represent a long step toward a general theory of international relations, but no one has shown how to take it. (Waltz 1990: 31–2)

The reason it makes sense to contemplate such an extension concerning actors is that Waltz uses actors to constitute his conception of structure.

Speaking about structure, you can proceed and begin to contemplate which kind of structures you want to include in your theory. Given that numerous existing theories are characterized by weak notions of structure, this element constitutes a real challenge for many would-be theorists. If you choose to include structures, however, your theory may potentially become more complex and intellectually interesting. If you choose to include both actors and structures, you are subsequently bound to reflect on the relations between them. In other words, you should consider your position concerning the agent–structure problem (cf. Giddens 1984; Wendt 1987; Hollis and Smith 1990).

Finally, it is time to think about your notion of processes. For some, processes are simply the outcome of dynamics between actors and structures (Hollis and Smith 1990). Others have specified notions of process variables (Nye 1988; Haas 1958; Buzan 1993). In any case, the omnipresence of discourses on processes, whether we talk about processes of globalization, European integration, de-colonization or climate change, appears to make it rewarding to think hard on the nature of processes and their respective roles in a theory of international relations.

7. Import options

Probably you have knowledge of theories that have been created or employed in other academic disciplines. In any case consider whether importing theories from other fields of study is possible, necessary or desirable. In other words, this step is about the art of grand-scale application and about taking advantage of knowledge of the developments within several academic disciplines. There are many examples of importing theory in this manner. The following five examples will suffice for illustrative purposes. First, in his endeavour to create neorealism, Kenneth Waltz draws heavily on microeconomics. In many ways, neorealism is microeconomics applied to international politics. The relationship between firms and markets mirrors the relations between states and the international system. Furthermore, the assumptions about actors are identical in the sense that states are assumed to be utility maximizers, rational actors engaged in instrumental or strategic action. Finally, a certain sense of timelessness characterizes both microeconomics and neorealism, whereas any sense of historical development has been ditched. Importing theory from economics is hardly limited to neorealism. Theories of strategy (Schelling 1960), game theory, rational choice, principal agent theory and numerous other theoretical orientations are all deeply inspired by developments within the field of economics.

By contrast, Alexander Wendt draws heavily on developments within sociology; specifically on inter-actionist sociological group theory and structuration theory as developed by sociologist Anthony Giddens (1984). When theorizing global society, Mathias Albert (2001) draws on the work of German sociologist Niklas Luhmann and his systems theory. The discipline of history has also been a very important contributor of inspiration. When conceptualizing historical structure, John Ruggie (1989) draws on the French *Annales* School. Similarly, Donald Puchala (2003) traces relations between history and international relations, and Robert Cox draws attention to the concept of historical structure. Moreover, most of the English School has a very close relationship to history; not least diplomatic history. Several English School studies are macro-historical investigations, for example, concerning the dynamics of states systems across time. As outlined in Chapter 2, international political theory draws – unsurprisingly – on political theory, political philosophy, the history of ideas and conceptual history. In summary, we can conclude that there is – and presumably always has been – a lively exchange of ideas between International Relations and other academic disciplines. This exchange is likely to continue, perhaps with your theory as the next example.

8. Teamwork

If possible, make the theorizing process a teamwork process. Obviously, this is not to say that individuals cannot theorize. Many have done so. However, theorizing in teams facilitates the thorough discussion of decisions, priorities and findings.

9. Consult other sources of inspiration

If you get the time, read key books and articles on the art or craft of theorizing, for example, the publications listed in 'Further reading' (below). There is no single path to theorizing, and reading provides much food for thought. Search the Internet for further inspiration, including key terms such as conceptualizing, theorizing, thinking theoretically, theory synthesis, theory building or related terms.

10. For which reason?

If theory, as Robert Cox has famously claimed, is always *for* someone and *for* some purpose (Cox 1981, emphasis added), then *who* is the special someone for your theory and which *purpose* does your theory intend to serve? Discuss the relevance and implications of Robert Cox's theorem. In case you do not agree with Cox, which arguments can you provide that run counter to his claim?

11. Problems abound ahead!

The final step is to attempt to accept the fact that to every solution there is a problem. In other words, you should expect that your theory will be criticized from different perspectives and for different reasons. If you choose a middle-of-the road theory, for instance, rest assured that those cruising either side of the road will criticize you for misrepresenting something and missing important insights about international relations. The same happens if you theorize in some radical fashion, now with the middle-of-the-roaders popping up as your critics. Theorizing is essentially a catch-22 situation, and you can just as well consider how you will handle criticism, possibly trying to pre-empt at least some kind of criticism. Pre-emptive means including specification of scope conditions, that is, your claims regarding when or where your theory is relevant, and where or when it is entirely irrelevant. James Rosenau and Mary Durfee (1995) rightly emphasize that you should be prepared to be proven wrong. This may well be a frustrating outcome, yet there is no guaranteed way of avoiding such negative experiences. Furthermore, the act of theorizing is in a certain sense risky business, as you are the sole person responsible for your creation. You cannot blame internal incoherence, misreadings or unintended applications on another distant theorist about whom you often know relatively little.

Conclusion

This chapter is based on the idea that DIY theorizing is both possible and desirable. In order to encourage you to theorize, a range of key aspects of theorizing has been introduced and discussed. Examples of how prominent theorists have tackled these aspects have been provided, and a comprehensive recipe has been outlined in the form of a DIY manual for theorizing. How you may want to make use of the tool-box and its tools is basically up to you. Even if the outcome of theorizing is not a theory of, say, international cooperation, the theorizing process will undoubtedly trigger a better understanding of existing theories. By means of DIY theorizing – the process of building your own theory – you will become familiar with existing theories in ways that are fundamentally different from just reading about them. You will know where theories come from, whether in historical or geographical terms. Who creates them? Furthermore, you will be prompted to explore the structure of a given theory as well as the deeper foundations upon which specific theories have been built, that is, their ontological and epistemological attributes. Finally, having completed the exercises, questions such as the following will acquire a different status and gain in terms of relevance. Which actors, structures and processes are the more important, historically as well as in the contemporary world?

Questions

- Which building blocks do you think are most important, perhaps even inescapable? Why?
- Why is theoretical synthesis a controversial way of theorizing?
- Do you believe that we should expect more non-Western theories in the future? How would this development have an impact on the discipline?
- Do you favour the development of a theory with Chinese characteristics? Is such a theory necessary?
- Do you agree that theories are always for someone and for some purpose? If you construct a theory, who is it for and for which purpose?
- Do you believe theorizing is an art or a craft? Why?
- Is theorizing 'fun'? Argue pro and con!
- Why do so relatively few international relations scholars engage in theorizing?

Further reading

Barkin, S. J. (2003) 'Realist Constructivism', *International Studies Review*, 5, 3: 325–42.
    An interesting article suggesting that constructivism and realism are not as incompatible as intuitive thinking might suggest.

Gerring, J. (1999) 'What Makes a Concept Good? A Critical Framework for Understanding Concept Formation in the Social Sciences', *Polity*, 31: 357–93.
    In this article Gerring outlines benchmarks for good conceptualization, an essential part of theory building.

Klotz, A. and C. Lynch, C. (2007) *Strategies for Research in Constructivist International Relations* (Armonk, NY: M. E. Sharpe).
    An invaluable guide to constructivist methodology.

Kruzel, J. and Rosenau, J. N. (eds) (1989) *Journeys through World Politics: Autobiographical Reflections of Thirty-four Academic Travellers* (Lexington, MA: Lexington).
    This book consists of intellectual autobiographies, each one providing various insights to the process of theorizing.

Neumann, I. B. and Wæver, O. (eds) (1997) *The Future of International Relations: Masters in the Making* (London: Routledge).
    A book focused on a range of theorists rather than their theories.

Rosenau, J. N. and Durfee, M. (1995) *Thinking Theory Thoroughly: Coherent Approaches to an Incoherent World* (Boulder, CO: Westview) (especially pp. 177–90).
    One of the few books dealing with the topic of thinking theoretically.

Shinko, R. E. (2006) 'Thinking, Doing, and Writing International Relations Theory', *International Studies Perspectives*, 7: 43–50.

In this article, Shinko addresses issue associated with experimental teaching focused on engaging students in processes of theorizing.

Websites for further information

www.theory-talks.org

A website devoted to interviews with an increasing number of international relations scholars – very useful for brief insights.

Chapter 10

Conclusion and Perspectives

Are textbooks simply supposed to reproduce simple popular images and well-established certainties? Are they supposed to 'box' theoretical richness into simple formats or reduce diversity to Mickey Mouse unity, for example, by claiming that 'realists argue' or 'constructivists claim'. Should founding myths be reproduced and heuristically convenient narratives outlined, for example, that the discipline has developed through a number of 'great debates' among grand theorists?

Any student can count to three or four and subsequently, with some effort, reproduce the main points about each 'great debate'. But is such a narrative sufficient to understand the development of the discipline, not to mention the contending perspectives and theoretical debates throughout the 20th century? As demonstrated elsewhere, the idealism–realism debate took quite a distinct route and form in continental Europe (Jørgensen 2000); elsewhere, it assumed no form and took no direction at all. Furthermore, Peter Wilson (1998) has convincingly argued that the idealism–realism debate was not really a debate but rather an act of admonition by self-righteous realists in need of some idealism bashing in order to establish themselves as the new holders of the dogma of the discipline. Finally, Brian Schmidt and David Long (2004) have argued that if ever there was such a debate, it was certainly not the first debate; indeed, previous debates were characterized by themes such as imperialism and internationalism. And all these qualifications concern just one self-image of the discipline – the 'great debates' image – cultivated in just some parts of the world. In other words, there are many good reasons to thoroughly reconsider how international relations theory ought to be introduced to newcomers to the field.

As mentioned in the introductory chapter, the aim of this book is to be just such a new introduction to international relations theory, acknowledging that there are numerous schools to introduce; many analytical dilemmas to handle; and an abundance of issues to address. In order to achieve this aim, it has been informed by five general guiding principles, and the present concluding chapter will be structured by revisiting these principles.

Conceptions of theory

Among the most important principles is the deliberate employment of a relatively broad notion of theory. As demonstrated consistently in previous chapters, this book does not subscribe to various narrow or monist conceptions of the nature of theory. On the contrary, a relatively broad notion of theory has been chosen, enabling a more pluralistic vision of the discipline than some perhaps are used to. In Chapters 2 through 7, we have seen how different theoretical traditions have clear leanings towards specific kinds of theory. Major parts of realism and liberalism, and certain branches of IPE, cling to explanatory theory, whereas English School and post-positivist theorists first and foremost engage in interpretive theory. Normative theory is unsurprisingly cultivated by international political theorists focusing on normative issues, although it is hardly difficult to identify normative dimensions in other traditions, including IPE, realism and liberalism. We have learned that much theoretical criticism is founded on critics cherishing one kind of theory, whereas the target of criticism is employing theory of a different nature. In other words, football players are being criticized for not playing volleyball. We have also seen that, despite frequent anxieties concerning scientific decay, it is perfectly possible to work rigorously within all three kinds of theory. To be sure, they employ different criteria for what it takes to be a good theory, yet that only augments our theoretical and analytical repertoire.

The challenge in the future will be to further cultivate and specify the three kinds of theory, including exploring the various connections between them and specifying their individual comparative advantages, that is, for which analytical tasks should we reach for which kind of theory? Or, to continue the theme of Chapter 9, which kind of theory should we build in order to analyze issues x, y and z?

Tree structure

In the chapters on theoretical traditions (Chapters 2 through 7), the book introduces theories of international relations, highlighting the 'tree structure' of different levels of thinking and reasoning, that is, traditions, currents of thought and a range of discrete and applicable theories. Indeed, the book insists on a relatively clear distinction between the three layers of theoretical reflection. It is most helpful to keep these layers of reflection separate, specifying what the purpose of each level is (and is not). For instance, warnings have been issued against attempting to apply theoretical traditions and currents of thought in empirical research, the primary reason being that no one has ever been able to demonstrate the usefulness of such an enterprise. Indeed, there are ample examples of analytical disasters, pure nonsense arguments and misplaced assertiveness regarding the outcome of such attempts. Readers are therefore strongly recommended only to apply applicable theories and to use theoretical traditions and currents of thought for other purposes.

Like deep structures, theoretical traditions are characterized by *longue durée* qualities. They emerge over time and do not necessarily have specific functional attributes as such. Once they have emerged, however, they assume certain functions, for example, as orientation points for navigation in the rich, dense undergrowth of theoretical reflection. Over time, they also form genealogies, providing answers to questions about where a given theoretical tradition comes from, how it has generally developed and the phases through which the present has been reached. Theoretical traditions can be seen as broad contours of major ways of conceiving of the world, reflections on international affairs and engaging the world (in contrast to, e.g., isolationism). They also represent major patterns of thinking and typologies or categorizations of international thought. Six such traditions have been selected for introduction, thus maintaining a balance between too many and too few.

Finally, it is important to emphasize that employing the term 'tradition' is not entirely unproblematic, for which reason we should pay brief attention to the problematic aspects. Brian Schmidt highlights a number of the problematic aspects of thinking in terms of traditions, for example, that such thinking 'serves as an unreflective orthodox regulatory ideal for research and teaching' (1998: 24). Hedley Bull has also voiced concern, especially about one specific example of making traditions the centre of attention. Thus, when commenting on Martin Wight's image of three traditions, Bull found that 'the branches of the tree are so weighted down with historical foliage that it is difficult to find the trunk' (Bull 1991: xxii). Despite these potentially problematic features of research traditions, they have been one of the backbones of this book. They represent a simple way of ordering a complex field of study and – as it is valid for any other solution – there are some problems to every solution.

'Shaping' by means of epistemological variation

The book has not only introduced different *kinds* of theory. It has also introduced different *forms* of theory, 'shaped' by means of underpinning epistemological commitments, such as positivism, rationalism and constructivism. This section summarizes 'applied epistemology', that is, the dimension of epistemology we will find in all theories of international relations. Though the form of theorizing may change, the substantive aspect of theoretical traditions often remains in place. During the 20th century, all major theoretical traditions have been cast in different epistemological modes or keys.

Hence, we can explore the variation characterizing individual traditions and currents of thought.

For instance, what appearance does realist theory assume when based on a so-called traditionalist, behaviouralist, positivist, rational choice or constructivist footing, respectively? Basically, realism has been shaped by means of five different epistemological commitments, that is, five different ways of mixing form and substance. More examples could be provided, but those included are sufficient to illustrate the argument. In the first versions of 20th-century realism, epistemological commitments were usually implicit and best characterized as a mixture. However, E. H. Carr's *The Twenty-Years' Crisis* (1939) was deliberately informed by Karl Mannheim's pronounced relativism. Second, realism was to some extent influenced by positivism and the registers of explanatory theory, best illustrated in Morgenthau's formulation of realism's 'six principles'. Subsequently, realism was given a new shape and presented in the form of game theory. Thomas Schelling (1960) was among the first to employ game theory in the study of international conflict. His contribution remains one of the finest examples of game theory employed in the study of world politics. In 2005, he received the Nobel Prize for his contribution. Third, Robert Gilpin emphasizes that 'I consider myself a soft realist because I think of realism as a philosophical position regarding the nature of man, society and politics. Realism is not a science, subject to the test of falsifiability, but rather a way of looking at the world' (2005: 361). Fourth, Vasquez has described how the change from traditionalism to behaviouralism first and foremost represented a change in form, whereas the realist state-centric approach was continued (Vasquez 1983; see also Hollis and Smith 1990; Smith 1995). Finally, in contrast to several realists who believe that constructivism is a competitor to realism (Mearsheimer 1995; Jervis 1998), Henry Nau (2002) has convincingly demonstrated that constructivism and realism work very well together as complementary perspectives on world politics. In addition to presenting his argument in general, Nau has carried out a major study of US foreign policy in which he has demonstrated the advantages of employing both perspectives. Barkin (2003) proceeds one step further than Nau, arguing that constructivist realist theories are perfectly possible. In other words, there is nothing inherently contradictory about realism and constructivism. The case of realism has here been used as an illustration of the general shaping principle. We could just as well have chosen one of the other theoretical traditions for this illustrative purpose.

In summary, our examination of the 'shaping' principle highlights the variation over time of epistemological strategies. Furthermore, it enables a crucially important distinction between form and substantive claims about international affairs, which in turn can be used to 'unpack' theoretical debates. Finally, the principle makes less superficial or misleading accounts of theories possible. Conflating form with substance has often been the source of an endless row of rather futile debates.

De-centric

The de-centric principle – the idea that theorists should reflect on and possibly transcend their own perspectives – has provided a novel geographical emphasis in the general account for the discipline and its theories (see also Chapter 1). It has been used to demonstrate a potentially disquieting, uneven distribution of the production of theoretical knowledge. The principle of de-centric perspectives on international affairs implies considerable disturbance to all strongly centric perspectives. More specifically, the de-centric perspective implies the inclusion of theoretical reflection from around the world. Though theoretical reflection is first and foremost cultivated in the West, important contributions with non-Western origins have also been identified. The de-centric perspective can also be used to apply theories to unusual or counter-intuitive cases. Because it has been described in previous chapters, we know now that offensive realism is a theoretical stance and, thus, characterized by certain features. Furthermore, we know it has been used to prescribe a certain US policy towards China. However, the de-centric principle leads us to ask which policy advice would offensive realists give the Chinese, Russian or Japanese ministries of foreign affairs, or the European Union?

Surely, there are problems when adopting de-centric perspectives. One such problem concerns the risk of 'nationalizing' non-Western theories, for example, by searching for or expecting Chinese theorizing with Chinese philosophical underpinnings *à la* Tao or Confucius, expecting Czech theoretical reflection being based on, say, Thomas Masaryk, Roman Imgarden, Czech linguistic structuralism or Vienna Circle positivism, or, expecting Iranian IR with Shiite Islamic characteristics. Actually, Morten Valbjørn reports from a conference that 'the most frequently cited sources among the attending Iranian scholars were . . . neither the Quran nor the works by Khomeini or Khatami but Wendt and Waltz' (Valbjørn 2008; for more, see Callahan 2004; Johnston 1996). It is sometimes possible to square the circle; in the present context by accepting the existence of universal theoretical traditions and, at the same time, acknowledging their locally distinct configurations.

A second potential problem would be an excessive de-centr*ism*, celebrating diversity for its own sake and downplaying, for example, quality. In turn, this raises the problem of contested notions of quality. Which criteria do we prioritize? Do these criteria apply worldwide – without any variation. If not, then why do certain criteria apply in some corners of the world but not in others?

A third problem is the idea that the relevance of individual theoretical traditions might vary by continent, region or country. Thus, in the African context, one of the authors of *Power, Wealth and Global Order: An International Textbook for Africa* argues that, 'realism and liberalism are less useful for understanding Africa's current place in the global economy than transformative theories that focus on the plight of the poor, marginalized states' (cited from Gordon 2002: 239). However, this is not necessarily the case. On the one hand theories of conflict are perhaps not eminently suited for studies of security dynamics in global zones of peace. On the other hand it seems that, contrary to what the editors of *Power, Wealth and Global Order: An International Textbook for Africa* believe, all major theoretical traditions are highly relevant to African students. Realist theories, such as alliance theory, power transition theory or hegemonic stability theory, seem indispensable to African students, whether applied to specific African international politics or international politics more generally. Given that African states are deeply embedded in international institutions, integration processes, patterns of interdependence and processes of democratization, liberal theories seem no less relevant.

In short, centric perspectives trigger contention and criticism. As they should. But the development of alternatives is no straightforward task, and each solution seems to carry its own problems. De-centric perspectives encourage critical inclusion, connecting hitherto unconnected IR communities and highlighting the fact that theoretical reflection is a genre of scholarship that has mainly been cultivated in the West thus far.

Major contemporary theoretical debates

Like other social science disciplines, International Relations has always been characterized by major theoretical debates. Some regard this as a sign of the discipline being immature, because they believe that mature disciplines are capable of producing cumulative knowledge, leading eventually to a kind of consolidated master perspective. Others regard the debates to be a necessary evil or, alternatively, actually demonstrating that the discipline is thriving. In any case, we can ask whether silence would be any better than debate.

New perspectives generally tend to be seen as better perspectives, not least by their proponents. The unavoidable burden of young theorists is therefore to explain how their new perspective adds value to the accumulated knowledge of the tradition represented by their older peers. What a chance – take it!

The theoretical debates represent the fault lines of different theoretical orientations, and these fault lines constitute patterns of continuity and change. In individual chapters on the various traditions, we have seen how the fault lines of intra-tradition debates have changed over time and in Chapter 8, we traced the patterns of inter-tradition debates. We have also seen that some debates are more potential than actual debates. Given the high degree of common interests, strong liberals should thus be prone to close encounters with English School solidarists. For some reason, however, this debate has not flourished.

Surely, there are examples of debates turned sour or generating a pattern of non-productive repetition. They degenerate into trench-like conflicts and contribute little to the development of the discipline. After all, what is the usefulness of people endlessly deploring the fact that cats do not bark? Despite the lack of benefits, many debates have been constants in otherwise changing configurations of encounters. In terms of density, the 20th-century debates are highly uneven. Some axes of conversation (or yelling) have been considerably more popular than others.

In summary, the challenge for us is to master the debates by being able to account for them. Subsequently, it is possible for us to engage in the debates by assuming a position and explaining why we are where we are and perhaps how we got there. Some might also want to contemplate the consequences of the fact that in academic affairs there is always a problem with every solution.

DIY theorizing

Diagnoses of contemporary developments are notoriously difficult, and this feature is also valid concerning trends in theorizing. Summaries of contemporary developments are necessarily marked by the major disadvantage that developments have not been sifted through the big merciless filter of history, that is, the social process through which simplified representations are being crystallized, thereby assuming a form that resembles some kind of order of affairs on which we largely agree. This explains why it is very difficult to predict where the discipline's next theoretical breakthroughs will occur. Historically, European émigrés introduced the continental European IR theory tradition to the American academic environment, thus making a significant contribution to the discipline (Söllner 1990). Subsequently, North America became a hothouse for theorizing international relations and, as demonstrated throughout the book, remains a premier centre for theoretical reflection. In the recent decades, European scholars have managed to put a significant mark on international theorizing, and their efforts have gained speed. When looking beyond American and European horizons, we can notice for instance how Song (2001) and Callahan (2001) discuss how IR in China ought to be developed. Song does not find IR with Chinese characteristics particularly attractive. In his view, Chinese IR scholars should adopt 'modern' theoretical positions and methodologies. Callahan does not find Chinese characteristics attractive either but makes a plea for a more cautious approach than uncritical import (see also Chan 1999). In 2007, the Oxford University Press launched a new journal entitled *Chinese Perspectives on International Relations*, indicating that we should begin to recognize Chinese scholarship as one of several emerging new global centres. Although focusing on German scholarship on international relations, Michael Zürn (1994) and Günther Hellmann (1994) essentially discuss the same dilemma between import and 'home-brew'. Actually, it is a global classic issue that also, for instance, Russian, Indian and Brazilian scholars address. The issue simply reflects the present somewhat uneven production of theoretical knowledge.

Against this background, the invitation to theorize is meant to encourage a more interactive and less 'iconic' approach to the teaching of IR theory. The book has been designed with a view of the idea that competence in theorizing should be extended from the few to the many. In line with Petr Drulak's (2003) argument, theoretical competence should be extended to areas in which such competence has been relatively less developed. The present book has been designed with precisely this objective in mind. The need for such extensions is based on the fact that, in major parts of the world, theory does not have the status of defining the discipline. In these parts of the world, theory does not have the same value as in, say, North America, Europe or Australia. Consequently, descriptive and quasi-normative studies are much more widespread. These comments lead to the principle of DIY theorizing.

The demand for new theories is linked to changes in time and space. As demonstrated throughout the 20th century, changing times trigger a demand for the development of new theories. It is thus no coincidence that realism emerged in the conflict-ridden Europe during the 1930s and 1940s, reigned during the Cold War and has experienced decline since the end of the Cold War. However, most of the existing theories were created during the Cold War, that is, in an international context that somehow might influence why given theories were created in the first place, but also influencing the characteristics of these theories. When the Cold War ended, it was therefore time to reconsider the portfolio of international relations theory (Kegley 1993; Allan and Goldman 1992). We now find ourselves in the 21st century, and it is most likely that the new context presents compelling reasons for creating new theories or adapting existing theories to new circumstances. To some degree, the political agenda of the 21st century is markedly different from the 20th-century agenda.

New spaces are also likely to trigger new trends in theorizing. While no space on the globe is novel as such, many are novel in the context of theories of international relations. As the craft of theorizing becomes less unevenly distributed worldwide, it becomes more likely that unevenly distributed experiences, assumptions and conceptualizations will trigger new trends in theorizing. Morten Valbjørn's (2008) exploration of the nexus between the general IR discipline and specific area studies represents a promising strategy for fruitful interaction between the quest for generalized broad knowledge (IR) and the competing quest for specific yet deep knowledge (area studies).

Contemporary research agendas

Particularly two important flows of influence determine the shape of research agendas on international affairs. One such flow consists of the kind of questions different people raise when certain events or developments in world politics make them wonder about possible explanations. During the WTO Cancun meeting on trade in 2003, several African diplomats asked why they should accept an agreement that was largely determined by the US and the EU. Similarly, Africans south of the Sahara ask what they can do in order to avoid becoming further marginalized in the world economy. After the 9/11 terrorist attacks in New York and Washington in 2001, many Americans asked 'Why do they hate us?'. This question is inevitably followed by a different kind of question: 'How do we best fight this new kind of threat?' Similarly, the rise of predominantly American power leads some people to ask, 'Is the international system still anarchic or has it become hierarchical?' or, 'Does it make sense to speak of an American empire?'. Current affairs politics is also connected to research agendas in a more structured fashion, as many research programmes are formulated by governments. They ask the questions which scholars subsequently aim at answering.

As we have seen in previous chapters, theoretical traditions, currents of thought and individual theories are closely linked. Combined, they produce the second flow of questions, thus contributing to constitute the contemporary research agenda. The chapters on theoretical traditions all include sections spelling out the questions people tend to ask when they work within a given tradition and, in turn, what they study when they analyze international affairs. For each tradition, the section functions as a guide to the FAQs.

In order not to neglect the nuances, diversity within traditions and the shared concerns of traditions will be identified. Two examples illustrate the logic. Feminist scholars begin by asking why (the variable of) gender has played virtually no role in IR theory for such a long time. Subsequently, they proceed by demonstrating instances of importance of gender in world politics. One of the functions of feminist theories is exactly to generate questions to be asked, that is, to provide the stuff that makes research agendas. For scholars working within the English School tradition, the point of departure is often the existence, expansion and dynamics of international society. Hence, they raise questions about how states behave – or should behave – in international society, about the proper balance between order and justice in international society, or the dilemmas characterizing humanitarian intervention, including the controversial temporary cancellation of national sovereignty and self-determination.

In summary, contemporary research agendas are constituted by the outcome of the turbulent encounters between these two major flows of influence. Research agendas are determined by the combined output of the questions asked and issues examined, no matter whether questions are related to events or developments within world politics or informed by theoretical reflection.

Questions

- How would you characterize the comparative advantages of the three major kinds of theory?
- Which theoretical traditions do you find to be the most and least attractive, respectively? Why?
- Do the theoretical traditions or currents of thought adequately address the contemporary agenda of world politics?
- Which benefits and costs of theoretical simplification would you nominate for a top-three ranking?
- What is 'shaping'? How has shaping influenced the development of the discipline?
- Did the de-centric perspectives change your world views? In which ways?
- Why is the discipline less international than one intuitively expects?
- Are you prepared to be proven wrong?

Further reading

Chan, G. (ed.) (1999) *Chinese Perspectives on International Relations: A Framework for Analysis* (Basingstoke: Palgrave Macmillan).

Crawford, M. A. and Jarvis, D. S. L. (eds) (2001) *International Relations – Still an American Science: Towards Diversity in International Thought?* (New York: State University of New York Press).

Jørgensen, K. E. and Knudsen, T. B. (eds) (2006) *International Relations in Europe: Traditions, Perspectives, Destinations* (London: Routledge).

Katzenstein, P., Keohane, R. and Krasner, S. (eds) (1999) *Exploration and Contestation in the Study of World Politics: A Special Issue of International Organization* (Cambridge, MA: MIT Press).

Tickner, A. B. and Waever, O. (eds) (2009) *International Relations Scholarship Around the World* (London: Routledge).

These five volumes reflect on contemporary developments within international studies around the world.

Bibliography

Acharya, A. and Buzan, B. (2005) 'Preface: Why is There No Non-Western International Relations Theory? Reflections On and From Asia', *International Relations of the Asia-Pacific*, 7, 3: 285–6.

Adler, E. (2005) *Communitarian International Relations: The Epistemic Foundations of International Relations* (London: Routledge).

Adler, E. and M. Barnett (1999) *Security Communities* (Cambridge: Cambridge University Press).

Albert, M. (2001) 'What Systems Theory Can Tell Us About Constructivism', in K. M. Fierke and K. E. Jørgensen, *Constructing International Relations* (New York: M. E. Sharpe).

Allan, P. and Goldman, K. (eds) (1992) *International Relations Theory After the Cold War* (The Hague: Kluwer).

Anderson, B. (1991) *Imagined Communities: Reflections on the Origin and Spread of Nationalism* (London: Verso).

Anderson, P. (1973) *Considerations on Western Marxism* (London: Verso).

Angell, N. (1909/2009) *The Great Illusion* (Oxford: Oxford University Press).

Aron, R. (1967) 'What is a Theory of International Relations?', *Journal of International Affairs*, 21: 185–206.

Arrighi, G. and Silver, B. (1999) *Chaos and Governance in the Modern World System* (Minneapolis: University of Minnesota Press).

Ashley, R. K. (1981) 'Political Realism and Human Interest', *International Studies Quarterly*, 25: 204–36.

Ashley, R. K. (1984) 'The Poverty of Neorealism', *International Organization*, 38, 2: 225–86.

Ashley, R. K. and Walker, R. B. J. (1990a) 'Reading Dissidence/Writing the Discipline: Crisis and the Question of Sovereignty in International Studies', *International Studies Quarterly*, 34, 3: 367–416.

Ashley, R. K. and Walker, R. B. J. (1990b) 'Speaking the Language of Exile: Dissident Thought in International Studies', *International Studies Quarterly*, 34, 3: 259–68.

Austin, J. L. (1976 [1962]) *How to Do Things with Words: The William James Lectures Delivered at Harvard University in 1955*, ed. J. O. Urmson (Oxford: Clarendon Press [1962]).

Axelrod, R. A. (1984) *The Evolution of Cooperation* (New York: Basic Books).

Aydinli, E. and Mathews, J. (2000) 'Are the Core and Periphery Irreconcilable? The Curious World of Publishing in Contemporary International Relations', *International Studies Perspectives*, 1, 3: 289–303.

Baldwin, D. A. (1993) *Neorealism and Neoliberalism: The Contemporary Debate* (New York: Columbia University Press).

Ball, T. (1995) *Reappraising Political Theory. Revisionist Studies in the History of Political Thought* (Oxford: Clarendon Press).

Banks, M. (1985) 'The Inter-Paradigm Debate', in M. Light and A. J. R. Groom (eds), *International Relations: A Handbook of Current Theory* (London: Frances Pinter).

Baran, P. A. (1957) *The Political Economy of Growth* (New York: Monthly Review Press).

Barkin, J. S. (2003) 'Realist Constructivism', *International Studies Review*, 5, 3: 325–42.

Barry, Brian M. (1989) *Theories of Justice* (Berkeley, CA: University of California Press).

Bartelson, J. (1995) *A Genealogy of Sovereignty* (Cambridge: Cambridge University Press).

Baudrillard, J. (1986) *America* (London: Verso).

Baudrillard, J. (1995) *The Gulf War Did Not Take Place* (Bloomington: Indiana University Press).

Baylis, J. and Smith, S. (eds) (2003) *The Globalization of World Politics: An Introduction to International Relations* (Oxford: Oxford University Press).

Behera, N. C. (2007) 'Re-imagining IR in India', *International Relations of the Asia-Pacific*, 7: 341–68.

Beitz, C. (1979) *Political Theory and International Relations* (Princeton, NJ: Princeton University Press).

Bellamy, A. J. (ed.) (2005) *International Society and its Critics* (Oxford: Oxford University Press).

Berger, P. (1986) 'Epilogue', in J. D. Hunter and S. C. Ainley (eds), *Making Sense of Modern Times: Peter L. Berger and the Vision of Interpretive Sociology* (London and New York: Routledge and Kegan Paul).

Booth, K. (1995) International Relations Theory Today' (University Park, PE: The Pennsylvania State University Press).

Bonanate, L. (1995) *Ethics and International Relations* (Oxford: Polity).

Boucher, D. (1998) *Political Theories of International Relations* (Oxford: Oxford University Press).

Brown, C. (1992) *International Relations Theory: New Normative Approaches* (New York: Columbia University Press).

Brown, C. (1997) *Understanding International Relations* (Basingstoke: Macmillan).

Brown, C. (2001) 'Fog in the Channel: Continental Relations Theory Isolated (Or an Essay on the Paradoxes of Diversity and Parochialism in IR Theory)', in M. A. Crawford and D. S. L. Jarvis (eds), *International Relations – Still an American Science: Towards Diversity in International Thought?* (New York: State University of New York Press): 203–19.

Brown, C. (2002a) 'On Morality, Self-Interest and Foreign Policy', *Government and Opposition*, 37: 173–89.

Brown, C. (2002b) *Sovereignty, Rights and Justice: International Political Theory Today* (Oxford: Polity).

Brown, C., Nardin, T. and Rengger, N. (eds) (2002) *International Relations in Political Thought: Texts from the Ancient Greeks to the First World War* (Cambridge: Cambridge University Press).

Buchanan, A. (2004) *Justice, Legitimacy and Self Determination: Moral Foundations for International Law* (Oxford: Oxford University Press).

Bull, H. (1966a) 'International Theory: The Case for a Classical Approach', *World Politics*, 18: 361–77.

Bull, H. (1966b) 'The Grotian Conception of International Society', in H. Butterfield and M. Wight (eds), *Diplomatic Investigations: Essays in the Theory of International Politics* (London: Allen & Unwin): 51–73.

Bull, H. (1969) 'International Theory: The Case for a Classical Approach', in K. Knorr and J. N. Rosenau (eds), *Contending Approaches to International Politics* (Princeton, NJ: Princeton University Press): 20–38.

Bull, H. (1972) 'The Theory of International Politics, 1919–1969', in B. Porter (ed.), *The Aberystwyth Papers* (London: Oxford University Press).

Bull, H. (1977/1995) *The Anarchical Society: A Study of Order in World Politics* (Basingstoke: Palgrave Macmillan and New York: Columbia).

Bull, H. (1982) 'Civilian Power Europe: A Contradiction in Terms', *Journal of Common Market Studies*, 21: 149–64.

Bull, H. (1986) *Interventions in World Politics* (Oxford: Oxford University Press).

Bull, H. (1991) 'Martin Wight and the Theory of International Relations', in M. Wight, *International Theory. The Three Traditions*, ed. by G. Wight and B. Porter (Leicester and London: Leicester University Press).

Bull, H. and A. Watson (eds) (1984) *The Expansion of International Society* (Oxford: Oxford University Press).

Bull, H., Kingsbury, B. and Roberts, A. (eds) (1992) *Hugo Grotius and International Relations* (Oxford: Clarendon Press).

Burchill, S. (2001) *Theories of International Relations* (Basingstoke: Palgrave Macmillan).

Burton, J. (1965) *International Relations: A General Theory* (Cambridge: Cambridge University Press).

Burton, J. (1968) *Systems, States, Diplomacy and Rules* (Cambridge: Cambridge University Press).

Burton, J. (1972) *World Society* (Cambridge: Cambridge University Press).

Bussmann, M. and Oneal, J. R. (2007) 'Do Hegemons Distribute Private Goods? A Test of Power-Transition Theory', *Journal of Conflict Resolution*, 51: 88–111.

Butterfield, H. and Wight, M. (eds) (1966) *Diplomatic Investigations. Essays in the Theory of International Politics* (London: Allen & Unwin).

Buzan, B. (1993) 'From International System to International Society: Structural Realism and Regime Theory Meet the English School', *International Organization*, 47, 3: 327–52.

Buzan, B. (2001) 'The English School: An Underexploited Resource in IR', *Review of International Studies*, 27, 3: 471–88.

Buzan, B. (2004) *From International to World Society? English School Theory and the Social Structure of Globalization* (Cambridge: Cambridge University Press).

Buzan, B. and Little, R. (2000) *International Systems in World History: Remaking the Study of International Relations* (Oxford: Oxford University Press).

Buzan, B. and Gonzales-Pelaez, A. (2005) 'A Viable Project of Solidarism? The Neglected Contributions of John Vincent's Basic Rights Initiative', *International Relations*, 17: 321–39.

Buzan, B. and Gonzales-Pelaez, A. (2009) *International Society and the Middle East: English School Theory at the Regional Level* (Basingstoke: Palgrave Macmillan).

Buzan, B., Held, D. and McGrew, A. (1998) 'Realism versus Cosmopolitanism', *Review of International Studies*, 24: 387–98.

Buzan, B., Jones, C. A. and Little, R. (1993) *The Logic of Anarchy: Neorealism to Structural Realism* (New York: Columbia University Press).

Buzan, B., Wæver, O. and de Wilde, J. (1998) *Security: A New Framework for Analysis* (Boulder, CO: Westview).

Callahan, W. A. (2001) 'China and the Globalisation of IR Theory: Discussion of Building International Relations Theory with Chinese Characteristics', *Journal of Contemporary China*, 10, 26: 75–88.

Callahan W. A. (2004) 'Nationalising International Theory: Race, Class and the English School', *Global Society*, 18: 305–23.

Campbell, D. T. (1996) 'Political Prosaics, Transversal Politics, and the Anarchical World', in M. Shapiro and H. Alker (eds), *Challenging Boundaries: Global Flows, Territorial Identities* (Minneapolis: University of Minnesota Press): 7–32.

Campbell, D. T. (1998) *Writing Security: United States Foreign Policy and the Politics of Identity*, revised edn (Minneapolis: University of Minnesota Press).

Caney, S. (2005) *Justice Beyond Borders: A Global Political Theory* (Oxford: Oxford University Press).

Carlsnaes, W. (2002) 'Foreign Policy', in W. Carlsnaes, T. Risse and B. A. Simmons (eds), *Handbook of International Relations* (London: Sage).

Carr, E. H. (1939) *The Twenty-Years' Crisis 1919–1939: An Introduction to the Study of International Relations* (London: Macmillan).

Carr, E. H (1961) *What is History?* (New York: Penguin).

Cerrutti, F. (2007) *Global Challenges for Leviathan: A Political Philosophy of Nuclear Weapons and Global Warming* (Lexington, MA: Lexington).

Chan, G. (1999) *Chinese Perspectives on International Relations: A Framework for Analysis* (Basingstoke: Palgrave).

Checkel, J. T. (1998) 'The Constructivist Turn in International Relations Theory', *World Politics*, 50, 2: 324–48.

Christiansen, T. and K. E. Jørgensen (1999) 'The Amsterdam Process: A Structurationist Perspective on EU Treaty Reform', *European Integration Online Papers*, available at http://eiop.or.at/eiop/texte/1999-001a.htm

Christiansen, T., Jørgensen, K. E. and Wiener, A. (eds) (2001) *The Social Construction of Europe* (London: Sage).

Clark, I. (2009) 'Towards an English School Theory of Hegemony', *European Journal of International Relations*, 15: 203–28.

Claude, I. L. (1962) *Power and International Relations* (New York: Random House).

Claude, I. L. (1993) 'The Tension Between Principle and Pragmatism in International Relations', *Review of International Affairs*, 19, 3: 215–26.

Cohen, A. P. (1985) *The Symbolic Construction of Community* (London: Routledge).

Cohen, B. (1977) *Organizing the World's Money: The Political Economy of International Monetary Relations* (New York: Basic Books).

Cohen, B. J. (2007) 'The Transatlantic Divide: Why are American and British IPE So Different?', *Review of International Political Economy*, 14: 197–219.

Connolly, W. (1984) *The Terms of Political Discourse*, 2nd edn (Princeton, NJ: Princeton University Press).

Cooper, R. (1968) *The Economics of Interdependence: Economic Policy in the Atlantic Community* (New York: McGraw-Hill).

Copeland, D. (2003) 'A Realist Critique of the English School', *Review of International Studies*, 29: 427–41.

Cox, R. W. (1981) 'Social Forces, States and World Orders: Beyond International Relations Theory', *Millennium: Journal of International Studies*, 10: 126–55.

Cox, R. W. (1983) 'Gramsci, Hegemony and International Relations: An Essay on Method', *Millenium: Journal of International Studies*, 12: 162–75.

Cox, R. W. (1987) *Production, Power and World Order: Social Forces in the Making of History* (New York: Columbia Press University).

Cox, R. W. (1989) 'Production, the State, and Change in World Order', in E. Czempiel and J. N. Rosenau, *Global Changes and Theoretical Challenges: Approaches to World Politics for the 1990s* (Lexington, MA: Lexington).

Crawford, M. A. and Jarvis, D. S. L. (eds) (2001) *International Relations – Still an American Science: Towards Diversity in International Thought?* (New York: State University of New York Press).

Cutler, C. (1991) 'The Grotian Tradition in International Relations', *Review of International Studies*, 7: 41–65.

de Cecco, M. (1974) *Money and Empire: The International Gold Standard 1890 –1914* (Oxford: Basil Blackwell).

Del Arenal, C. (1992) *Introducción a las relaciones internacionales* (Madrid: Tecnos).

de Mesquita, B. B. (2006) 'Game Theory, Political Economy, and the Evolving Study of War and Peace', *American Political Science Review*, 100: 637–42.

Der Derian, J. (1987) *On Diplomacy* (Oxford: Blackwell).

Der Derian, J. (1988) 'Introducing Philosophical Traditions in International Relations', *Millennium – Journal of International Studies*, 17: 189–93.

Der Derian, J. (1989) 'The Boundaries of Knowledge and Power in International Relations', in J. Der Derian and M. Shapiro (eds), *International/Intertextual Relations* (Lexington, MA: Lexington): 3–11.

Der Derian, J. and Shapiro, M. (eds) (1989) 'Postmodern Readings of the World Politics', in J. Der Derian and M. Shapiro (eds), *International/Intertextual Relations: Postmodern Readings of World Politics* (Lexington, MA: Lexington).

Deutsch, K. W. (1978) *The Analysis of International Relations* (Englewood Cliffs, NJ: Prentice-Hall).

Deutsch, K. W. (1989) 'A Path among the Social Sciences', in J. Kruzel and J. N. Rosenau, *Journeys through World Politics: Autobiographical Reflections of Thirty-four Academic Travelers* (Lexington, MA: Lexington).

Deutsch, K. W., Burrell, S. A. and Kann, R. A. (1957) *Political Community and the North Atlantic Area* (Princeton, NJ: Princeton University Press).

de Wilde, J. (1991) *Saved from Oblivion* (Boston, MA: Dartmouth Publishing Co.).

Dickinson, G. L. (1916/2008) *The European Anarchy* (Gloucester: Dodo Press).

Diez, T. and Steans, J. (2005) 'A Useful Dialogue? Habermas and International Relations', *Review of International Studies*, 31: 127–40.

Diez, T. and Whitman, R. (2002) 'Analysing European Integration: Reflections on the English School', *Journal of Common Market Studies*, 40: 43–67.

Donaldson, T. (1995) 'International Deontology Defended: A Response to Russell Hardin', *Ethics and International Affairs*, 9: 147–54.

Donnelly, J. (2000) *Realism and International Relations* (Cambridge: Cambridge University Press).

Dougherty, J. E. and Pfaltzgraff, R. L. (2001) *Contending Theories of International Relations: A Comprehensive Survey* (New York: Longman).

Doyle, M. (1983a) 'Kant, Liberal Legacies, and Foreign Affairs: Part 1', *Philosophy and Public Affairs*, 12: 205–34.

Doyle, M. (1983b) 'Kant, Liberal Legacies, and Foreign Affairs: Part 2', *Philosophy and Public Affairs*, 12: 323–53.

Doyle, M. (1986) 'Liberalism and World Politics', *American Political Science Review*, 80: 1151–69.

Drinkwater, D. (2005) *Sir Harold Nicolson and International Relations: The Practitioner as Theorist* (Oxford: Oxford University Press).

Drulak, P. (2003) *Teorie mezinárodních vztahu°* (Praha: Portál).

Dûchene, F. (1972) *Europe in World Peace* (London: Fontana/Collins).

Dunn, J. (1990) *Interpreting Political Responsibility* (Princeton, NJ: Princeton University Press).

Dunn, K. C. and Shaw, T. M. (eds) (2001) *Africa's Challenge to International Relations Theory* (Basingstoke: Palgrave Macmillan).

Dunne, T. (1995) 'The Social Construction of International Society', *European Journal of International Relations*, 1, 3: 367–89.

Dunne, T. (1998) *Inventing International Society: A History of the English School* (Basingstoke: Palgrave Macmillan).

Dunne, T. (2003) 'Society and Hierarchy in International Relations', *International Relations* 16: 303–20.

Edkins, J. (1999) *Post-structuralism and International Relations: Bringing the Political Back In* (Boulder, CO: Lynne Rienner).

Elman, C. (1996) 'Horses for Courses: Why Not a Neorealist Theory of Foreign Policy?', *Security Studies*, 6: 7–53.

Elman, C. and Elman, M. F. (eds) (2003) *Progress in International Relations Theory: Appraising the Field* (Cambridge, MA: MIT Press).

Europa (2009) http://ec.europa.eu/trade/issues/global/gsp/eba/index_en.htm

Evans, P. and Sahnoun, M. (2001) *The Responsibility to Protect: Report of the International Commission on Intervention and State Sovereignty* (Ottawa: Government of Canada, Department of Foreign Affairs).

Evans, P., Jacobson, H. and Putnam, R. (1993) *Double-edged Diplomacy: International Bargaining and Domestic Politics* (Berkeley, CA: University of California Press).

Fearon, D. (1998). 'Domestic Politics, Foreign Policy, and Theories of International Relations', *Annual Reviews of Political Science*, I: 289–313.

Feng, L. and Ruizhuang, Z. (2006) 'The Typologies of Realism', *The Chinese Journal of International Politics*, 1: 109–34.

Ferguson, A. (1998) 'Resisting the Veil of Privilege: Building Bridge Identities as an Ethico-politics of Global Feminism', *Hypathia*, 13, 3: 95–113.

Ferguson, Y. H. (1998). 'Hedley Bull's The Anarchical Society Revisited: States or Polities in Global Politics?', in B. A. Roberson (ed.), *International Society and the Development of International Relations Theory* (London: Pinter).

Ferguson, Y. H. and Mansbach, R. W. (1988) *The Elusive Quest: Theory and International Politics* (Columbia: University of South Carolina Press).

Fierke, K. M. (2001) 'Critical Methodology and Constructivism', in K. M. Fierke and K. E. Jørgensen (eds), *Constructing International Relations: The Next Generation* (Armonk, NY: M. E. Sharpe).

Finnemore, M. (1996) *Defining National Interests in International Society* (Ithaca, NY: Cornell University Press).

Finnemore, M. (2001) 'Exporting the English School?', *Review of International Studies*, 27: 509–13.

Finnemore, M. and Sikkink, K. (1998) 'International Norm Dynamics and Political Change', *International Organization*, 52, 4: 887–917.

Finnemore, M. And Sikkink, K. (2001) 'Taking Stock: The Constructivist Research Program in International Relations and Comparative Politics', *Annual Review of Political Science*, 4: 391–416.

Frank, A. G. (1967) *Capitalism and Underdevelopment in Latin America* (New York: Monthly Review Press).

Frei, C. (2001) *Hans J. Morgenthau: An Intellectual Biography* (Baton Rouge, LA: Louisiana State University Press).

Frey, B. (1984) 'The Public Choice View of International Political Economy', *International Organization*, 38: 199–223.

Frieden, J. and Martin, L. L. (2003) 'International Political Economy: Global and Domestic Interactions', in Katznelson, I. and Milner H. V. eds., *Political Science: The State of the Discipline* (New York: W.W. Norton).

Friedrichs, J. (2004) *A House With Many Mansions: European Approaches to International Relations Theory* (London: Routledge).

Frost, M. (1986) *Towards a Normative Political Theory of International Relations* (Cambridge: Cambridge University Press).

Frost, M. (1996) *Ethics in International Relations: A Constitutive Theory* (Cambridge: Cambridge University Press).

Fukuyama, F. (1992) *The End of History and the Last Man* (New York: Free Press).

Gallie, W. B. (1955) 'Essentially Contested Concepts', *Proceedings of the Aristotelian Society*, 56: 167–98.

Garst, D. (1995) 'Thucydides and Neorealism', *International Studies Quarterly*, 33: 3–27.

Gaus, G. F. and Kukathas, C. (2004) *Handbook of Political Theory* (London: Sage).

Geertz, C. (1993) *The Interpretation of Cultures* (London: Fontana).

George, A. and Bennett, A. (2005) *Case Studies and Theory Development in the Social Sciences* (Boston: MIT Press).

Gerring, J. (1999) 'What Makes a Concept Good? A Critical Framework for Understanding Concept Formation in the Social Sciences', *Polity*, 31: 357– 93.

Giddens, A. (1984) *The Constitution of Society. Outline of the Theory of Structuration* (Cambridge: Polity).

Giesen, K. G. (1992) *L'ethique des relations internationals: les theories anglo-americaines contemporaines* (Bruxelles: Bruylant).

Giesen, K. G. (2006) 'France and Other French-speaking Countries (1945–1994)', in K. E. Jørgensen and T. B. Knudsen (eds), *International Relations in Europe: Traditions, Perspectives and Destinations* (London: Routledge).

Gilpin, R. G. (1981) *War and Change in World Politics* (Cambridge: Cambridge University Press).

Gilpin, R. G. (1986) 'The Richness of the Tradition of Political Realism', in R. O. Keohane (ed.), *Neorealism and Its Critics* (New York: Columbia University Press): 301–21.

Gilpin, R. (1987) *The Political Economy of International Relations* (Princeton, NJ: Princeton University Press).

Gilpin, R. (2003) 'War is Too Important to Be Left to Ideological Amateurs', *International Relations*, 19, 1: 5–18.

Gilpin, R. (2005) 'Conversations in International Relations: Interview with Robert Gilpin', *International Relations*, 19: 361–72.

Glaser, C. L. (1995) 'Realists as Optimist: Cooperation as Self-Help', in M. E. Brown, S. M. Lynn-Jones and S. E. Miller (eds), *The Perils of Anarchy: Contemporary Realism and International Security* (Cambridge: MIT Press).

Goldstein, J. and Keohane, R. O. (1993) *Ideas and Foreign Policy. Beliefs, Institutions, and Political Change* (Ithaca and London: Cornell University Press).

Gong, G. (1984) *The Standard of 'Civilization' in International Society* (Oxford: Clarendon Press).

Gordon, D. (2002) 'Interpreting *Power, Wealth and Global Order*: Assessing Regional Approaches to International Relations Textbooks', *International Studies Perspectives*, 3: 235–41.

Grieco, J. M. (1990) *Cooperation Among Nations: Europe, America and Non-tariff Barriers to Trade* (Ithaca, NY: Cornell University Press).

Grieco, J. M. (1997) 'Realist International Theory and the Study of World Politics', in M. W. Doyle and J. G. Ikenberry (eds), *New Thinking in International Relations Theory* (Boulder, CO: Westview).

Griffiths, M. (1992) *Realism, Idealism and International Politics* (London: Routledge).

Griffiths, M. (1999) *Fifty Key Figures in International Relations* (London: Routledge).

Guzzini, S. (1998) *Realism in International Relations and International Political Economy: The Continuing Story of a Death Foretold* (London: Routledge).

Guzzini, S. (2000) 'A Reconstruction of Constructivism in International Relations', *European Journal of International Relations*, 6, 2: 147–82.

Haacke, J. (2005) 'The Frankfurt School and International Relations: On the Centrality of Recognition', *Review of International Studies*, 31: 181–94.

Haas, E. B. (1953) 'The Balance of Power as a Guide to Policy-Making', *Journal of Politics*, XV: 370–98.

Haas, E. B. (1958) *The Uniting of Europe: Political, Social, and Economic Forces 1950–57* (Stanford, CA: Stanford University Press).

Haas, E. B. (1990) *When Knowledge is Power: Three Models of Change in International Organizations* (Berkeley, CA: University of California Press).

Habermas, J. (1984) *The Theory of Communicative Action: Reason and the Rationalization of Society*, vol. 1 (Boston: Beacon Press)

Habermas, J. (1999) *From Kant to Hegel and Back Again: The Move Towards Detranscendentalization* (Oxford: Blackwell).

Haggard, S. and Simmons, B. (1987) 'Theories of International Regimes', *International Organization*, 41: 491–517.

Hansen, L. (1997) 'A Case for Seduction? Evaluating the Poststructuralist Conceptualization of Security', *Cooperation and Conflict*, 32, 4: 369–97.

Hardin, R. (1995) 'International Deontology', *Ethics & International Affairs*, 9: 133–47.

Hasenclever, A., Meyer, P. and Rittberger, V. (1997) *Theories of International Regimes: Cambridge Studies in International Relations* (Cambridge: Cambridge University Press).

Haslam, J. (1999) *The Vices of Integrity: A Biography of E. H. Carr* (London: Verso).

Hassner, P. (1968a) 'Change and Security in Europe, Part I: The Background', *Adelphi Papers*, 45 (London: IISS).

Hassner, P. (1968b) 'Change and Security in Europe, Part II: In Search of a System', *Adelphi Papers*, 49 (London: IISS).

Hawtrey, R. G. (1952) *Economic Aspects of Sovereignty* (London: Longmans).

Held, D. (1995) *Democracy and the Global Order* (Cambridge: Polity).

Held, D. (2003) *Cosmopolitanism: A Defence* (Cambridge: Polity).

Hellmann, G. (1994) 'Für ein problemorientierte Grundlagenforschung: Kritik und Perspektiven der Disziplin "Internationale Beziehungen" in Deutschland', *Zeitschrift für Internationale Beziehingen*, 1: 65–90.

Hellmann, G. (ed.) (2003) '*The Forum*: Are Dialogue and Synthesis Possible in International Relations?', with contributions by Gunther Hellmann, Friedrich Kratochwil, Yosef Lapid, Andrew Moravcsik, Iver Neumann, Steve Smith, Frank Harvey and Joel Cobb, *International Studies Review*, 5: 123–53.

Hermann, M. (1998) 'One Field, Many Perspectives: Building the Foundations for Dialogue', *International Studies Quarterly*, 42: 605–24.

Herz, J. H. (1950) 'Idealist Internationalism and the Security Dilemma', *World Politics*, 5: 157–80.

Herz, J. H. (1951) *Political Realism and Political Idealism* (Chicago: University of Chicago Press).

Hettne, B. (1995) *Development Theory and the Three Worlds* (Harlow: Longman).

Heywood, A. (2004) *Political Ideologies: An Introduction* (Basingstoke: Palgrave Macmillan).

Hinnebusch, R. and Ehteshami, A. (eds) (2002) *The Foreign Policies of Middle East States* (Boulder, CO: Lynne Rienner).

Hobson, J. A. (1902) *Imperialism: A Study* (London: Allen & Unwin).

Hoffman, M. (1987) 'Critical Theory and the Inter-Paradigm Debate', *Milllennium*, 16, 2: 233–6.

Hoffmann, S. (1977) 'An American Social Science: International Relations', *Daedalus*, 106: 41–60.

Hoffmann, S. and R. Keohane (1990) 'Conclusions: Community Politics and Institutional Change', in William Wallace (ed.), *Dynamics of European Integration* (London: Pinter).

Holden, G. (2006) 'The Relationship between Anglo-Saxon Historiography and Cross-community Comparisons', in K. E. Jørgensen and T. B. Knudsen (eds), *International Relations in Europe: Traditions, Perspectives and Destinations* (London: Routledge).

Hollis, M. and Smith, S. (1990) *Explaining and Understanding International Relations* (London: Clarendon).

Holsti, K. J. (2001) 'Along the Road of International Theory in the Next Millennium: Four Travelogues', in M. A. Crawford and D. S. L. Jarvis (eds) (2001) *International Relations – Still an American Science: Towards Diversity in International Thought?* (New York: State University of New York Press).

Hooper, C. (2001) *Manly States: Masculinities, International Relations and Gender Politics* (New York: Columbia University Press).

Hughes, M. (1990) *Nothing If Not Critical: Selected Essays on Art and Artists* (New York: Penguin).

Humrich, C. (2006) 'Germany', in K. E. Jørgensen and T. B. Knudsen (2006) *International Relations in Europe: Traditions, Perspectives and Destinations* (London: Routledge).

Huntington, S. P. (1993). 'The Clash of Civilizations?', *Foreign Affairs*, 72: 22–49.

Hurrell, A. (2002) 'Norms and Ethics in International Relations', in W. Carlsnaes, T. Risse and B. A. Simmons (eds), *Handbook of International Relations* (London: Sage).

Hurrell, A. (2004) 'America and the World: Issues in the Teaching of US Foreign Policy', *Perspectives on Politics*, 2: 101–12.

Hutchings, K. (1999) *International Political Theory: Rethinking Ethics in a Global Era* (London: Sage).

Huysman, J. (1996) *Making/Unmaking European Disorder: Meta-Theoretical, Theoretical and Empirical Questions of Military Stability after the Cold War* (Leuven: Katholieke Universiteit Leuven).

Inoguchi, T. and Bacon, P. (2001) 'The Study of International Relations in Japan: Towards a More International Discipline', *International Relations of the Asia-Pacific*, 1, 1: 1–20.

Jackson, R. (2000) *The Global Covenant: Human Conduct in a World of States* (Oxford: Oxford University Press).

Jackson, R. (2005a) 'Pluralism', in Martin Griffiths (ed.), *The Encyclopedia of International Relations and Global Politics* (London: Routledge).

Jackson, R. (2005b) 'Solidarism', in Martin Griffiths (ed.), *The Encyclopedia of International Relations and Global Politics* (London: Routledge).

Jackson, R. and G. Sørensen (2003) *Introduction to International Relations* (Oxford: Oxford University Press).

James, A. M. (1986) *Sovereign Statehood: The Basis of International Society* (New York: Palgrave).

Janis, I. L. (1982) *Groupthink: A Psychological Study of Policy Decisions and Fiascos* (Boston: Houghton Mifflin).

Jay, M. (1973) *The Dialectical Imagination: A History of the Frankfurt School and the Institute of Social Research 1923–1950* (Berkeley, CA: University of California Press).

Jepperson, R. L., Wendt, A. and Katzenstein, P. (1996) 'Norms, Identity and Culture in National Security', in P. J. Katzenstein (ed.), *The Culture of National Security. Norms and identity in World Politics* (New York: Columbia University Press): 33–75.

Jervis, R. (1976) *Perception and Misperception in International Politics* (Princeton, NJ: Princeton University Press).

Jervis, R. (1998) 'Realism in the Study of World Politics', *International Organization*, 52, 4: 971–91.

Jones, R. E. (1981) 'The English School of International Relations: A Case for Closure', *Review of International Studies*, 7, 1: 1–13.

Jones, R. W. (2001) *Critical Theory and World Politics* (Boulder, CO: Lynne Rienner).

Johnston, A. I. (1996) 'Cultural Realism and Strategy in Maoist China', in P. J. Katzenstein (ed), *The Culture of National Security. Norms and Identity in World Politics* (Ithaca, NY: Cornell University Press).

Jørgensen, K. E. (2000) 'Continental IR Theory: The Best Kept Secret', *European Journal of International Relations*, 6, 1: 9–42.

Jørgensen K. E. (2001) 'Four Levels and a Discipline', in K. M. Fierke and K. E. Jørgensen (eds), *Constructing International Relations. The Next Generation* (Armonk, NY: M. E. Sharpe).

Jørgensen, K. E. (2003/4) 'Towards a Six Continents Social Science: International Relations', *Journal of International Relations and Development*, 6, 4: 330–43.

Jørgensen, K. E. and Knudsen, T. B. (2006) *International Relations in Europe: Traditions, Perspectives and Destinations* (London: Routledge).

Kagan, R. (2003) *Of Paradise and Power: America and Europe in the New World Order* (New York: Knopf).

Kahler, M. (1993) 'International Relations: Still an American Science?', in L. B. Miller and M. J. Smith (eds), *Ideas and Ideals: Essays in Honor of Stanley Hoffmann* (Boulder, CO: Westview).

Kaiser, K. (1969) 'Transnationale Politik', in E. O. Czempiel (ed.), *Die anachronistische Souveränität* (Opladen: Westdeutscher Verlag).

Kant, I. (1795/1983) *Perpetual Peace: A Philosophical Essay*, trans. by T. Humphrey (Cambridge, MA: Hackett).

Karns, M. P. and Mingst, K. A. (1990) *The United States and Multilateral Institutions: Patterns of Changing Instrumentality and Influence* (London: Routledge)

Katzenstein, P. J. (1978) *Between Power and Plenty: Foreign Economic Policies of Advanced Industrial States* (Madison: University of Wisconsin Press).

Katzenstein, P. J. (ed.) (1996) *The Culture of National Security: Norms and Identity in World Politics* (New York: Columbia University Press).

Katzenstein, P. J. and Sil, R. (2004) 'Rethinking Asian Security: A Case for Analytical Eclecticism', in J. J. Suh, P. J. Katzenstein and A. Carlson (eds), *Rethinking Security in East Asia: Identity, Power and Efficiency* (Stanford: Stanford University Press): 1–33.

Katzenstein, P. J., Keohane, R. O. and Krasner, S. D. (1998) 'International Organization and the Study of World Politics', *International Organisation*, 52, 4: 645–85.

Katzenstein, P. J., Keohane, R. and Krasner, S. (eds) (1999) *Exploration and Contestation in the Study of World Politics: A Special Issue of International Organization* (Cambridge, MA: MIT Press).

Kegley, C. W. (1993) 'The Neoidealist Moment in International Studies? Realist Myths and the New International Realities,' *International Studies Quarterly*, 37: 131–46.

Kennan, G. (1995) 'On American Principles', *Foreign Affairs*, 74, 2: 116–26.

Keohane, R. O. (1984) *After Hegemony: Cooperation and Discord in the International Political Economy* (Princeton, NJ: Princeton University Press).

Keohane, R. O. (1986) *Neorealism and Its Critics* (New York: Columbia University Press).

Keohane, R. O. (1988) 'International Institutions: Two Approaches', *International Studies Quarterly*, 32: 379–96.

Keohane, R. O. (1989) *International Institutions and State Power: Essays in International Relations Theory* (Boulder, San Francisco and London: Westview).

Keohane, R. O. (1990) 'Multilateralism: An Agenda for Research', *International Journal*, 45, 4: 731–64.

Keohane, R. O and Nye, J. S. (1971) *Transnational Relations and World Politics* (Cambridge, MA: Harvard University Press).

Keohane, R. O. and Nye, J. S. (1977) *Power and Interdependence: World Politics in Transition* (Boston: Little, Brown).

Keohane, R. O. and Nye, J. S. (1985) 'Two Cheers for Multilateralism', *Foreign Policy*, 60: 148–67.

Keohane, R. O. and Nye, J. S. (1987) 'Power and Interdependence Revisited', *International Organization*, 41: 725–53.

Keohane, R. O., Nye, J. and Hoffmann, S. (1993) *After the Cold War: International Institutions and State Strategies in Europe, 1989–1991* (Cambridge, MA: Harvard University Press).

Kindleberger, C. (1973) *The World in Depression, 1929–1939* (Berkeley and Los Angeles: University of California Press).

King, G., Keohane, R., and Verba, S. (2004) *Designing Social Inquiry* (Princeton, NJ: Princeton University Press).

Kingsbury, B. and Roberts, A. (1992) 'Introduction: Grotian Thought in International Relations', in H. Bull, B. Kingsbury and A. Roberts (eds), *Hugo Grotius and International Relations* (Oxford: Clarendon Press): 1–64.

Kissinger, H. (1957) *A World Restored: Castlereagh, Metternich and the Restoration of Peace, 1812–1822* (Boston: Houghton Mifflin).

Klotz, A. and Lynch, C. (1998) 'Conflicted Constructivism? Positivist Leanings vs Interpretivist Meanings', paper presented at the International Studies Association Annual Meeting, Minneapolis, MN.

Klotz, A. and C. Lynch (2007) *Strategies for Research in Constructivist International Relations* (Armonk, NY: M. E. Sharpe).

Knudsen, T. B. (1999) *Humanitarian Intervention and International Society: Contemporary Manifestations of an Explosive Doctrine* (Aarhus: University of Aarhus, Department of Political Science)

Knudsen, T. B. (2000) 'Theory of Society or Society of Theorists?', with T. Dunne in 'The English School', *Cooperation and Conflict*, 35, 2: 193–203.

Knudsen, T. B. (2005) 'The English School: Sovereignty and International Law', in J. Sterling-Folker (ed.), *Making Sense of International Relations Theory* (Boulder CO: Lynne Rienner): 311–26.

Kowert, P. and J. Legro (1996) 'Norms, Identity, and their Limits: A Theoretical Reprise', in P. J. Katzenstein (ed.), *The Culture of National Security: Norms and Identity in World Politics* (New York: Columbia University Press): 451–97.

Krasner, S. D. (1983) *International Regimes* (Ithaca: Cornell University Press).

Kratochwil, F. (1982) 'On the Notion of Interest in International Relations', *International Organization*, 36: 1–30.

Kratochwil, F. (1989) *Rules, Norms, Decisions: On the Conditions of Practical and Legal Reasoning in International and Domestic Affairs* (Cambridge, MA: Cambridge University Press).

Kratochwil, F. (1993) 'The Embarrassment of Changes: Neo-Realism as the Science of *Realpolitik* without Politics', *Review of International Studies*, 19: 1–18.

Kratochwil, F. (2006) 'History, Action and Identity: Revisiting the "Second" Great Debate and Assessing its Importance for Social Theory', *European Journal of International Relations*, 12: 5–29.

Kratochwil, F. and Mansfield, I. (1994) *International Organization* (New York: HarperCollins).

Kratochwil, F. and Ruggie, J. G. (1986) 'International Organization: A State of the Art on the Art of the State', *International Organization*, 40, 4: 753–75.

Krause, K. and Williams, M. (1997) *Critical Security Studies: Concepts and Strategies* (London: Taylor and Francis).

Kruzel, J. and Rosenau, J. N. (eds) (1989) *Journeys through World Politics: Autobiographical Reflections of Thirty-four Academic Travellers* (Lexington, MA: Lexington).

Kubálková, V., N. Onuf and P. Kowert (1998) 'Constructing Constructivism', in V. Kubálková, N. Onuf, and P. Kowert (eds), *International Relations in a Constructed World* (Armonk, NY: M. E. Sharpe): 3–21.

Lake, D. A. (2006) 'International Political Economy: A Maturing Inter-discipline', in B. R. Weingast and D. A. Wittman (eds), *The Oxford Handbook of Political Economy* (Oxford: Oxford University Press).

Lake, D. A. and Powell, R. (1999) *Strategic Choice and International Relations* (Princeton, NJ: Princeton University Press).

Lapid, Y. (1989) 'The Third Debate: On the Prospects of International Theory in a Post-positivist Era', *International Studies Quarterly*, 33: 235–54.

Laudan, L. (1977) *Progress and Its Problems* (Berkeley and Los Angeles: University of California Press).

Leander, A. (1997) 'Bertrand Badie: Cultural Diversity Changing International Relations?', in I. B. Neumann and O. Wæver (eds), *The Future of International Relations: Masters in the Making* (London: Routledge).

Legro, J. and Moravcsik, A. (1999) 'Is Anybody Still a Realist?', *International Security*, 24, 2: 5–55.

Lepgold, J. (1998) 'Is Anyone Listening? International Relations Theory and the Problem of Policy Relevance', *International Studies Quarterly*, 18, 1: 41–74.

Lijphart, A. (1974) 'The Structure of the Theoretical Revolution in International Relations', *International Studies Quarterly*, 18: 41–74.

Linklater, A. (1982) *Men and Citizens in the Theory of International Relations Theory* (London: Macmillan).

Linklater, A. (1990) *Beyond Realism and Marxism: Critical Theory and International Relations* (Basingstoke: Palgrave Macmillan).

Linklater, A. (1993) 'Liberal Democracy, Constitutionalism and the New World Order', in R. Leaver and J. L. Richardson (eds), *The Post-Cold War Order: Diagnoses and Prognoses* (St Leonard's: Allen and Unwin).

Linklater, A. (1998) *The Transformation of Political Community: Ethical Foundations of the Post-Westphalian Era* (Columbia: University of South Carolina Press).

Linklater, A. and Suganami, H. (2006) *The English School of International Relations: A Contemporary Reassessment* (Cambridge: Cambridge University Press).

Little, R. (2000) 'The English School's Contribution to the Study of International Relations', *European Journal of International Relations*, 6: 395–422.

Long, D. and P. Wilson (1995) *Thinkers of the Twenty Years' Crisis: Inter-War Idealism Reassessed* (Oxford: Oxford University Press).

Luhmann, N. (1997) *Die Gesellschaft der Gesellschaft*, 2 vols (Frankfurt: Suhrkamp).

Lyotard, J.-F. (1984) *The Postmodern Condition* (Minneapolis: Columbia University Press).

Maier, C. (1987) *Changing Boundaries of the Political: Essays on the Evolving Balance Between the State and Society, Public and Private in Europe* (Cambridge: Cambridge University Press).

Manners, I. (2002) 'Normative Power Europe: A Contradiction in Terms?', *Journal of Common Market Studies*, 40: 235–58.

Manners, I. (2003) 'Europaian Studies', *Journal of Contemporary European Studies*, 11, 1: 67–83.

Manning, C. A. W. (1962) *The Nature of International Society* (London: London School of Economics).

Martin, L. (2007) 'Neoliberalism', in T. Dunne, M. Kurki and S. Smith (eds), *International Relations Theories: Discipline and Diversity* (Oxford: Oxford University Press).

McCarty, N. and Meirowitz, A. (2007) *Political Game Theory: An Introduction* (Cambridge: Cambridge University Press).

Mearsheimer, J. J. (1990) 'Back to the Future: Instability in Europe After the Cold War', *International Security*, 15, 1: 5–56.

Mearsheimer, J. J. (1995) 'The False Promise of International Institutions', *International Security*, 19, 3: 5–49.

Mearsheimer, J. J. (2003) *The Tragedy of Great Power Politics* (New York: W.W. Norton and Co.).

Mearsheimer, J. J. (2006) 'Conversations in International Relations Part I and II', *International Relations*, 20: 105–25/231–45.

Mearsheimer J. J. and Walt, S. M. (2003) 'An Unnecessary War', *Foreign Policy*, 134: 50–9.

Meinecke, F. (1924) *Die Idee der Staatsräson in der neueren Geschichte* (München: Verlag von R. Oldenbourg).

Milliken, J. (2001) 'Discourse Study: Bringing Rigor to Critical Theory', in K. M. Fierke and K. E. Jørgensen (eds), *Constructing International Relations: The Next Generation* (London: Sharpe).

Mitrany, D. (1943) *A Working Peace System* (London: Royal Institute of International Affairs).

Molloy, S. (2003) 'The Realist Logic of International Society', *Cooperation and Conflict*, 38: 83–100.

Moravcsik, A. (1998) *The Choice for Europe: Social Purpose and State Power from Messina to Maastricht* (London: UCL Press).

Moravcsik, A. (2003a) 'Liberal International Relations Theory', in C. Elman and M. Fendius Elman (eds), *Progress in International Relations Theory: Appraising the Field* (Cambridge, MA: MIT Press).

Moravcsik, A. (2003b) 'Theory Synthesis in International Relations: Real not Metaphysical', *International Studies Review*, 5: 131–6.

Morgenthau, H. J. (1946) *Scientific Man vs Power Politics* (Chicago: University of Chicago Press).

Morgenthau, H. J. (1948) *Politics Among Nations* (New York: Knopf), 2nd edn 1954.

Morgenthau, H. J. (1984) 'Fragment of an Intellectual Autobiography: 1904–1932', in K. Thompson and R. J. Myers (eds), *Truth and Tragedy. A Tribute to Hans J. Morgenthau* (New Brunswick and London: Transaction).

Mueller, J. (1990) *Retreat from Doomsday: The Obsolescence of Major War* (New York: Basic Books)

Müller, H. (2001) 'International Relations as Communicative Action', in K. M. Fierke and K. E. Jørgensen (eds), *Constructing International Relations: The Next Generation* (London: Sharpe).

Murphy, C. N. and Nelson, D. R. (2001) 'International Political Economy: A Tale of Two Heterodoxies', *British Journal of Politics and International Relations*, 3: 393–412.

Murphy, C. and Tooze, R. (eds) (1991) *The New International Political Economy* (Boulder, CO: Lynne Rienner).

Nardin, T. (1983) *Law, Morality and the Relations of States* (Princeton, NJ: Princeton University Press.)

Nardin, T. (2006) 'International Political Theory and the Question of Justice', *International Affairs*, 82: 440–65.

Nau, H. R. (2002) *At Home Abroad: Identity and Power in American Foreign Policy* (Ithaca and London: Cornell University Press).

Neufield, M. (1993) 'Interpretation and the "Science" of International Relations', *Review of International Studies*, 19: 39–61.

Neuman, I. B. and Wæver, O. (1997) *The Future of International Relations: Masters in the Making* (London: Routledge).

Nicholson, M. (1996) *Causes and Consequences in International Relations: A Conceptual Study* (London: Pinter).

Niebuhr, R. (1932) *Moral Man and Immoral Society: A Study of Ethics and Politics* (New York: Charles Scribner's Sons).

Nossall, K. (2001) 'Tales that Textbooks Tell: Ethnocentricity and Diversity in American Introductions to International Relations', in M. A. Crawford and S. L. Darryl (eds), *International Relations – Still an American Science: Towards Diversity in International Thought?* (New York: State University of New York Press).

Nye, J. (1970) 'Comparing Common Markets: A Revised Neo-Functionalist Model', *International Organization*, 24, 4: 796–835.

Nye, J. (1990) *Bound to Lead: The Changing Nature of American Power* (New York: Basic Books).

Nye, J. (1988) 'Neorealism and Neoliberalism', *World Politics*, 40, 2: 235–51.

Onuf, N. G. (1989) *World of Our Making: Rules and Rule in Social Theory and International Relations* (Columbia, SC: University of South Carolina Press).

Onuf, N. G. (2001) 'The Politics of Constructivism', in K. M. Fierke and K. E. Jørgensen (eds), *Constructing International Relations. The Next Generation* (Armonk, NY: M. E. Sharpe).

Orend, B. (2001) *Michael Walzer on War and Justice* (Montreal: McGill-Queen's University Press).

Organski, A. F. K. (1958) *World Politics* (New York: Alfred A. Knopf).

Organski A. F. K. and Kugler, J. (1980) *The War Ledger* (Chicago: University of Chicago Press).

Oudeshook, P. (1995) *Game Theory and Political Theory* (Cambridge: Cambridge University Press).

Parsons, Craig (2007) *How to Map Arguments in Political Science* (Oxford: Oxford University Press).

Patterson, L. (1997) 'Agricultural Policy Reform in the European Community: A Three Level Game Analyses', *International Organization*, 51: 135–65.

Peterson, V. S. (ed.) (1992) *Gendered States: Feminist (Re-)Visions of International Political Theory* (Boulder, CO: Lynne Rienner).

Philips, N. (2005) '"Globalizing" the Study of International Political Economy', in N. Philips (ed.), *Globalizing International Political Economy* (Basingstoke: Palgrave Macmillan).

Pogge, T. (2002) *World Poverty and Human Rights* (Cambridge: Polity Press).

Polanyi, K. (1944/2001) *The Great Transformation* (Boston, MA: Beacon).

Posen, B. (2004) 'ESDP and the Structure of World Power', *The International Spectator*, 39: 5–17.

Price, R. (1995) 'A Genealogy of the Chemical Weapons Taboo', *International Organization*, 49, 1: 73–103.

Puchala, D. (1997) 'Some Non-Western Perspectives on International Relations', *Journal of Peace Research*, 34, 2: 129–34.

Puchala, D. (2003) *Theory and History in International Relations* (New York: Routledge).

Putnam, R. D. (1988) 'Diplomacy and Domestic Politics: The Logic of Two-level Games', *International Organization*, 42: 427–60.

Rawls, J. (1971) *A Theory of Justice* (Cambridge, MA: Belknap).

Rengger, N. J. (1990) 'The Fearful Sphere of International Relations', *Review of International Studies*, 16: 361–8.

Rengger, N. J. (1999) *International Relations, Political Theory and the Problem of Order: Beyond International Relations Theory?* (London: Routledge).

Rengger, N. J. (2001) 'Negative Dialectic? The Two Modes of Critical Theory in World Politics', in R. Wyn Jones (ed.), *Critical Theory and World Politics* (London: Lynne Rienner).

Rengger, N. J. (2006) 'Theorizing World Politics for a New Century', *International Affairs*, 82, 3: 427–30.

Risse, T. (2000) '"Let's Argue": Communicative Action in World Politics', *International Organization*, 54: 1–39.

Risse-Kappen, T. (1995) *Bringing Transnational Relations Back In: Nonstate Actors, Domestic Structures and International Institutions* (Cambridge: Cambridge University Press).

Roberts, A. and Kingsbury, B. (eds) (1988) *United Nations – Divided World: The UN's Roles in International Relations* (Oxford: Clarendon).

Rosenau, J. N. (1980) *The Study of Global Interdependence: Essays on the Transnationalisation of World Affairs* (New York: Nichols).

Rosenau, J. N. (1990) *Turbulence in World Politics: A Theory of Change and Continuity* (Princeton, NJ: Princeton University Press).

Rosenau, J. and Durfee, M. (1995) *Thinking Theory Thoroughly: Coherent Approaches to an Incoherent World* (Boulder, CO: Westview).

Ruggie, J. G. (1982) 'International Regimes, Transactions, and Change: Embedded Liberalism in the Postwar Economic Order', *International Organization* 36: 195–231.

Ruggie, J. G. (1983) 'Continuity and Change in the World Polity: Towards a Neo-realist Synthesis', *World Politics* 35:261-285.

Ruggie, J. G. (1989) 'International Structure and International Transformation: Space, Time, and Method', in E.-O. Czempiel and J. Rosenau (eds), *Global Changes and Theoretical Challenges. Approaches to World Politics for the 1990s* (Lexington, MA: Lexington).

Ruggie, J. G. (1991) 'Embedded Liberalism Revisited: Institutions and Progress in International Economic Relations', in E. Adler and B. Crawford (eds), *Progress in Postwar International Relations* (New York: Columbia University Press).

Ruggie, J. G. (1993) 'Territoriality and Beyond: Problematizing Modernity in International Relations', *International Organization*, 47, 1: 139–74.

Ruggie, J. G. (1998a) 'What Makes the World Hang Together? Neo-Utilitarianism and the Social Constructivist Challenge', *International Organization*, 52, 4: 855–85.

Ruggie, J. G. (1998b) *Constructing the World Polity: Essays on International Institutionalization* (London and New York: Routledge).

Ruggie, J. G. (2003) 'Taking Embedded Liberalism Global: The Corporate Connection', in D. Held and M. Koenig-Archibugi (eds), *Taming Globalization: Frontiers of Governance* (Cambridge: Polity Press).

Russett, B. (1989) 'Democracy and Peace', in B. Russett and H. Starr (eds), *Choices in World Politics: Sovereignty and Interdependence* (New York: Freeman): 245–61.

Said, E. (1979) *Orientalism* (New York: Vintage).

Schieder, S. and Spindler, M. (eds) (2003) *Theorie der Internationalen Beziehungen* (Opladen: Barbara Budrich).

Schimmelfennig, F. (2003) *The EU, NATO and the Integration of Europe: Rules and Rhetoric* (Cambridge: Cambridge University Press).

Schmidt, B. C. (1998) *The Political Discourse of Anarchy: A Disciplinary History of International Relations* (New York: State University of New York Press).

Schmidt, B. C. (2002) 'On the History and Historiography of International Relations', in W. Carlsnaes, T. Risse and B. A. Simmons (eds), *Handbook of International Relations* (London: Sage).

Schmidt, B. C. (2006) 'Epilogue', in K. E. Jørgensen and T. B. Knudsen (eds), *International Relations in Europe: Traditions, Perspectives and Destinations* (London: Routledge).

Schmidt, B. C. and Long, D. (2005) *Imperialism and Internationalism in the Discipline of International Relations* (New York: State University of New York Press).

Scholte, J. A. (2000) *Globalization: A Critical Introduction* (Basingstoke: Palgrave Macmillan).

Schonfield, A. (ed.) (1976) *International Economic Relations of the Western World* (Oxford: Oxford University Press).

Schwarzenberger, G. (1941) *Power Politics: An Introduction to the Study of International Relations and Post-war Planning* (London: J. Cape).

Schelling, T. (1960) *The Strategy of Conflict* (Oxford: Oxford University Press).

Schuman, F. (1937) *International Politics: An Introduction to the Western State System*, 2nd edn (New York: McGraw-Hill).

Schweller, R. (1994) 'Bandwagoning for Profit: Bringing the Revisionist State Back In', *International Security*, 19, 1: 72–107.

Schweller, R. (1996) 'Neorealism's Status-Quo Bias: What Security Dilemma?', *Security Studies*, 5, 3: 90–121.

Schweller, R. (2003) 'The Progressiveness of Neoclassical Realism', in C. Elman and M. Fendius Elman (eds), *Progress in International Relations Theory* (Cambridge, MA: MIT Press).

Schweller, R. and Priess, D. (1997) 'A Tale of Two Realisms: Expanding the Institutions Debate', *Mershon International Studies Review*, 41: 1–32.

Searle, J. (1969) *Speech Acts* (Cambridge: Cambridge University Press).

Searle, J. (1995) *The Construction of Social Reality* (New York: Free Press).

Shapcott, R. (2001) *Practical Reasoning: Constructivism, Critical Theory and the English School*, paper presented to the 4th Pan-European Conference on International Relations, 8–10 September, University of Kent at Canterbury.

Shinko, R. (2006) 'Thinking, Doing, and Writing International Relations Theory', *International Studies Perspectives*, 7: 43–50.

Singer, D. (1961) 'The Level-of-Analysis-Problem in International Relations', *World Politics*, XIV, 1: 77–92.

Sjöstedt, G. (1977) *The External Role of the European Community* (Hampshire: Saxon House).

Sloan, G. R. (1988) *Geopolitics in United States Strategic Policy 1890–1987* (London: Wheatsheaf).

Smith, M. J. (1986) *Realist Thought from Weber to Kissinger* (Baton Rouge, LA: Louisiana State University Press).

Smith, S. (1985) *International Relations: British and American Perspectives* (Oxford: Blackwell).

Smith, S. (1992) 'The Forty Years' Detour: The Resurgence of Normative Theory in International Relations', *Millennium*, 21: 489–506.

Smith, S. (1995) 'The Self-Images of a Discipline: A Genealogy of International Relations Theory', in K. Booth and S. Smith (eds), *International Relations Theory Today* (Pennsylvania: Pennsylvania State University Press): 1–37.

Smith, S. (1996) 'Positivism and Beyond', in S. Smith, K. Booth and M. Zalewski (eds), *International Theory: Positivism and Beyond* (Cambridge: Cambridge University Press).

Smith, S. (2001) 'Social Constructivisms and European Studies', in T. Christiansen, K. E. Jørgensen and A. Wiener (eds), *The Social Construction of Europe* (London: Sage).

Smith, S. and Baylis, J. (2003) *The Globalization of World Politics: An Introduction to International Relations* (Oxford: Oxford University Press).

Smith, S., Booth, K. and Zalewski, M. (eds) (1996) *International Theory: Positivism and Beyond* (Cambridge: Cambridge University Press).

Smith, T. (1979) 'The Underdevelopment of Development Literature: The Case of Dependency Theory', *World Politics*, 31: 247–88.

Snyder, G. H. (1984) 'The Security Dilemma in Alliance Politics', *World Politics*, 36: 461–95.

Snyder, G. H. (1990) 'Alliance Theory: A Neorealist First Cut', *Journal of International Affairs*, 44: 103–23.

Snyder, G. H. (1997) *Alliance Politics* (Ithaca, NY: Cornell University Press).

Snyder, J. (1991) *Myths of Empire: Domestic Politics and International Ambition* (Ithaca, NY: Cornell University Press).

Söllner, Alfons (1990) 'Vom Staatsrecht zur "political science"? Die Emigration deutscher Wissenschaftler nach 1933, ihr Einfluss auf die Transformation einer Disziplin', *Politische Vierteljahresschrift*, 31: 627–54.

Song, X. (2001) 'Building International Relations Theory with Chinese Characteristics', *Journal of Contemporary China*, 10, 26: 61–74.

Sørensen, G. (1991) 'A Revised Paradigm for International Relations: The "Old" Images and the Postmodernist Challenge', *Cooperation and Conflict*, XXVI: 85–166.

Spegele, R. (1987) 'Three Forms of Political Realism', *Political Studies*, 35: 189–210.

Steiner, Z. (2003) 'Views of War: Britain Before the "Great War" – and After', *International Relations*, 17: 7–33.

Sternberg, F. (1926) *Der Imperialismus*, Berlin.

Strange, S. (1970) 'International Economics and International Relations: A Case of Mutual Neglect?' *International Affairs*, 46: 304–15.

Strange, S. (1987) 'The Persistent Myth of Lost Hegemony', *International Organization*, 41: 551–74.

Strange, S. (1994) 'Wake Up Krasner, the World *has* Changed', *Review of International Political Economy*, 1: 209–20.

Strange, S. (1999) 'The Westfailure System', *Review of International Studies*, 25: 345–54.

Suganami, H. (1983) 'The Structure of Institutionalism: An Anatomy of British Mainstream International Relations', *International Relations*, 7, 5: 362–81.

Suganami, H. (1989) *The Domestic Analogy and World Order Proposals* (Cambridge: Cambridge University Press).

Suganami, H. (2001a) 'C. A. W. Manning and the Study of International Relations', *Review of International Studies*, 27: 91–107.

Suganami, H. (2001b) 'Alexander Wendt and the English School', *Journal of International Relations and Development*, 4: 403–23.

Sylvester, C. (2001) *Feminist International Relations* (Cambridge: Cambridge University Press).

Tammen, R. L. (2000) *Power Transitions: Strategies for the 21st Century* (New York: Chatham House).

Tammen, R. L. and Kugler, J. (2007) 'Power Transition and Chino–US Conflicts', *The Chinese Journal of International Politics*, 1: 35–56.

Taylor, C. (1978) 'Interpretation and the Sciences of Man', in R. Beckler and A. R. Drengson (eds), *Philosophy of Society* (London: Methuen).

Thies, C. (2002) 'Progress, History and Identity in IR Theory', *European Journal of International Relations*, 8: 147–85.

Thomas, S. M. (2001) 'Faith, History and Martin Wight: The Role of Religion in the Historical Sociology of the English School of International Relations', *International Affairs*, 77: 905–31.

Thompson, K. (1993) *Traditions and Values in Politics and Diplomacy: Theory and Practice* (Baton Rouge, LA: Louisiana State University Press).

Thompson, K. and Myers, R. J. (eds) (1984) *Truth and Tragedy. A Tribute to Hans J. Morgenthau* (New Brunswick and London: Transaction).

Tickner, A. B. (2003) 'Hearing Latin American Voices in International Relations Studies', *International Studies Perspectives*, 4, 4: 325–50.

Tickner, A. B. and Wæver, O. (eds) (2009) *International Relations Scholarship Around the World* (London: Routledge).

Underhill, G. R. D. (2003) 'State, Market, and Global Political Economy: Genealogy of an (Inter?) Discipline', *International Affairs*, 76: 805–24.

Valbjørn, M. (2008) *A 'Baedeker' to IR's Cultural Journey Before, During and After the Cultural Turn: Explorations into the (Ir)relevance of Cultural Diversity, the IR/Area Nexus and Politics in an (Un)Exceptional Middle East* (Aarhus: Politica).

van Evera, S. (1997) *Guide to Methods for Students of Political Science* (Ithaca, NY: Cornell University Press).

van Munster, R. (2009) *Securitising Immigration* (Basingstoke: Palgrave Macmillan).

Vasquez, J. (1983) *The Power of Power Politics: A Critique* (New Brunswick, NJ: Rutgers University Press).

Vasquez, J. (1995) 'The Post-Positivist Debate', in K. Booth and S. Smith (eds), *International Relations Theory Today* (Cambridge: Polity).

Vasquez, J. (1997) 'The Realist Paradigm and Degenerative versus Progressive Research Programs: An Appraisal of Neotraditional Research on Waltz's Balancing Proposition', *American Political Science Review*, 91: 899–912.

Vasquez, J. (1998) *The Power of Power Politics: From Classical Realism to Neotraditionalism* (Cambridge: Cambridge University Press).

Vincent, R. J. (1974) *Non-Intervention and International Order* (Princeton, NJ: Princeton University Press).

Vincent, R. J. (1986) *Human Rights and International Relations* (Cambridge: Cambridge University Press).

Vincent, R. J. (1990) 'Grotius, Human Rights and Intervention', in H. Bull, B. Kingsbury and A. Roberts (eds), *Hugo Grotius and International Relations* (Oxford: Clarendon): 241–56.

Vincent, R. J. and Wilson, P. (1993) 'Beyond Non-Intervention', in I. Forbes and M. Hoffmann (eds), *Political Theory, International Relations, and Ethics of Intervention* (Basingstoke: Palgrave Macmillan).

Wæver, O. (1994) 'Resisting the Temptation of Post Foreign Policy', in W. Carlsnaes and S. Smith (eds), *European Foreign Policy: The EC and Changing Perspectives in Europe* (London: Sage).

Wæver, O. (1995) 'Securitization and Desecuritization', in R. Lipschutz (ed.), *On Security* (New York: Columbia University Press).

Wæver, O. (1996a) 'The Rise and Fall of the Inter-paradigm Debate', in S. Smith and M. Zalewski (eds), *International Theory: Positivism and Beyond* (Cambridge: Cambridge University Press): 149–85.

Wæver, O. (1996b) 'European Security Identities', *Journal of Common Market Studies*, 34: 103–32.

Wæver, O. (1998) 'The Sociology of a Not So International Discipline: American and European Developments in International Relations', *International Organization*, 52, 4: 687–727.

Wæver, O. (1999) 'American Constructivism and the ES', paper presented to BISA Annual Conference, 20–2 December, University of Manchester.

Walker, R. B. J. (1987) 'Realism, Change and International Political Theory', *International Studies Quarterly*, 31: 65–86.

Walker, R. B. J. (1993) *Inside/Outside: International Relations as Political Theory* (Cambridge: Cambridge University Press).

Wallace, W. (1996) 'Truth and Power, Monks and Technocrats: Theory and Practice in International Relations', *Review of International Studies*, 22, 3: 301–21.

Wallace, W. and D. Allen (1977) 'Political Cooperation: Procedure as Substitute for Policy', in H. Wallace, W. Wallace and C. Webb (eds), *Policy-Making in the European Community* (Chichester: John Wiley and Sons).

Wallerstein, I. (1974) *The Modern World System: Capitalist Agriculture and the Origins of the European World Economy in the Sixteenth Century* (New York and London: Academic).

Walt, S. M. (1987) *The Origins of Alliances* (Ithaca, NY: Cornell University Press).

Walt, S. M. (1998) 'International Relations: One World, Many Theories', *Foreign Policy*, 110: 29–46.

Waltz, K. N. (1959) *Man, the State and War: A Theoretical Analysis* (New York: Columbia University Press).

Waltz, K. N. (1964) 'The Stability of a Bipolar World', *Daedalus*, 93, 3: 881–909.

Waltz, K. N. (1979) *Theory of International Politics* (Reading, MA: Addison-Wesley).

Waltz, K. N. (1990) 'Realist Thought and Neorealist Theory', *Journal of International Affairs*, 44, 1: 21–37.

Waltz, K. N. (1993) 'The Emerging Structure of International Politics', *International Security*, 18: 44–79.

Waltz, K. N. (1996) 'International Politics Is Not Foreign Policy', *Security Studies*, 6: 54–7.

Waltz, K. N. (1998) 'Interview with Ken Waltz', *Review of International Studies*, 24: 371–86.

Waltz, K. N. (1999) 'Globalization and Governance', *PS: Political Science and Politics* 32: 693-77.

Waltz, K. N. (2000a) 'Structural Realism after the Cold War', *International Security*, 25: 5–41.

Walzer, M. (1977) *Just and Unjust Wars: A Moral Argument with Historical Illustrations* (New York: Basic Books).

Watson, A. (1984) 'European International Society and its Expansion', in H. Bull and A. Watson (eds), *The Expansion of International Society* (Oxford: Oxford University Press): 13–32.

Watson, A. (1987) 'Hedley Bull, States Systems and International Societies', *Review of International Studies*, 13: 147–53.

Watson, A. (1992) *The Evolution of International Society: A Comparative Historical Analysis* (London: Routledge).

Weber, C. (1994) 'Good Girls, Little Girls, and Bad Girls: Male Paranoia in Robert Keohane's Critique of Feminist International Relations', *Millennium*, 23: 337–49.

Weber, C. (1995) *Simulating Sovereignty: Intervention, the State and Symbolic Interchange* (Cambridge: Cambridge University Press).

Weber, C. (1998) 'Reading Martin Wight's "Why is there No International Theory?" as History', *Alternatives*, 23: 451–69.

Weingast, B. R. and Wittman, D. A. (eds) (2006) *The Oxford Handbook of Political Economy* (Oxford: Oxford University Press).

Weldes, J. (1996) 'Constructing National Interests', *European Journal of International Relations*, 2, 3: 275–318.

Wendt, A. (1987) 'The Agent–Structure Problem in International Relations Theory', *International Organization*, 41: 335–70.

Wendt, A. (1991) 'Bridging the Theory/Meta-theory Gap in International Relations', *Review of International Studies*, 17: 383–92.

Wendt, A. (1992a) 'Anarchy is What the States Make of It: The Social Construction of Power Politics', *International Organization*, 46, 2: 391–426.

Wendt, A. (1992b) 'Bridging the Theory/Metatheory Gap in International Relations', *Review of International Studies*, 17: 383–92.

Wendt, A. (1992c) 'Levels of Analysis vs Agents and Structures: Part III', *Review of International Studies*, 18, 2: 181–5.

Wendt, A. (1994) 'Collective Identity Formation and the International State', *American Political Science Review*, 88, 2: 384–96.

Wendt, A. (1995) 'Constructing International Politics', *International Security*, 20, 1: 71–81.

Wendt, A. (1999) *Social Theory of International Politics* (Cambridge: Cambridge University Press).

Wendt, A. and Duvall, R. (1989) 'Institutions and International Order', in E.-O. Czempiel and J. N. Rosenau (eds), *Global Changes and Theoretical Challenges: Approaches to World Politics for 1990s* (Lexington, MA: Lexington): 51–73.

Wheeler, N. J. (1992) 'Pluralist or Solidarist Conceptions of International Society: Bull and Vincent on Humanitarian Intervention', *Millennium*, 21, 3: 463–87.

Wheeler, N. J. (2000) *Saving Strangers: Humanitarian Intervention in International Society* (Oxford: Oxford University Press).

Wheeler, N. J. and Dunne, T. (1996) 'Hedley Bull's Pluralism of the Intellect and Solidarism of the Will', *International Affairs*, 72, 2: 91–107.

Wight, M. (1946/1977) *Power Politics* (Leicester: Leicester University Press).

Wight, M. (1960) 'Why is There No International Theory?', *International Relations*, 2: 35–48.

Wight, M. (1966) 'Western Values in International Relations', in H. Butterfield and M. Wight (eds), *Diplomatic Investigations: Essays in the Theory of International Politics* (London: George Allen & Unwin): 89–131.

Wight, M. (1969) 'Why is There No International Theory?', in H. Butterfield and M. Wight (eds), *Diplomatic Investigations. Essays in the Theory of International Politics* (Cambridge, MA: Harvard University Press).

Wight, M. (1991) *International Theory: The Three Traditions*, ed. by G. Wight and B. Porter (Leicester: Leicester University Press).

Williams, M. C. (2005) *The Realist Tradition and the Limits of International Relations* (Cambridge: Cambridge University Press).

Wilson, P. (1998) 'The Myth of the "First Great Debate"', *Review of International Studies*, 24: 1–15.

Wivel, A. (2003) 'The Power Politics of Peace: Exploring the Link between Globalization and European Integration from a Realist Perspective', *Cooperation and Conflict*, 39: 5–25.

Wolfe, R. and Mendelsohn, M. (2004) 'Would Citizens Support a New Grand Compromise?', in S. F. Bernstein and L. W. Pauly (eds), *Global Liberalism and Political Order: Toward a New Grand Compromise* (New York: State University of New York Press).

Young, O. R. (1983) 'Regime Dynamics: The Rise and Fall of International Regimes', *International Organization*, 36: 277–97.

Zacher, M. W. and Matthew, R. A. (1995) 'Liberal International Theory: Common Threads, Divergent Strands', in C. W. Kegley, *Controversies in International Relations: Realism and the Neoliberal Challenge* (New York: St Martin's Press).

Zehfuss, M. (2002) *Constructivism in International Relations: The Politics of Reality* (Cambridge: Cambridge University Press).

Zhao, S. (1991) 'Metatheory, Metamethod, Meta-data-analysis: What, Why, and How?', *Sociological Perspectives*, 34, 3: 377–90.

Zimmern, A. (1936) *The League of Nations and the Rule of Law, 1918–1935* (London: Macmillan).

Zimmern, A. (1939) *L'Ensignement Universitaire des Relations Internationales* (Paris: Institut International de Cooperation Intellectuelle).

Zürn, M. (1994) 'We Can Do Much Better! Aber muss es auf Amerikanisch sein? Zum Vergleich der Disziplin "Internationale Beziehungen" in den USA und in Deutschland', *Zeitschrift für Internationale Beziehungen*, 1, 1: 91–114.

Glossary

This glossary contains an explication of key technical terms, having meanings which are specific to International Relations theory. In case a concept is characterized by multiple, contested meanings, the variety of meanings is introduced.

Abandonment. When an ally abandons a military or diplomatic alliance and, thereby, the commitments constituting the core of the alliance. Prior to World War 2, France abandoned its alliance with Czechoslovakia. The United Kingdom, fearing entrapment, did not support France's commitments. *See also* **entrapment.**

Agent–structure problem. A meta-theoretical problem concerning the dilemmas analysts face when in prioritizing either agents (actors) or structures. *See also* **structuration theory.**

Alliance. A formal agreement or coalition between two or more states to cooperate in military or security matters. Military alliances often play a role in **balance of power** politics. Liberal theorists regard alliances as an example of international institutions.

Anarchy. Absence of political authority. The international system is anarchical as there is no higher political authority (e.g. no world government); states are fully sovereign entities. According to English School theorists, the anarchical society can be an orderly society; according to liberal theorists, anarchy can be moulded, hence for them it is a matter of degree, not of kind. *See also* **hierarchy.**

Balance of power. A key concept among especially realist and English School theorists; characterized by several meanings. For some it refers to a condition of an almost mechanical power equilibrium between states. Others assume that balances between states are created by state leaders. Still others see it as an inherent feature of international politics, i.e. beyond the will of state leaders. Reflections on balance of power might be used by decision-makers as a rational basis or justification for a given foreign policy. Critics of the concept emphasize that the numerous meanings of the concept diminish its analytical utility in studies of international relations. *See also* **balance of threat.**

Balance of threat. A version of **balance of power** theory. However, theorists claim that it is not power *per se* that tend to be balanced. It is the degree of threat a state assign to a given opponent power.

Balancing. When a state or an alliance consciously balances military opponents, i.e. engages in balance of power politics. Some make a distinction between hard and soft balancing. It is contested whether soft balancing can take place within alliances.

Bandwagoning. When weaker powers align with the stronger power rather than opposing it by means of balancing (for instance, by means of forming an alliance).

Bilateralism. Bilateral relations are relations between two states. Bilateralism refers to the web of such relations. *See also* **unilateralism** and **multilateralism.**

Bipolarity. A structural concept referring to a systemic distribution of power, specifically when there are only two great powers (or superpowers) in the international system.

During the Cold War, the United States and the Soviet Union constituted a bipolar structure in the international system. The contemporary international system is considered **unipolar**, or, increasingly, **multipolar**.

Buck-passing. Refers to a pronounced reluctance to counter a given emerging threat while hoping that other states will do something about it. When encountering the emerging Nazi Germany, the Western powers passed the buck to one another. President Truman is said to have a sign on his desk, 'The buck stops here', meaning that there was no one further up to refer an issue to.

Chain-ganging. Similar to a chain reaction; states are chain-ganged into war by alliance partners, since alliance commitments force states into war even if they have no special interest in the war in question. By contrast, *see* **buck-passing**.

Civil society. A classical concept within political philosophy, denoting an intermediate realm between the state and the individual; the network of societal institutions, e.g. political parties, free markets, trade unions, non-state media, interest groups, NGOs, etc. Totalitarian states are characterized by an almost complete absence of a civil society.

Classical approach. Also called the traditional approach – a mode of thinking about international relations emphasizing the role of international law, diplomatic history and philosophy, in contrast to behaviouralist approaches which employ the language of variables, propositions, formal hypothesis testing and frequently also the use of statistical analysis.

Communitarianism. Political, philosophical and ethical stance emphasizing the common origins of moral codes and individual identities; in international relations associated with nationalism, respectively with the idea of a pluralist international society; communitarians perceive the nation-state as the primary site of moral obligations and as the primary limit to the expansion of the moral community. In contrast, *see* **Cosmopolitanism**.

Convention. Agreement or jointly accepted principle of action; solution to recurrent coordination games; an arbitrary equilibrium.

Cosmopolitanism. A term derived from the Greek word *kosmopolites*. Philosophical approach outward in orientation and avoiding local and ethnocentric prejudices; initial expression of cosmopolitanism attributed to Diogenes, who proclaimed himself to be a 'citizen of the world'. Definitions of cosmopolitanism vary, yet principles of individuality and universality are core elements. In international relations cosmopolitanism is linked to liberalism and the argument that no morally significant boundaries separate human beings.

Defensive realism. Strand of realism whose theorists assume that states strive for an 'appropriate' or sufficient amount of power. Moreover, they stress that seeking superior power is not a rational response to external systemic pressures. According to defensive realists the prime strategy for survival is balancing against those states which are increasing their relative power.

Democratic peace theory. Argues that spread of democracy will lead to greater security as democratic states tend not to fight other democratic states. Instead democracies are believed to settle mutual conflicts of interests without the use of threat or force since internal shared norms and institutions matter. Democratic peace theory is based on a Kantian logic stressing the three elements of republican democratic representation, transnational interdependence and ideological commitment to human rights.

Deterrence. Psychological effect on an opponent resulting in a decision not to take some action, such as attacking or starting a war; achieved either through fear of disciplinary punishment or through rational calculation that pursuing this action will not lead to the accomplishment of the intended objectives or respectively that the involved costs will be to high.

Diplomacy. The process or the art of communication among states (or their representatives) in international politics; the tools of diplomacy include positive inducements, persuasive tactics, compromise, threats and coercion. Diplomacy in foreign policy relates to a state's political or policy element in conducting its foreign relations.

Double standards. Refers to equal cases being treated differently; or that a state demands from others what it would never dream about delivering itself. *See also* **exceptionalism.**

Duty. The duties of states are often called 'deontology'. Within the same family of terms, we find notions such as obligation, responsibility and commitment.

Entrapment. The process of being dragged into a conflict over an ally's interests that one does not share, or only share to some degree; entrapment occurs when states value the preservation of an alliance more than the costs of fighting for the ally's interest.

Epistemology. Derived from the Greek word *episteme* meaning knowledge; refers to theories of knowledge and the question as how we come to know what we think we know about the world; denotes a pursuit that leads us to adopt various methods/methodologies for testing our propositions of theoretically derived expectations.

Exceptionalism. Political reasoning according to which a given state is exceptional, for which reason double standards are all right; the state is definitely beyond comparison.

First-image. In the three **levels of analysis** format, first-image theories focuses on explanations situated at the level of individuals/ human nature. Causes of conflict are seen in the intervention of governments nationally and internationally disturbing the natural order. Determinants of peace are individual liberty, free trade, interdependence and prosperity. *See also* **second** *and* **third images.**

First-order theory. Substantive theories about international relations; theories which can be applied in empirical studies; *See also* **second-order theory.**

Game theory. A mathematical interaction theory that has been widely applied in a range of scientific disciplines, including economics, political science and international relations. Being mathematical, it is a form of theory that is as formal as it probably gets. The theory concerns strategic interaction among rational players and assigns paramount importance to preferences and outcomes.

Geopolitics. Study of the influence of geographical factors on politics and state behaviour, dealing with the question of how location, population, climate, natural resources and physical landscape determine a state's foreign policy options as well as its position in the hierarchy of states.

Hegemony. Refers to a system regulated by a dominant leader; to relations of dominance with a major power exercising hegemony over countries within its sphere of influence; to control, power, or influence used by the leading state over other states.

Hierarchy. A system that is characterized by higher and lower levels of political authority; national political systems and empires are hierarchical. Realist power transition theorists regard the international system hierarchical. *See also* **anarchy.**

Identity. Relates to 'Who am I or with whom do I identify?' In International Relations the answer is sometimes linked to terms of identification with a nation which may/may not be associated with a state; thus, identity can be transnational, cf. the examples of religious, gender or class identification. Some theorists focus on state identity, i.e. the key characteristics a state has or wants to be recognized for.

Imperialism. In its classic meaning a position of superiority or dominance with regard to foreign territories; a policy of acquiring foreign territory through force, especially associated with the establishment of colonies staffed by personnel (administrators, military troops, missionaries) from the imperial country during the 19th century, known as colonialism.

Institutionalization. Refers to the expansion of international law and the significant increase in the number of international institutions as well as their scope. According to neoliberal institutionalism, the degree of systemic institutionalization tempers the effects of anarchy and influences the scope of cooperation and conflict.

Interaction capacity. Relates to physical and social technologies determining possibilities for transportation and communication within any social system. The use of airplanes during World War 1 increased interaction capacity significantly and blew the roof off the nation-state.

Interdependence. A situation whereby actions or events in one state or part of the world affect people elsewhere; interdependence exists only when there is a degree of mutual dependence or reciprocal ties among the parties concerned. Interdependence is frequently *asymmetric*, i.e. one party is more affected than the other; thus, it can exist among states or involve other actors, such as *transnational* companies, organizations or individuals, with means of interaction that overcome boundaries of states and their societies.

Interests. Represent that which is of importance to a unit, e.g. a state, a class, a group or an individual, and usually includes, as a minimum, its survival. *National* interest relates to matters of importance to a state; can be defined in more or less narrow terms and in more or less contrast to common interests.

International community. References to the international community often have legitimizing functions, for instance when a powerful coalition of states claims that 'the international community' cannot accept the behaviour of state X. The coalition could have said 'we' but that would connote self-interest rather than common interest. Sometimes, the United Nations is seen as embodying the international community.

International governmental organizations. Multilateral institutions set up by states to pursue common objectives that usually cannot be achieved by means of unilateral or bilateral action (reduction of transaction costs), cf. the United Nations, WTO or ILO. Members of international organizations are states which distinguishes them from **transnational** or **non-governmental organizations** (NGOs).

International institutions. A generic term comprising international organizations, regimes and conventions.

International law. Refers to laws which transcend borders and apply to states (international law narrowly conceived), individuals (natural persons as in international humanitarian law) or to organizations and corporations (legal persons, for instance, in international business law). Sources of international law are **conventions** and **treaties** which bind states to these formal agreements even when their contracting governments change.

International regime. An international agreement comprising sets of rules and principles agreed by states in order to coordinate and manage their relations in a particular issue area. Some regime rules have the binding character of international law while others are informal yet followed by states because they make many frequent transactions a habit or are perceived as generally being in the state's self-interest. Examples include international monetary regimes and international export control regimes, e.g. the Missile Technology Control Regime (MTCR).

International society. A key concept in English School theory, an association of member states interacting across international orders, sharing common purposes, organizations and standards of conduct; also referring to a global social framework of shared norms and values based on state sovereignty as political independence is a core value of an international society.

Intervention. Interference in internal affairs of another state through diplomatic, military, economic or other means. English School solidarists explain humanitarian military interventions by reference to human security concerns and the growth of solidarist norms.

Just war. A theory stating the conditions under which states may go to war rightfully (*jus ad bellum* – justice of war), for instance with just reason, as in self-defence in response to aggression; refers also to waging war by using means that are proportional to the ends sought, and when actions are taken with the right intention to achieve legitimate military objectives and to reduce destruction and collateral death.

Justice (international). One of many essentially contested terms. However, according to a common understanding, just(ice) refers to fair, right or equitable for individuals, states or regions. An international order might be just or not; the distribution of power or wealth might be considered just or unjust.

Levels of analysis. An analytical means to organize thinking about and analysis of world politics where individuals, groups, societies and states as well as the overall international system represent separate foci, each illuminating an aspect of international relations; helps scholars to be systematic and focused when analyzing international politics or international political economy. The number of levels varies yet is often between three and five.

Meta theory. Theoretical reflections on theory, meaning (**second-order**) theory about (**first-order**) theory.

Methodology. Refers to operational procedures in an academic study of a given topic; modes of analysis and research, e.g. the use of historical or comparative case studies, statistics in causal modelling, interpretive strategies in discourse analysis, procedures for framing an argument within international political theory or formal hypothesis testing.

Multilateralism. Refers to three or more states cooperating on international issues or functional aspects of international relations (security, trade or environmental management) instead of either unilateral efforts by a single state or bilateralism; a way to achieve mutual gains by developing mutually acceptable institutions and norms.

Multipolarity. Relates to the distribution of power among three or more of the great powers (or poles) in the international system/society; a systemic, structural state of affairs.

Ñon-governmental organizations (NGOs). Transnational organizations characterized by an autonomous standing *vis-à-vis* governments and a diversified membership; work in favour of specific and often narrowly conceived political, economic or social objectives that may have a positive or negative impact on different segments of society. NGOs can include, among others, multinational corporations, labour unions, media companies, churches and religious organizations.

Norms. An often used, yet essentially vague, term in perpetual need of specification; comprises legal, moral and sociological norms. Legal norms emerge when states decide to codify or formalize moral or sociological norms, a process that might be triggered or promoted by norm-entrepreneurs. Sociological norms are associated with custom or habit and therefore not the direct outcome of intended action. If norms are not socially reproduced, they might well erode.

Offensive realists. Oppose the view of **defensive realists** claiming that states only seek an 'appropriate' amount of power, sufficient for balance of power purposes. Advocates of offensive realism argue that since states face an uncertain international environment, security requires the acquisition of as much power as possible.

Ontology. A branch of philosophy dealing with issues related to the existence of things and thereby to one's world-view, meaning the essence of things as well as the properties of existence in the world; frequently theorists make a distinction between material and social ontology. *See also* **epistemology.**

Order. Sustained pattern of social arrangements, comprising both a structural and functional dimension; the former referring to how things are arranged and to the nature of relationship between the constituent parts; the latter relating to the purpose of the arrangement. Examples include the social order (of societies) and the international order (of states).

Peace. Various definitions exist ranging from simply absence of war, a situation of security, stability and order, or harmonious relations between states or other actors.

Pluralism. Concept of international society where sovereign states are the basic units cultivating their own values and interests; states coexist and interact on a basis of self-interest, expediency, out of mutual recognition and regard for common norms and practices as well as political and commercial reciprocity; a current of thought within the English School. *See also* **solidarism.**

Positivism. A philosophy of science; within the social sciences a specific methodology concerned with knowledge building based on four assumptions: (i) unity of sciences, (ii) distinction between facts and values, where facts are neutral among theories, (iii) the social world displays regularities that can be discovered by theorists in the same way scientists discover regularities in nature, and (iv) the way to determine the truth of statements is by appeal to neutral facts, meaning the employment of empiricist epistemologies.

Post-positivism. Theoretical tradition rejecting positivism as an appropriate philosophy of science, epistemology and methodology for the study of international relations. Post-positivist currents of thought include, among others, poststructuralism, social constructivism and critical theory.

Process variables. Analysts making use of process variables argue that not all important explanatory factors are either unit or system factors. Examples of process variables include Glenn Snyder's extension of neorealism (relationships, interactions and structural modifiers) and John Ruggie's notion of dynamic density.

Rationalism. In International Relations theory, rationalism refers to two fundamentally different things: for theorists within the international society tradition, rationalism is simply a synonym for their tradition, situated as it is 'middle-of-the-road'-like between *realism* and *revolutionism* (i.e. *liberalism*). These theorists recognize anarchy as the defining characteristic of the international system yet, significantly, add that an international society has developed through centuries and characterized by common rules and institutions. Second, rationalism refers to rational-choice-like approaches and perspectives, usually imported from economics.

Reason. Analysts make an important distiction between causes of action (as in causal analysis) and reasons for action. The latter refers to justifications for a given action, usually provided to make the action legitimate; reason also refers to the rational thinking of human beings. Not least, liberal theorists make strong assumptions about human reason.

Reflectivism. Sometimes used as a synonym for constructivism. Opposed to purely rationalist and objectivist stances, reflectivists take into consideration the role of social ontologies and social institutions.

Regionalism. Refers to state-led regional cooperative frameworks; institution-building among groups of countries at a regional level; some regard so-called 'new regionalism' a political-institutional response to uneven processes of economic globalization.

Republican states. In contrast to dictatorships or old-time kingdoms, republican states are characterized by constitutions that make citizens' consent matter for decisions on war. As citizens tend to be more sceptical as regards the benefits of war, rulers are somewhat reluctant to wage war; hence, republican states are more inclined to peace than non-republican states. This reasoning can be traced back to philosopher Immanuel Kant's reflections on conditions for a perpetual peace. *See also* **democratic peace theory**.

Responsibility. Refers to a kind of future *duty*, i.e. credited prospectively in a forward-looking sense, to a person or state who is obligated/socially entrusted either on customary, legal or moral grounds with a specific type of action. Responsibility might exist with reference to international law or be self-inflicted due to, for instance, identity or an ethical stance.

Rights. Entitlements to perform or not to perform certain actions, or to live or not to live in given states.

Sanctions. Punitive measures used as an instrument of power; can be imposed on and by any actor in world politics, such as states, governments, governing elites as well as intergovernmental organizations or ordinary groups of consumers; includes any measure that interrupts normal intercourse in global politics, e.g. economic sanctions, boycotts or embargoes.

Second image. Within a three levels of analysis perspective, 'second-image' refers to the state level, for instance when explaining the causes of war or the conditions of peace. In second-image perspectives the causes of war are explained by means of characteristics of states, including their domestic institutions and policy-making processes. *See also* **second image reversed**.

Second image reversed. The opposite analytical perspective to **second-image** theories. Analysts employing a second image reversed approach focus on how factors external to a state might constitute the state, including influencing the state's basic institutions and policy-making processes.

Second-order theory. Theoretical reflection that is independent of substantive international relations issues. Examples include the **agent–structure problem** and the distinction between objectivist and subjectivist perspectives. *See also* **meta-theory**.

Society. Analytical definitions vary significantly due to different emphasises on different key features such as autonomy, degree of organization, changing boundaries of state and society. *See also* **civil society** *and* **international society**.

Solidarism. Concept of international society in which sovereign states jointly pursuit common purposes which serve as their ultimate *raison d'être*; in world politics a collective process of cooperative and coordinated activities which leads to joint destinations. *See also* **pluralism**.

Sovereignty. Claim to political authority based on autonomy and territory that is historically associated with the modern state. Internally, it refers to the right claimed by states to exercise exclusive political authority over a defined territory, including also the claim to a right to autonomy. Externally, it relates to relations with other states. Some make a distinction between formal (legal) sovereignty and the actual capacity to make a state sustainable (in contrast to failed states).

State. A legal-political entity consisting of a territory with defined boundaries, a relatively fixed population (with or without a common identity), a sovereign government or administration exercising supreme authority, and of recognition as a sovereign state by other sovereign states.

State-centric. A perspective that gives primacy to (nation-)states and their national governments as the major or only players in world politics. Most statistics are fairly state-centric.

Structuration theory. Theory proposed as a solution to the agent–structure problem; emphasizes the mutual constitution of agents and structures: in terms of operational analytical procedure, a strategy of bracketing is often suggested, i.e. first agents > structures, then structures > agents (or vice versa).

System. A set of interrelated parts or an arrangement of units connected in such a way as to form a unity; systems can be used as abstract concepts, taxonomies or frameworks by theorists to organize research and analysis. Use of the term varies, for instance **international** systems being composed of states *vis-à-vis* world capitalism as an economic and political system constituted by classes with conflicting interests.

Third image. In the three levels of analysis framework, the third image refers to the systemic level; systemic properties, for instance the structure of the international system, the global capitalist system or the global cultural environment have significant impact on the identity or behaviour of states.

Transnationalism. Transnationalism refers to interactions and coalitions across state boundaries which involve various non-governmental actors, such as multinational corporations or organized criminals. Sometimes transnationalism comprises non-governmental as well as transgovernmental links. The term *transnational* can be used to label an actor, e.g. a *transnational* actor, or to describe a pattern of behaviour, for instance an international organization operating across state boundaries, thus acting *transnationally*.

Treaty. An explicit and formal agreement or contract between two or more states specifying norms, rules and principles, e.g. trade arrangements, the pursuit of collective security, arms control, health standards and environmental protection, etc. Treaties in international law are considered binding despite the non-existence of an international enforcing authority *per se*.

Unilateralism. Denotes a specific foreign policy strategy; decisions are taken by a given state without consulting bilateral or multilateral partners; also called a going-it-alone strategy. *See also* **multilateralism** *and* **bilateralism**.

Unipolarity. Refers to an international distribution of power where there is clearly only one dominant power or 'pole', a world that is subject to the influence of only one great power is *unipolar*; essentially balance of power dynamics is absent.

Universal. Associated with terms such as general, global, common, complete, worldwide, collective, entire, etc.

Values. Political values include preferences with regard to security, equality, freedom, liberty, peace, stability and order.

War. The engagement in military conflicts, usually for some political purpose. Whereas armed conflict between states is *interstate* war, armed conflict within a given state is *civil* war; war involving irregular and usually non-uniformed fighters is *guerrilla* war. Realist and liberal scholars are primarily concerned with the causes of war. Within the international society tradition (the English School) war is considered a fundamental institution of international society.

Westphalian order. Refers to the Peace of Westphalia (1648), the first explicit expression of a European society of states with its own diplomatic practices and an emerging body of formal international law; served as a prototype for subsequent developments of international society; the Westphalian international society is based on three principles: (i) kings and emperors are sovereign within their own realm; (ii) those who rule determine the religion of their realm; and (iii) a balance of power system preventing in principle any hegemonic power from emerging. The (European) international society was subsequently gradually extended and eventually globalized.

World politics. Those stressing the importance of politics beyond state-centric international politics tend to employ the term, or, alternatively, global politics. In this context 'beyond' means including states but also international (or transnational) governmental or non-governmental organizations, other groupings and intellectual leaders. 'Beyond' also means including more issue areas than classic war and peace-related issues, for instance values, human rights, demographic or environmental issues.

World society. Refers to a society of individuals, not states. Notably, sociologist Niklas Luhmann's conception of world society is influenced by his general systems theory.

World system. A term primarily related to the work of Immanuel Wallenstein. He focuses on capitalism as a world economic system; his theory is influenced by Marxist understandings of capitalism as a global system.

Index